THE

GOSPEL ACCORDING TO ST. JOHN

THE
GOSPEL ACCORDING TO ST. JOHN

*An Inquiry into
Its Genesis and Historical Value*

BY

DR. HANS HINRICH WENDT
PROFESSOR OF THEOLOGY IN THE UNIVERSITY OF JENA

TRANSLATED BY
EDWARD LUMMIS, M.A.

WIPF & STOCK · Eugene, Oregon

Wipf and Stock Publishers
199 W 8th Ave, Suite 3
Eugene, OR 97401

The Gospel According to St. John
An Inquiry into Its Genesis and Historical Value
By Wendt, Hans Hinrich
ISBN 13: 978-1-60608-379-6
Publication date 01/29/2009
Previously published by T & T Clark, 1902

PREFACE TO THE GERMAN EDITION

IN the year 1886, in my *Lehre Jesu*,[1] i. pp. 215-342, I attempted to establish the hypothesis that in the Fourth Gospel, and specifically in the discursive passages, a source consisting of older written notes or memoirs had been employed. Since that time a long series of important disquisitions have appeared with regard to that Gospel, all of which I have been at pains to study. In almost all of them my hypothesis is curtly rejected. I have not, however, been shaken in my conviction of the correctness of my main idea, either by these works or by the treatise of Dr. E. Haupt (*Studien und Kritiken*, 1893, pp. 217-250), which deals with my hypothesis in detail: a paper for which I take this opportunity of recording my especial thanks to my esteemed colleague of Halle. I have not found any effectual confutation of the reasons which I put forward, or any better explanation of the remarkable phenomena in the Fourth Gospel which appear to me to be due to the employment of a written source. But I have found in these works much that directly confirms and supports, sometimes, indeed, even necessitates, my hypothesis. A strong desire has grown upon me, in consequence, to explain and justify my hypothesis once more, in a new and better form, and with greater detail than was admissible in

[1] Authorised English Translation — *The Teaching of Jesus* (Edinburgh, T. & T. Clark).

the scheme of that larger work, and to compare it with the recent labours of other writers. It is my hope and aim to show, in the following pages, that my hypothesis affords a really satisfactory solution of the important and difficult Johannine problem.

H. H. WENDT.

JENA, 4*th March* 1900.

PREFACE TO THE ENGLISH EDITION

THE hypothesis proposed in this book, with reference to the structure and origin of the Gospel according to John, first forced itself upon my mind when, at the beginning of my academic work, I sought to form an independent judgment, apart from the influence of theological tradition, concerning the Fourth Gospel. The composition of this Gospel presents many peculiarities and difficulties, for which, as it seemed to me, no satisfactory explanation could be found, except on the assumption that two layers of tradition lie side by side,—an older material, and the additions of a more recent redactor. I found this hypothesis of great help in the understanding of the Gospel, both in detail and as a whole; and reached the conviction that only by its aid could a true estimate of the value of the Gospel be attained.

I first gave literary expression to my hypothesis in the first part of the German edition of my *Lehre Jesu* (Göttingen, 1886), pp. 215-342. Therein I sought to justify the manner and method in which I made use of the Fourth Gospel in my presentment of the substance of Jesus' teaching. In the English edition, *The Teaching of Jesus*, the first part of the German edition, which investigates the original records used as sources in the Gospels, was not included.

Since then several important treatises on the Fourth

Gospel have appeared, from which I have tried to learn. Having repeatedly to lecture on this subject, I have been under the necessity of continually testing my hypothesis, and the conflicting explanations of other writers, by means of a detailed interpretation of the Gospel. This careful testing process has not shaken my conviction of the correctness of my hypothesis: for I have not found that the critics who reject it offer any effectual refutation of the reasons upon which I base it, or any better explanation of those difficulties in the Gospel which first constrained me to adopt it.

When I had occasion recently to prepare a new German edition (published at Göttingen in the autumn of this year) of the *Lehre Jesu*, I thought it better to detach from that work the detailed critical discussion of the Johannine problem. For I wished to establish my hypothesis concerning the Fourth Gospel, and compare it with the recent labours of other men, in a more exhaustive way than the scheme of that larger work would admit. Thence arose this special treatise on the Gospel according to John. It is my hope that it may prove a useful contribution to the great theological effort which has been devoted to a problem, as difficult as it is interesting and important.

It gives me great pleasure that this book should now appear in an English translation. I hope that in this form it will be found by many, who have given a friendly reception to the English edition of my *Teaching of Jesus*, a welcome supplement to that work. My sincere thanks are tendered to the publishers of this volume, and in particular to the translator.

H. H. WENDT.

JENA, 10th *November* 1901.

CONTENTS

INTRODUCTION

	PAGE
THE CRITICAL PROBLEM	1

CHAPTER I

EXAMINATION OF THE NARRATIVE PLAN OF THE FOURTH GOSPEL IN THE LIGHT OF THE SYNOPTIC RECORD

A. The True Synoptic Standard 7
B. The Relation of the Johannine Narrative to the Synoptic Tradition.
   1. The Festal Journeys of Jesus to Jerusalem . . . 9
   2. The Date of Jesus' Death 12
   3. The Testimony of the Baptist concerning Jesus . . . 14
   4. The Publication of Jesus' Messiahship 18
   5. The Signs of Jesus 21
C. The Literary Dependence of the Fourth Gospel on the Synoptics.
   1. The Acquaintance of the Fourth Evangelist with the Synoptic Literature in general 32
   2. The detailed Coincidences of the Fourth with the Synoptic Gospels 34
   3. Final Inferences 47

CHAPTER II

INDICATIONS OF THE USE OF A WRITTEN SOURCE IN THE FOURTH GOSPEL

A. The Question of the Sources of the Gospel 49
B. Differences between the point of view of the Evangelist and that of the Discourses of Jesus.
   1. The Distinction between the "Signs" and the "Works" of Jesus 58
   2. Misinterpretations of Particular Sayings of Jesus . . 66

	PAGE
C. Disturbance of the Original References and Contexts	72
1. Discrepancy between Narrative and Discourse in Chapter v.	73
2. Discrepancy between Narrative and Discourse in Chapter vi.	75
3. The Detachment of vii. 15–24 from Chapter v.	85
4. Severance of Connected Passages in Chapters vii. and viii.	92
5. Severance of xii. 44–50 from xii. 35 and 36a	96
6. Disruption of the Context in xiii. 12–20	99
7. Displacement in the Farewell Discourse, Chapters xiii.–xvi.	101

CHAPTER III

Inquiry into the Composition of the Source

A. General Principles in the Determination of Passages from the Source	108
B. The Passages from the Source in Detail.	
1. Source-components in the Prologue, i. 1–18	110
2. Source-components in i. 19–iv. 54	117
3. Source-components in Chapter v. and Chapter vi.	128
4. Source-components in Chapters vii. and viii.	142
5. Source-components in Chapters ix. and x.	148
6. Source-components in Chapter xi.	153
7. Source-components in Chapter xii.	158
8. Source-components in Chapters xiii.–xvii.	161
9. Source-components in Chapters xviii.–xx.	164
C. The Character of the Source as a whole	166

CHAPTER IV

The Source of the Fourth Gospel in its Relation to other Literature

A. The Johannine Epistles	171
B. Christian Writers of the Second Century.	
1. Ignatius	175
2. Justin	178

CHAPTER V

The Historical Value of the Source as a Record

A. The Relation of the Historical Notices in the Source to the Synoptic Tradition	182
B. The Relation of the Discourses of Jesus in the Source to the Synoptic Tradition	
1. The Characteristic Form of the Discourses	186
2. The General Religious Attitude and Conception in the Discourses	188
3. The Sayings of Jesus concerning Himself	193
4. The Absence of Predictions after the Event	201

CHAPTER VI

THE AUTHOR OF THE SOURCE

PAGE

A. Signs of the Authorship of the Apostle John
    1. The Personal Statements of the Author of the Source . . 207
    2. The Hints of the Fourth Evangelist 211
    3. The Tradition as to the Residence of John in Asia Minor . 214

B. Apparent Reasons against the Authorship of the Apostle
    1. The Whilom Fisherman an Author 220
    2. The Relation of the Apostle to Alexandrian Speculation about the Logos 223

CHAPTER VII

THE GENESIS OF THE FOURTH GOSPEL

A. The Main Portion, Chapters i.-xx.
    1. The Apostolic Tradition in the Subapostolic Rendering . 235
    2. The Specific Aims and Prepossessions of the Evangelist . 242

B. The Appendix, Chapter xxi. 248

CONCLUSION 254

SYNOPSIS OF THE PASSAGES IN THE GOSPEL WHICH ARE PROBABLY DERIVED FROM THE SOURCE 256

INDEX OF PASSAGES CITED FROM THE JOHANNINE BOOKS.
    The Gospel according to St. John 257
    The Epistles of St. John 260

THE GOSPEL ACCORDING TO ST. JOHN

INTRODUCTION

THE CRITICAL PROBLEM

HOW far does the Fourth Gospel contain a credible record concerning the historic Jesus Christ? This is the cardinal question on which a critical view of the Fourth Gospel must hinge. The living interest which Christian theology takes in a problem of literary criticism, like this "Johannine Problem," is rooted in the desire of Christendom for the fullest and most exact knowledge possible of the historic life and ministry of Jesus. Even if the Fourth Gospel contains no trustworthy records of the history of Jesus, or if the possible elements of sound tradition in it cannot be clearly distinguished from the untrustworthy matter around them, it must still retain a high historic value as a precious document of sub-apostolic Christianity; it retains its value for the soul, as a treasury of the deepest Christian thought and meditation. But it loses in that case the highest historic value of all, which would attach to an authentic document concerning the history of Jesus Himself, an authentic record of Jesus' own words.

In the answers which they give to this cardinal question

theological inquirers of the present day are widely at variance.[1] The one school look upon the Johannine narrative as a trustworthy history. They hold that by the Johannine scheme, and that alone, the remainder of the Gospel records are disposed in due order; that without the Johannine conception they cannot be interpreted aright.[2] The other school hold with equal definiteness that the Fourth Gospel is a "philosophic poem with a special religious intention," and, "as a source for the history of the Christ in the flesh, almost worthless."[3] Between these opposite verdicts there are many intermediate positions. On the one hand, even those inquirers who accept the Johannine account in general as historically credible may yet believe that its objective truth has been modified in several respects by the evangelist's ideal point of view, and the speculative licence which he allowed himself;[4] or they suppose that the credible record of the evangelist is interspersed with

[1] To obtain an insight into the earlier development and present state of this problem, see H. Holtzmann, *Einleitung in das N. T.*, 3rd ed. 1892, pp. 433 sqq.; E. Schürer, "Ueber den gegenwärtigen Stand der johann. Frage" (*Vorträge d. theol. Konferenz zu Giessen V.*), 1889; A. Meyer, *Th. R.*, 1899, pp. 255 sqq., 295 sqq., 333 sqq. In what follows I intentionally confine myself to the citation of the more modern literature.

[2] So recently especially P. Ewald, *Das Hauptproblem der Evangelienfrage und der Weg zu seiner Lösung*, 1890; O. Wuttig, *Das johann. Evang. u. seine Abfassungszeit*, 1897, pp. 98 and 106; Th. Zahn, *Einleitung in d. N. T.*, 1899, ii. pp. 551 sqq.

[3] So A. Jülicher, *Einleitung in d. N. T.*, 1894, pp. 258 sq. (§ 31, 4); substantially to the same effect: O. Pfleiderer, *Das Urchristentum*, 1887, pp. 695 sqq., 742 sqq.; Osc. Holtzmann, *Das Johannesev.*, 1887, pp. 97 sq.; H. Holtzmann, *Einleitung in d. N. T.*, 3rd ed. 1892, pp. 441 sqq.; *Neutest. Theol.*, 1897, ii. pp. 351 sqq.; C. Weizsäcker, *Das apost. Zeitalter*, 2nd ed. 1892, pp. 517, 520 sqq.; *The Apostolic Age*, 1894, vol. ii. pp. 206 sqq., especially pp. 225 f., 234 sqq.

[4] So especially B. Weiss, *Einleitung in d. N. T.*, 3rd ed. 1897, §,52, 7; and in Meyer's *Kommentar zum Ev. Joh.*, 8th ed.; *Einl.* § 3, 3; cf. also H. Köhler, *Von der Welt zum Himmelreich*, 1892, pp. 65 sq., 150 sqq.; F. Loof's "Die Auferstehungsberichte und ihr Wert" (*Hefte zur Chr. W.*, No. 33), 1898, pp. 33 sqq.

interpolations of inferior value.[1] On the other hand, even among those critics who regard the Gospel as concerned, on the whole, more with religious instruction than historic accuracy, there are some who make the reservation that echoes of a true, historic record are to be heard in it, so that it may be called a mixture of truth and poetry.[2]

The cardinal question, How far may the contents of this Gospel be believed? has closely bound up with it the further question, Was it written by the Apostle John? If we answer Yes, that will not prevent us from supposing that the picture which the apostle drew from memory has been, in many of its strokes, erased or overlaid. On the other hand, it is possible to acknowledge in this Gospel an original record of the highest value, even though it is not the Apostle John, but some other eye-witness of the events recorded,—perhaps the presbyter John of Asia Minor,—who is taken for its author or sponsor.[3] But at any rate it is only by deriving the Gospel directly or indirectly from one who saw and heard the things therein recorded that we can establish the historical value of his record. A reader who is sure that the Gospel was written by the Apostle John will need no further guarantee for the substantial credibility of its text. On the other hand, one who is convinced that its contents are generally untrustworthy will look upon this as a decisive argument against an apostolic origin for the Gospel.

The problem can therefore be approached on two sides. We may either search, first of all, the Gospel itself, for such

---

[1] So recently H. Delff, *Das vierte Evang.*, 1890.

[2] So C. Weizsäcker (in his earlier period), *Untersuchungen über die evang. Geschichte*, 1864, pp. 238 sqq., and C. Hase (in his later period), *Geshhichte Jesu*, 1876, pp. 49 sqq.; cf. also H. Holtzmann, *Einleitung in d. N. T.*, 3rd ed. 1892, pp. 445 sq.

[3] So F. von Uechtritz, *Studien über den Ursprung, die Beschaffenheit und Bedeutung d. Evangeliums nach Joh.*, 1876, pp. 202 sqq.; Delff, *op. cit.* pp. 1 sqq.; W. Bousset, "Die Offenbarung Johannis" (Meyer's *Komm.* xvi., 5th ed.), 1896, pp. 44 sqq.

indications as it may yield as to its origin; secondly, the oldest external notices on the same subject; thirdly, the earliest traces of its being known and used, and seek in this way to decide whether the Gospel can actually be derived from the Apostle John or some other eye-witness of the events it sets forth: if so, it will of course possess a claim to be believed, at least in the main. Or else we may try, by examining the Gospel itself, to judge how far it is worthy of belief, and so decide how far it is likely to be the authentic work of an apostle. A sound criticism, even when it has set out on one of these ways of investigation, must not altogether disregard the other. Still, a great deal depends upon whether we begin by taking account of external testimony or of internal credibility, and to which of the two ways of investigation we assign the graver significance.

The first way seems at first the safer, for the data of external testimony are actual facts, whose recognition does not appear so dependent on our subjective conception as is the distinction between what is possible and impossible, probable and improbable, in the contents of the Gospel. Such tokens of his own personality as are given by the evangelist himself, the notices concerning the residence in Asia Minor of the Apostle John and his authorship of the Gospel, as well as the traces that the Fourth Gospel was in familiar use in the second Christian century, have been, and still are, the object of a most thorough investigation. Both the defenders and the assailants of its authenticity have devoted themselves with intense diligence to this investigation.[1] There can hardly be, in the extant Christian

[1] Cf. especially E. Luthardt, *Der johanneische Ursprung des vierten Evangeliums*, 1874, pp. 34 sqq. (*St. John the Author of the Fourth Gospel* [Edin.: T. & T. Clark, 1875, pp. 9 sqq.]); A. Thoma, *Zw. Th.*, 1875, pp. 490 sqq.; A. Hilgenfeld, *Einleitung in d. N. T.*, 1875, pp. 44 and *passim*, 695 sqq.; H. Holtzmann, *Zw. Th.*, 1871, pp. 336 sqq.; 1875, pp. 40 sqq.; 1877, pp. 187 sqq.; Th. Zahn, *Geschichte des neutest. Kanons*, 1888, i. pp. 150

literature of the second century, any direct or indirect references to John or to the Fourth Gospel which have not already been considered from several standpoints, and elucidated in their bearing upon the Johannine problem. But these thorough investigations have not yet led, so far as I see, to any decisive and convincing result, either such as evidently confirms or such as certainly precludes the apostolic authenticity of the Gospel. The statements, or rather the hints, in the Gospel itself with regard to its author are so peculiarly phrased as to admit of various interpretations. The oldest records which attest the residence of the Apostle John in Asia Minor and his authorship of this Gospel wear a very definite aspect, but they leave room none the less for certain doubts, which are not altogether captious. The points of contact between the oldest Christian literature and the thoughts and words of the Fourth Gospel are certainly numerous: until the middle of the second century, however, they are not precise enough to exclude the question whether the influence which they exhibit is really that of the Fourth Gospel, or rather of some "Johannine" tradition and school of thought which already existed before the Gospel appeared. In fact, the conclusions which we are inclined to draw from this external testimony, or to adopt when drawn, depend practically on the judgment which we have already passed on the internal value and credibility of the Gospel.

For this reason we must begin our treatment of the Johannine problem with the internal criticism of the Gospel. A well-founded verdict on the greater or less credibility

sqq. and *passim*; 1889, ii. pp. 32 sqq. and *passim*; *Einleitung in d. N. T.*, 1899, ii. pp. 445 sqq.; E. Abbot, *The Authorship of the Fourth Gospel*, 1888; E. von der Goltz, "Ignatius v. Ant." (*T. U.* xii. 3), 1894, pp. 118 sqq.; A. Resch, "Ausserkanon. Paralleltexte zu den Evangelien, H. 4 (*T. U.* x. 4), 1896; W. Bousset, *op. cit.*; A. Harnack, *Chronologie der altchristl. Litteratur*, 1897, i. pp. 656 sqq.; W. Beyschlag, *St. Kr.*, 1898, pp. 71 sqq.

of its contents must first be sought. The chief fault of the internal ciriticism which has hitherto been bestowed upon the Gospel seems to me to be a tendency towards a too hasty generalisation, by which conclusions derived from one, or but a few, points or sections are extended to the whole Gospel narrative. To arrive at the truth we must distinguish, to a much greater degree than is generally practised, between different constituents in the text. There are certain indications, pointing to such a distinction, which have not yet, in my judgment, been adequately weighed and considered. As soon as the distinction is made, a clear light is thrown upon the obscurities of the external testimony.

CHAPTER I

EXAMINATION OF THE NARRATIVE PLAN OF THE FOURTH GOSPEL IN THE LIGHT OF THE SYNOPTIC RECORD

A. THE TRUE SYNOPTIC STANDARD

OUR inquiry whether, and to what extent, the account in the Fourth Gospel can be appraised as a trustworthy record need not be regulated by prepossessions, either of dogma or caprice. There is an objective standard at hand for our use. It is to be found in the oldest notices, other than these, which relate to the ministry and preaching of Jesus. We must test the Johannine record by the synoptic standard.

But what is the true synoptic standard? Is it to be found in the contents of the synoptic Gospels as a whole, without distinction? In those places where the synoptic account differs from the Johannine, may we assume as self-evident that the synoptic narrative is the true and authentic one? In order to make a right use of the synoptic Gospels as a standard we shall require a scientific understanding of the relations in which these Gospels stand to one another, and of the degree of credibility which is to be assigned to their separate notices. The criticism of the Synoptics is therefore an important part of our equipment when we begin to criticise the Fourth Gospel.

In spite of the great similarity of the contents of the three Gospels, the synoptic record cannot be treated as a

homogeneous whole. Account must be taken of many by
no means unimportant differences between them. Moreover, we cannot treat the three synoptic Gospels as three
equal, independent pieces of testimony. Their extensive
agreement, not only in the general outline of their narrative, but also in detailed expositions, an agreement which
makes the outstanding isolation of the Johannine account
so striking, is to be explained by the literary connection
which exists between them, and by their use of common
sources. Thanks to the century of critical labour which
has been devoted to the synoptic writers, we are able by
this time to treat a certain theory of their inter-relations as
established. Of our three Gospels, Mark [1] is the oldest;
the two others are founded on Mark: but both make use,
as a primary source, of another collection of speeches and
detached sayings of Jesus—probably the "Logia" of the
Apostle Matthew. It must be admitted that this "two-
source theory," as it is called, does not yield at all points a
satisfactory solution of the synoptic problem. There remain difficulties which must be solved by supplementary
hypotheses. .But with regard to a great number of very
important points this theory does really afford a clear and
firm conclusion. And it is of value for those points which
come into special prominence in the comparison of the
Johannine record with that of the Synoptics.

If by the help of this criticism we distinguish between
a primary and a secondary element, between an older and
a more recent tradition in the first three Gospels, it follows
that in our inquiry into their relation to the Fourth Gospel
we must pay special heed to the question whether the
Johannine account agrees with the older elements in the
synoptic tradition,—this is, with Mark, and with the

---

[1] For convenience the names Matthew, Mark, Luke, John are used
as the names of the Gospels. When used personally they will be
qualified by some title, such as "The Apostle John."

"Logia" which can be disengaged from our First and Third Gospels. It will not be enough to ask whether there are many single incidents and sayings in which such an agreement can be traced. If the Fourth Gospel is really founded on an independent apostolic record, some considerable difference in the matter recorded is only what we should expect — is indeed a sign of its independence. The way in which our question must be framed is this: Does the general historical conception which pervades the Fourth Gospel agree with that which is to be found throughout the older synoptic tradition; or are there any decisive features in which it departs from that general conception, and betrays a kinship with the secondary elements in the synoptic record?

B. THE RELATION OF THE JOHANNINE NARRATIVE TO THE SYNOPTIC TRADITION

1. *The Festal Journeys of Jesus to Jerusalem*

When we begin to compare the historical conception of Jesus' public ministry in John with that of the Synoptics our attention is instantly caught by a difference with respect to the scene of Jesus' activity. The Fourth Gospel notices several journeys of Jesus to Jerusalem to keep a feast (ii. 13, v. 1, vii. 10, x. 22, xii. 1). Most of the speeches and discussions which it records take place in Jerusalem. In the Synoptics, on the other hand, the chief part of Jesus' public ministry took place on the soil of Galilee. They speak (if we leave out of sight Luke ii. 22 sqq. and 41 sqq.) of but one stay made by Jesus in Jerusalem, that which ended in His death.

Is the synoptic testimony on this point a concurrence of several independent witnesses? Strictly speaking it is only the historical outline of Mark which is so strikingly at variance with that of the Fourth Gospel. Our first and third evangelists, in giving this outline, are only following Mark. At the same time, however, they record the utterance of Jesus, derived from the Logia (Matt. xxiii. 37; Luke xiii. 34), "O Jerusalem, Jerusalem ... how often would I have gathered thy children together," etc. This utterance is a very important piece of evidence in favour of the Johannine view. It is, of course, possible to hold that Jesus is here using the words "children of Jerusalem," in the sense of Galatians iv. 25, to mean the people of Israel in general. But it is much more natural to suppose that He meant the inhabitants of Jerusalem, and was referring to the fact that He had often preached among them. Again, the section from the Logia (Luke ix. 51–56), with which the long Logia episode in Luke (ix. 51–xviii. 14) begins, relates to a journey of Jesus through Samaria to Jerusalem. It is true that by the introductory words (Luke ix. 51a) this is represented as the last journey. But that note of time belongs, without question, to the evangelist Luke, who interpolated the Logia into Mark's narrative. Since Mark recounts only one journey of Jesus to Judæa, Luke naturally selected the beginning of that journey (Mark x. 1) as the appropriate place in Mark's chronological framework for the introduction of this passage. In the source itself, however,—in which we have still to read of the sending-out of the disciples (Luke x. 1 sqq.) and their return (x. 17), and afterwards how Jesus "went through the cities and villages, teaching" (xiii. 22),—it seems certain that the journey to Jerusalem which is here meant was not the last (cf. xvii. 11).

Galilee was doubtless the chief scene of Jesus' activity, but that does not preclude the possibility that Jesus may in His preaching journeys have visited Jerusalem several times. During the first period of His ministry He was clearly seeking to spread far and wide among the people of

Israel the glad tidings, so rousing and attractive, that the kingdom of God was at hand. To this end He went preaching from place to place (Mark i. 38 sq.). When He found His own strength inadequate to the great field of labour He sent out His disciples, that they too might carry forth those glad tidings to the "lost sheep of the house of Israel." Would He, during this expansive period of His ministry, have held Himself far aloof from Jerusalem, the centre of the worship, the scriptural learning, the pious hopes of the Israelitish nation? Since Mark's account of these preaching journeys of Jesus is nowhere characterised by much detail,—for instance, he does not allude to His mighty work in Chorazin and Bethsaida (Matt. ii. 21; Luke x. 13),—it cannot seem strange that he should omit to record the transient earlier visits of Jesus to Jerusalem.[1] On the other hand, it is easily intelligible that another independent narrator should be led to dwell especially upon the abode of Jesus in the chief city, and His conflicts with the Jews who lived there. Moreover, in the Fourth Gospel Jerusalem is by no means represented as the scene of any long, continuous ministry on Jesus' part. His visits there are short visits for the sake of the Feast. Mention is made, besides, of His public appearance in Galilee (ii. 1–12, iv. 43–54) and the long stay which He made there (vi. 1–vii. 10).

What is to be thought of the definite number of the festal visits to Jerusalem mentioned in the Fourth Gospel, and of the historicity of the separate events which are assigned to each of them, is a question apart, and one, as

[1] Recollections of an earlier stay which Jesus had made at Jerusalem may perhaps underlie the notices of the disputes of Jesus (Mark xii. 13–37). These disputes, whose style and manner hardly suits the situation indicated in Mark xii. 12 and xiv. 1 sqq., plainly form, in the older record which Mark has reproduced, a continuation of the contests in Mark ii. 1–iii. 6. Cf. the close connection of xii. 13 with iii. 6. See my *Lehre Jesu*, i. pp. 25 sq.

we shall see later, which must be considered from various sides. For the moment we will only recall the one point, that the cleansing of the Temple, according to the fourth evangelist (ii. 13–22), belonged to Jesus' first festal visit to Jerusalem, whereas according to Mark xi. 15–18 (and parallels) it belonged to His last stay there. To harmonise the two accounts by assuming that Jesus cleansed the Temple twice, is out of the question. Such a demonstrative act, the expression of a holy zeal, can only once be morally justified. With which of the two different accounts does the greater probability lie? Decidedly with Mark. In Mark the cleansing of the Temple is an effective part of the development of that conflict between Jesus and the chief priests, in His last visit to Jerusalem (Mark xi. 27–xii. 12), which brought about the end. In the Fourth Gospel, on the contrary, it stands at the beginning of Jesus' work as an isolated occurrence, disconnected, without sequel. It is easy to understand the evangelist's reason for placing this incident at the beginning of his narrative. It contains the record of an oracular prediction, the fulfilment of which was intended to confirm the faith of the disciples (ii. 22). It seemed appropriate that this utterance should follow immediately after the narrative of the sign in Cana, by which Jesus awakened that faith for the first time (ver. 11).

But after due weight has been given to every consideration which can be urged against this point and many other points of the Johannine account, there is nothing to justify us in refusing to acknowledge that Jesus may really have made several visits to Jerusalem. Such a theory is, as we saw, actually supported by some indications in the older synoptic tradition.

2. *The Date of Jesus' Death*

A similar conclusion will be reached with regard to the difference about the date of Jesus' death. According to the fourth evangelist Jesus was crucified on that day on the evening of which the Jews ate the Passover, that is, on the 14th Nisan (xviii. 28).[1] But according to the synoptic view, based on Mark, Jesus kept the Passover meal with His disciples on the evening before His death (Mark xiv. 12 sqq. and parallels), so that His death would be on the 15th Nisan. This is a case where the record in the Fourth Gospel may claim the greater internal probability.[2] How are we to explain the haste with which events were hurried forward after the arrest of Jesus? He was arrested late in the evening; tried by night before the Sanhedrin; taken at daybreak before Pilate; the execution itself followed immediately on the sentence, and the burial upon the death. It can only be understood if we suppose that the arrest of Jesus, which was made possible by Judas' treachery, happened on the evening of the 13th Nisan: the utmost haste would then be needed to bring the whole trial, execution, and burial to an end before the beginning of the Feast,—that is, before sunset on the 14th Nisan. On the other hand, it is most improbable that strict formalists such as were the Jewish leaders would bring about the arrest on the evening of the 14th Nisan after the solemn Passover meal; and would hold the trial, wring from Pilate the final sentence, and press for an immediate crucifixion, all upon the ensuing first day of the Feast, for which a full Sabbath observance was prescribed by the law (Ex. xii. 16). The notice in Mark (xv. 46), that Joseph of Arimathea bought fine linen to enwrap the body of Jesus, is a piece of evidence furnished by Mark itself in favour of the Johannine record. At midnight on the 15th Nisan such a purchase can hardly have been possible.

[1] Cf. E. Schürer, *Ueber φαγεῖν τὸ πάσχα*, J. xviii. 28, Giessen, 1883.
[2] Cf. the opinion of O. Holtzmann, *Das Johannesevangelium*, p. 35.

3. *The Testimony of the Baptist concerning Jesus*

There are, however, other points in reference to which the accuracy of the Fourth Gospel must decidedly be contested. These points are all concerned with the attestation and acknowledgment of Jesus' Messiahship,—a matter, surely, of substantial importance in any representation of the Messianic appearance and work of Jesus. The difference of the Johannine from the synoptic account in these points does not obtrude itself in a merely superficial examination of the three Gospels, but, if we distinguish in the manner indicated above between the older and the more recent elements in the synoptic tradition, it then becomes clear that the Johannine narrative stands in contradiction to the older element, and is an extension of the more recent tradition.

The first of these points touches the witness which was borne by the Baptist to the Messiahship of Jesus. In the Fourth Gospel the Baptist is represented several times, with special emphasis, as the person who was to make Him known. Even in the prologue allusion is made to the mission of the Baptist, to bear witness of the light that was coming into the world (i. 6–8), and to the matter of his testimony (ver. 15). Then we are told how the Baptist bore record of the meaning of his own person and his baptism (19–34). He was not the Messiah, nor was he Elias, nor that prophet; none, in fact, of the bearers of revelation, and of the salvation of God in the last days, who had been announced in the Old Testament. His work was only to make straight the ways for a greater that was to come (vv. 19–27). The object of his baptism was to make this greater one known to the Israelites (ver. 31). In order that he might recognise Him when He came, for He was as yet unknown to John, God had marked Him out by a sign: it should be He upon whom the Spirit would be seen descending (ver. 33). At the baptism of Jesus he saw this sign (ver. 32). Accordingly, he testifies to the Israelites that He who was to come is standing unrecognised among them (vv. 26 sq.). On the following day, when he sees Jesus he points Him out openly as the man whom he had meant,[1] and as the Son of God (ver. 34), and speaks in the same breath both of the death of this "Lamb of God" to take away sin, and of His pre-terrestrial existence (vv. 29 sq.). Thus the first members of the trusted circle of Jesus' disciples were disciples of the Baptist (vv. 35 sqq.). Once again, at a later time, the Baptist testifies to the heavenly origin and saving efficacy of this Messiah Jesus (iii. 27–36).

What is here represented in the Fourth Gospel is incompatible with the older synoptic tradition concerning the Baptist. According to Mark the Baptist preached that after him a mightier should come who should baptize with the Holy Spirit (i. 7 sq.). Beyond question he meant the Messiah, but Mark gives no indication that the Baptist recognised Jesus and made Him known as this coming Messiah. And again, he does not depict what happened to Jesus at the baptism as a revelation concerning Him vouchsafed to John. It is Jesus alone who sees the heavens opened and the Spirit descending upon Him. It is to Him alone that the word of revelation from Heaven which attests His Messiahship is addressed (vv. 9–11).[2]

---

[1] The theory of the narrative is here that, as a result of the sign which he saw at the baptism of Jesus, the Baptist did indeed know the aspect of the Messiah, but did not yet know His name. So it happens that on the first day he can only give the assurance that Messiah is actually already there (vv. 26 sq.). But on the second day, when he sees Jesus, he is able to point Him out, and so make Him known to the others.

[2] There is no inconsistency between this conception of the Baptist, which occurs at the beginning of the Gospel, and the later notice (Mark xi. 29 sqq.), in which Jesus is asked "By what authority doest thou these things?" and will not give an answer unless His questioners first reply to a question of His: "The baptism of John, was it from

There is a perfect agreement between this story as told in Mark and the account from the Logia of the embassy which the Baptist sent from prison to Jesus with the question, " Art thou He that cometh, or look we for another?" (Matt. xi. 2–6; Luke vii. 18–23). This question is only intelligible on the supposition that the Baptist did not conceive until he was in prison, and then only doubtfully, the possibility that Jesus might be the Messiah whom he had proclaimed. The explanation that the Baptist had indeed recognised and testified to the Messiahship of Jesus, as is recorded in the Fourth Gospel, but afterwards fell into doubt because the manner of Jesus' appearance did not accord with his expectations of the Messiah, is excluded. Doubt of such a kind would be psychologically inconceivable if the Baptist had first obtained his knowledge of the Messiahship of Jesus through an express divine revelation, and if he had himself acclaimed Jesus as the Lamb of God which taketh away the sins of the world, and thereby confessed the necessity for Messianic suffering in fulfilment of Isa. liii. Such an assumption would also be inconsistent with Jesus' eulogy, uttered after that embassy, of the unshrinking firmness of the Baptist (Matt. xi. 7; Luke vii. 24). Another reason which excludes the idea that the Baptist had recognised and proclaimed to others the Messiahship of Jesus is to be found in Jesus' criticism of the Baptist, which follows in the same Logia passage; the sense is that John is outside the kingdom of God, and therefore though

Heaven, or of men?" The object of this counter-question cannot have been to cite the Baptist's testimony to His Messiahship as a proof of His divine authority. In that case Jesus would have asked—not whether the baptism but—whether the preaching of John was from Heaven or of men; and in ver. 31, instead of the aorist ἐπιστεύσατε He would have used the present. His aim was rather to test His questioners' capacity for judging whether His authority were divine or human. When they themselves confessed that they were incapable of judging the origin and nature of the Baptist's work, they must also be incompetent, declared Jesus (ver. 33), to judge His own.

among those born of women there hath not arisen a greater than he, yet he stands below the least in the kingdom of God (Matt. xi. 11–14; Luke vii. 28). If the Baptist had been, as the fourth evangelist represents, the first to recognise and acknowledge, and lead others to acknowledge, Jesus' Messiahship, he could hardly have been spoken of as standing himself outside the kingdom of God. He would have been the first and a specially prominent member of the kingdom.

The view of the relation of the Baptist to Jesus which we discover in Mark and in the Logia, is further confirmed by an account which comes from quite another source: when Paul came to Ephesus there were in that city disciples of John who were not disciples of Jesus, and who did not yet know of the existence of the Holy Spirit, though the Baptist had proclaimed that it would be bestowed by the coming Messiah (Acts xix. 1–7).[1] If the teaching of the Baptist had actually consisted in making Jesus manifest as Messiah, the separate existence of such disciples of John would be inconceivable. Their discipleship to the Baptist would necessarily have led them to attach themselves to Jesus and associate with Him.

It soon, however, began to be regarded by Christendom as self-evident that the Baptist, the prophet who prepared the way for Messiah (Luke i. 76), must have known Jesus explicitly as such. This idea was already to be met with in the more recent synoptic tradition. How characteristic are the modifications with which Matthew reproduces Mark's account of the baptism of Jesus! The insertion of the Baptist's astonished question, "I have need to be baptized of thee, and comest thou to me?" (Matt. iii. 14), presupposes that John knew Jesus as the Mightier one whose

[1] For the origin of this account in the Acts and on the relation of John's disciples here to Apollos (Acts xviii. 24 sqq.), cf. my commentary on the Acts (Meyer's *Komm.* iii.), 8th ed., 1899, pp. 308 sq.

coming he had preached. And the voice from Heaven (iii. 17) here takes the form not of an address to Jesus, but of an announcement about Him: it is conceived, that is to say, as a revelation to the Baptist concerning Jesus. In Luke, at the very beginning of the narrative, the mother of the Baptist and the mother of Jesus speak, even before the birth of their children, of what has been revealed by angels about their nature and significance (Luke i. 39–55); and, before the history of the Baptist's appearance begins, the presumption is established that he must have known of Jesus' Messiahship. This view, which obtains in the more recent synoptic tradition, is yet further developed in the fourth Gospel.

4. *The Publication of Jesus' Messiahship*

There is another important point with regard to which the Johannine account, when compared with the synoptic, must be called in question: this relates to Jesus' own avowal of His Messiahship, and its recognition by others. According to the Fourth Gospel the first disciples of Jesus, immediately after the Baptist's testimony, expressed their clear recognition of His Messianic office (i. 41, 45). From Nathanael, who at first doubted, Jesus evokes an acknowledgment at their first meeting (i. 49). Again, to the Samaritan woman, and afterwards to the man blind from his birth, He makes Himself directly known as Messiah (iv. 25 sq.; ix. 35–38). His Messiahship is also openly recognised by considerable classes of people; by the dwellers in that Samaritan city after His abode there for two days (iv. 42), and by the Galilean multitude after they had seen the miracle of the feeding (vi. 14 sq.).

How do these notices stand towards what is represented in Mark? According to Mark the Messiahship of Jesus, which was made known to Himself at His Baptism by the divine revelation, remained hidden, during the greater part of His public ministry, from other men, because Jesus purposely withheld its publication. He began His career by preaching that the kingdom of God was at hand, but did not point to Himself as its Messiah (i. 14 sq.). Only those who were possessed by evil spirits understood at that time what Jesus was. But Jesus forbade them to make Him known (i. 24 sq. 34, iii. 11 sq.). All other men asked in astonishment who He could be, and raised various conjectures about Him (i. 27, iii. 21 sq., iv. 41, vi. 14 sq., viii. 28). It was concealed, at first, even from the Twelve that Jesus was Himself the Messiah. Peter's confession on the way to Cæsarea Philippi was the first definite recognition among them of His Messiahship (viii. 29). And even the Twelve were charged by Jesus to tell no man of Him (ver. 30). It is the epoch-making novelty of Peter's confession which accounts for the date of the new teaching; then it was that Jesus "began to teach them" that He must needs suffer, and die by violence (vv. 31 sqq.). As soon as they recognised His Messianic office, for fear they should attach false hopes to it, they must be intrusted with the knowledge of that which was, according to Jewish ideas, strangely discrepant with the Messianic idea. The first public proclamation of Jesus as Messiah by His Galilean adherents ensued at His entry into Jerusalem, and not before (xi. 9 sq.). It was by His sufferance of the blind man's salute before Jericho, "Thou son of David" (x. 46–52), and by the fulfilment, in the manner of His entry, of the prophecy in Zach. ix. 9, that His disciples were stirred up to prepare for Him such Messianic homage. But Jesus Himself never publicly put forth His claim to be the Messiah until His trial before the High Priest (xiv. 61 sq.). After the previous hearing of witnesses had led to no result (vv. 55–59), this confession of Jesus Himself had the effect of breaking off the examination of witnesses as superfluous, and bringing about His condemnation forthwith (vv. 63 sq.). This makes it clear that Jesus had not up to that time openly professed the title of Messiah. Such a claim, which was regarded as blasphemous, could not be brought home to Him, and no one had expected that He Himself would now make it before the Sanhedrin.

In Mark then we have a logically consecutive account, with which those Johannine notices cannot be reconciled. If the confession of Peter had the epoch-making significance which Mark assigns to it, it is impossible that Jesus' Messiahship had been recognised by the Twelve from the beginning. And if Jesus withheld the direct announcement of His Messiahship so strictly as Mark represents, He cannot have proclaimed it outright between whiles, as the Fourth Gospel says He did to the Samaritan woman. The reason for Jesus' abstinence from the title of Messiah must have lain in His knowledge that it would immediately arouse ideas and hopes, concerning the nature and scope of His ministry, such as He could not and would not fulfil. His first object was therefore to teach the true nature of the kingdom of God. Then those who listened to His preaching would be able to understand aright and to observe for themselves that He was the God-sent, Messianic mediator, who should bring this kingdom of salvation to pass. If we consider this educational aim of Jesus in connection with His abstinence from the Messianic title, we cannot believe that He occasionally lapsed in an inconsequent way into another kind of behaviour.

The later tradition, however, treats it as self-evident that Jesus appeared openly as Messiah from the beginning, and found, and willingly accepted, a public recognition of His Messiahship. Matthew relates that before the confession of Peter, Jesus had been hailed with the Messianic style " Son of David" by two blind men (ix. 27), by the multitude after the healing of a demoniac (xii. 23), even by the heathen Canaanitish woman (xv. 22), and that after the miraculous walking on the water He had been worshipped by His disciples as "Son of God" (xiv. 33). A comparison of Matt. xii. 23 with Luke xi. 14, of Matt. xv. 22 with Mark vii. 25 sq., of Matt. xiv. 33 with Mark vi. 51 sq., shows that our first evangelist has in these places freely modified his subject-matter in accordance with his presupposition of the early recognition of Jesus' Messiahship. It is this same presupposition which reveals itself in these notices in the Fourth Gospel.

5. *The Signs of Jesus*

A third important point of difference between the Johannine and the older synoptic account relates to the miracles of Jesus. In the Johannine narrative the "Signs" of Jesus play a peculiarly important part. That evangelist tells us at the end, that he has, out of the multitude of Jesus' signs, written those which are to be found in his book, in order that the readers may believe that Jesus is the Messiah, the Son of God (30 sq.). In the same spirit he has already made it prominent, both in his detailed account of single signs and in his remarks about the ministry of Jesus in general, that the signs of Jesus were the ground of belief in Him (ii. 11, 23, iv. 45, 53 sq., vi. 2, 14 xi. 45, xii. 11, 18).

What is the meaning of the term "Signs," $\sigma\eta\mu\epsilon\hat{\iota}\alpha$, in the Fourth Gospel? The most important element in the concept is this, that the signs are *miraculous* events, such as cannot be explained by the ordinary course of nature or by ordinary human powers. Herein lies, according to the evangelist's view, their significance as credentials of Jesus' Messiahship. The word $\sigma\eta\mu\epsilon\hat{\iota}o\nu$ has in itself, of course, a more general sense. Etymologically the words $\sigma\eta\mu\epsilon\hat{\iota}\alpha$ and $\tau\epsilon\rho\alpha\tau\alpha$ are clearly distinct. But in the usage of the New Testament the term σημεῖον prefers the special sense of "miraculous sign," and this special sense prevails throughout the Fourth Gospel. Yet the root-meaning of "sign" is by no means eliminated; it is not by accident that in the Fourth Gospel the expression σημεῖα is constantly used, and not τέρατα.[1] The σημεῖα of Jesus are to be actual guides and tokens—tokens of something which has a religious significance, His divine glory and Messiahship (ii. 11). But, on the other hand, it still remains that they are *wonderful* occurrences, and that in their wonderful character their evidential force is specially to be found.

The fact that the miraculous is so essential a part of the concept does not of course prevent the signs of Jesus from being at the same time works of love. He uses them to help the needy, the sick, the sorrowing. Yet it is not always by sympathy with actual need that He is led, according to the Fourth Gospel, to perform a miracle. At the marriage in Cana the lack which was supplied by the miraculous wine was a lack, after all, only of a luxury, and the quantity supplied, fifteen to eighteen firkins (ii. 6), far exceeded what was required. In the miracle of the feeding, too, as told in this Gospel (vi. 5 sqq.), there is no mention of any real need among the crowd that was fed. In the conception of the evangelist the element in the "Signs" of Jesus which manifests His glory and accredits His Messiahship is not that they are tokens of His love, but that they are tokens of His wonderful power. By their side, with a similar attesting force, but without the title σημεῖα to denote them, there stand certain tokens of the wonderful knowledge of Jesus. By means of these also Jesus gave, in single cases, overwhelming testimony to His Messiahship, and evoked belief in Himself (i. 49 sq., ii. 22, iv. 16–19, 29, 39).

Our conclusion that the chief matter concerning the signs of Jesus in the Fourth Gospel is their wonderful

---
[1] The collocation σημεῖα καὶ τέρατα occurs only once, iv. 48.

character is not affected by the perception that several of the great signs recorded appear as it were allegories of the spiritual events of which Jesus speaks in the discourses bound up with them.[1] The miraculous bodily healing, which Jesus wrought on the sick man at the Pool of Bethesda (v. 1–16), seems like a material image of the gift of eternal life, of which He speaks in v. 20–27; the miraculous bodily feeding of the multitude (vi. 1–13), an image of the food which abideth unto eternal life (vi. 27–58); the opening of the eyes of the man blind from his birth (ix. 1 sqq.), an image of the gift of sight to the spiritually blind (ix. 39–41); the raising of Lazarus to the earthly life, an image of that resurrection to eternal life which, in speech with Martha, Jesus promises to all that believe (xi. 23 sqq.). We are not, however, to suppose that the evangelist looked upon these signs as being, first and chiefly, symbolic performances, or a mere introduction to the analogous spiritual events, which are, in that case, the actually important events, and the really valid tokens of Jesus' Messiahship. In such a conclusion we should be misled. Even those signs, the record of which appears to have a symbolic meaning, are certainly looked upon at the same time as miracles in the realistic sense. It is on account of their wonderful nature that they are called signs, not on account of their allegorical reference to higher spiritual events. Their significance for the arousing of belief does not lie in their connection with what Jesus says about the analogous spiritual events, but in the miracles themselves, before Jesus discourses upon them, and without reference to what He says (cf. vi. 14, ix. 24–38, xi. 45, xii. 11). In this way the signs of Jesus considered in general, and not only the single miracles which take a symbolic character through their connection with

[1] Cf. Haupt. *St. Kr.*, 1893, pp. 240 sqq., and especially H. Holtzmann, *Neut. Theologie*, ii. pp. 376 sq.

Jesus' discourses, are treated as a means for begetting faith in Jesus. On the other hand, such an incident as the washing of feet (xiii. 1 sqq.), which has an entirely symbolic character and illustrates in the most significant manner the religious lesson with which Jesus follows it, is nevertheless no σημεῖον in the sense of the fourth evangelist, because it is not a miraculous display of His higher power.

But the point which we must now, in our criticism of the Fourth Gospel, especially consider, is not the concept of the σημεῖα, which has no other sense here than in the other Gospels, nor yet the general fact that Jesus performs miracles, but the manner in which He performs them. According to this Gospel, Jesus from the beginning of His ministry worked many miraculous signs so publicly that they were seen of many (ii. 23, iii. 2, iv. 45, vi. 2). So it befell that not only were His miracles acknowledged with astonishment by the multitude (vi. 14, vii. 31, x. 21, xi. 45, xii. 17-19), but even His enemies, the Jewish hierarchs, could not assail the notorious fact of their real occurrence (ix. 13-34, xi. 47, xii. 37). Not only was it, as a matter of fact, in consequence of His wonderful signs that men believed in Jesus (ii. 11, 23, iv. 53, vi. 14, xi. 45, xii. 11); it was with an eye to this effect that Jesus Himself performed them. He said to the crowds that sought Him on the day after the miraculous feeding,

Verily, verily, I say unto you, ye seek me, not because ye saw signs, but because ye ate of the loaves and were filled" (vi. 26). That is, He upbraids them for seeking Him only on account of their practical advantage in what He did, and for failing to appreciate its miraculous character, and to believe on Him, as they ought to have done, for the sake of the miracle. This intention of Jesus to accredit Himself by a public display of miraculous power comes out most clearly in the story of the raising of Lazarus. When He hears of His friend's sickness, He deliberately defers the journey to

Bethany (which His love for Lazarus would have urged Him to undertake at once), in order that He may give so much the grander proof of His miraculous power, and therein of His glory (xi. 6, 15); and His manner of bringing to pass the miracle of raising a man dead for four days becomes a demonstration before the many Jews assembled at the grave (xi. 38–46).

Does this style and character of Jesus' thaumaturgy accord with the account in the older synoptic record? In that also the preaching of the kingdom of God by Jesus was accompanied by wonderful deeds. He healed sick people and drove out demons (Mark i. 34, 39, iii. 10; Luke xiii. 32). He exhorted His disciples to do the like, when He sent them forth in His lifetime to spread the tidings of the coming of the kingdom (Luke x. 9; Matt. x. 8; cf. Mark iii. 15, vi. 7, 13). The refreshment and deliverance of the wretched was to be a sign that the time of salvation, foretold in the Old Testament, was now come (Matt. xi. 5 sq.; Luke iv. 17–21). In this work of help and healing Jesus knew that He and His disciples were not restrained by natural law. He trusted in God, and was sure that to him who trusted, with God's almighty help, all things, even the most wonderful, were possible (Mark ix. 23, xi. 22–24; Luke xvii. 5 sq.). But the real significance of these deeds lay, for Him, not in their wonderful character, but in that they were tokens of helpful and healing love for those that needed help and healing. So He associates with them, as a sign of the dawn of the Messianic day of salvation, His preaching of the Gospel to the poor, which has nothing miraculous in its character (Matt. xi. 5; Luke iv. 18 sq.). In the eyes of others His healing of the sick did not show itself as primarily thaumaturgic, but as a labour of help and service, begotten of love; this is clear from His repeated conflicts with the Pharisees about healing on the Sabbath day. The mere utterance of a command,

"Be thou healed," and the miraculous recovery following upon such a command, could not have been construed even by the straitest standard as a breach of the Sabbath rest. But Jesus' doings among the sick appeared to the Pharisees as the labour of a physician, and so came under the conception of "work" forbidden on the Sabbath (Luke xiii. 14 sq.). Jesus' own reason for refusing to relinquish this work was that He knew God desired mercy, and not sacrifice (Matt. xii. 7). Such deeds, however, as bore a strikingly miraculous character Jesus sought, as appears from several notices in Mark, to screen from publicity. He refused to do them before many witnesses, and forbade people to speak of them (Mark i. 43 sq., v. 37–43, vii. 33–36, viii. 22–26; cf. Matt. ix. 30). He would not that He should be sought and believed in for the sake of the miraculous. Those who asked of Him a sign from heaven, received, according to the concurrent account of Mark (viii. 11 sq.) and the Logia (Matt. xii. 38 sq.; Luke xi. 16, 29), a flat refusal. His miraculous help was for those, and those only, who put faith in Him and His tidings of the kingdom of God (Mark vi. 5 sq.). Jesus must clearly have recognised that those who made their faith conditional upon some preliminary display of miracle could not in this way attain a faith of the right kind: not the true salvation of the kingdom of God.

Signs of the same attitude of Jesus towards His miracles are preserved even in the Fourth Gospel. We shall take account of them later. We must first, however, establish that the style and character of Jesus' thaumaturgy as generally depicted in the Fourth Gospel differs substantially from that ascribed to Him in the synoptic sources. It is impossible to combine these two demeanours, and hold that both are truly ascribed to Him, without depriving Jesus of all claim to any fixed principle. If Jesus performed His signs, as a rule, in the fullest publicity, if His desire and object in them was to awaken belief in His Messiahship, so that men might seek Him for their sake (John vi. 26), what sense would there be in His making occasional efforts in single cases to suppress the publication of His miracles, and roughly upbraiding those who asked Him for a sign? He can only have observed one or the other, not both, of these two attitudes.

On this point, however, the representation in the Fourth Gospel does not stand alone. The secondary synoptic tradition has no comprehension of any shrinking on Jesus' part from the publication of His miracles. This is seen in several single cases, where the older record is altered by the later hand. From Mark's narrative of the raising of the daughter of Jairus (v. 37–43) Matthew omits the statement that Jesus only permitted a very small circle of witnesses, and also the charge "that no man should know this" (ix. 23–26). In the place of Mark's account of the secret healing of a deaf-mute, whereof Jesus "charged them that they should tell no man" (vii. 32–36), Matthew tells of a great, public healing of the multitude (xv. 29–31). The account in Mark of the healing of a blind man, which likewise was performed apart from other men (viii. 22–26), is passed over by both the collateral narratives. In the account in the Logia of Jesus' answer to the messengers of the Baptist,—that they should tell how in his ministry the prophetic promises of salvation (Isa. xxxv. 5 sq., lxi. 1) were being fulfilled (Matt. xi. 2–6),—Luke interpolates the notice that "in that hour he cured many of all kinds of sufferers" (vii. 21). And in order to give to Jesus' expression, "the dead are raised up,"—which was certainly used by Jesus Himself in a metaphorical sense (cf. Luke xv. 24, 32; John v. 21, 24–27),—the force of a reference to a notorious miracle, Luke inserts, before the Baptist's embassy, the story of the raising of the dead at Nain, which happened in full publicity (Luke vii. 11–17). There is a special tendency in the secondary synoptic record to multiply the miracles of Jesus. Where Mark records that of the sick who were brought to Him Jesus healed many, the later narrators say that He healed all (cf. Mark i. 34 with Matt. viii. 16, Luke iv. 40; Mark iii. 10 with Matt. iv. 24, xii. 15, Luke vi. 17–19). Where Mark speaks only of the teaching of Jesus, they either substitute or add a healing (cf. Mark. ii. 2 with Luke v. 17*b*; Mark vi. 34 with Matt. xiv. 14, Luke ix. 11; Mark x. 1 with Matt. xix. 2; Mark xi. 17 sq. with Matt. xxi. 14). Where Mark relates that at the arrest of Jesus one of the bystanders cut off the ear of the High Priest's servant with a sword (xiv. 47), Luke adds that Jesus touched the ear and healed it (xxii. 51). The sub-apostolic generation of Christians regarded Jesus' miracles as most important tokens of His Messiahship, and thought it self-evident that Jesus worked those miracles on every occasion before all people. Our fourth evangelist, by the strong emphasis which he lays on Jesus' thaumaturgy, ranges himself with this sub-apostolic conception.

It is also very characteristic how the fourth evangelist, with obvious intention, seeks to repel certain doubts which necessarily arise when the chief stress is laid on Jesus' miracles, and the decisive proof of His Messiahship is found in them. How does it fit in with Jesus' miraculous higher knowledge, that He was deceived in Judas Iscariot, and admitted him into the circle of the Twelve? that He was outwitted by Judas' treachery? that He betook Himself to Jerusalem, into the midst of a hostile hierarchy? How does it fit in with His miraculous higher power, that He was overpowered by His enemies without a struggle? to these questions the evangelist gives answers such as are not contained in the synoptic tradition. Jesus was not really deceived in Judas. He always knew him as the devil that should betray Him (vi. 64, 70 sq.). Nor was He surprised by his betrayal; on the contrary, He had not only, at His last meeting with the Twelve, plainly pointed Judas out as the betrayer (xiii. 11, 18 sq., 21–30), but had even Himself urged Judas to do his treacherous work more quickly than he had intended (xiii. 27). In the account of the Last Supper, where Jesus speaks of the traitor, the progress from the primary to the secondary synoptic tradition, and thence to the Johannine version, is very plain. According to Mark xiv. 18-21 Jesus says that one of the Twelve, one of His table companions, one that dips with Him in the same dish (BC*: εἰς τὸ ἓν τρύβλιον), will betray Him. Doubtless Jesus means Judas; but it is clear that He does not specially indicate him in these words, since all who sat at the table ate from the same dish. In Matt. xxvi. 21 sqq., however, there is an interpolation made in the reproduction of this account from Mark (vv. 21-24): Judas asked Jesus the question, "Is it I, Rabbi?" and Jesus answered, "Thou hast said" (v. 25). Here then Judas is directly indicated as the traitor. In this sense, next, the whole scene is altered in the Fourth Gospel. Here also Jesus says no more at first than that it is one of those who were there (xiii. 21). But then, instead of the words "one that dips with me in the dish," which leave the person of the betrayer undetermined, we have this answer to the disciple whom Jesus loved, "he it is for whom I shall dip the sop, and give it him," and the statement that He gave the sop to Judas (vv. 25 sq.). Judas is thus clearly made known as the traitor. Jesus then addresses to him a further charge, to proceed with his betrayal (ver. 27).—Just as He was not deceived in Judas, so neither was He, according to the fourth evangelist, deceived in the inhabitants of Jerusalem. At the very beginning, when many in Jerusalem had faith in Him, He for His part put no faith in them, because He knew what was in man (ii. 23-25). He explained the removal of the scene of His ministry from Judæa to Galilee, at a time when He had found nothing but acknowledgment in Jerusalem and Judæa, by the remark that a prophet has no honour in his own home;

that is, assuming Jesus to have been born in Bethlehem, that He would find no honour in Judæa (iv. 44).[1] It is not, however, against His will that Jesus is overpowered by His enemies. The evangelist brings clearly out that their murderous intentions were repeatedly frustrated, because the time which Jesus had Himself fixed was not yet come (vii. 30, 44, viii. 20*b*, x. 39). When at last the hour struck in which, according to His Father's decree, He should drink the cup of suffering (xviii. 11), even then the large band sent to arrest Him,—which was made up not only, as in the synoptic account (Mark xiv. 43 and parallels), of servants of the Jewish rulers, but besides them of the Roman cohort (ἡ σπεῖρα) under the command of a chiliarch (John xviii. 3, 12; cf. Acts xxi. 31),—showed itself unable

[1] The taking of πατρίς (iv. 44) as meant for Judæa seems to me required by the context. Jesus' remark is given as an explanation of His departing from Samaria not towards Judæa, but towards Galilee. If by πατρίς Galilee were meant, and if the sense were that Jesus thought He could remain in Galilee unnoticed in retirement, whereas He found at the hands of the inhabitants a friendly reception (ver. 45), there would surely be a disjunctive particle at the beginning of ver. 45 to mark the contrast between Jesus' expectation and the event. The circumstance that according to the synoptic tradition (Mark vi. 4; Matt. xiii. 57; Luke iv. 24) Jesus' saying about a prophet's lack of honour in his own country referred to Nazareth, does not prove that the fourth evangelist may not have thought that so generally expressed a dictum referred first and properly to the proper native land of Jesus, Judæa, and was uttered by Him with that intent. The fourth evangelist was acquainted with our First and Third Gospels, as may certainly be discovered from many points of literary contact, into which we shall go more exactly hereafter. He must therefore have known of the tradition of Jesus' birth at Bethlehem. He does indeed relate in i. 46 sq., vii. 41 sq., 52 how the Messiahship of Jesus was called in question because He passed for a Galilean of Nazareth, whereas the Messiah ought, according to the promise, to be a Bethlehemite. But we cannot conclude from this that the fourth evangelist really thought that Jesus had failed, in this point, to correspond with the promise. He may have taken the birth at Bethlehem for granted, as a fact well known to Christians through the earlier Gospel writings, and have meant to bring out, by those notices in i. 46 sq., vii. 41 sq., 52, that the usual designation of Jesus as "Jesus of Nazareth" had been a hindrance to the faith of the Jews, who did not know of His birth in Bethlehem.

to do Him any harm until He gave Himself up of His own free will into their power (xviii. 4–8).

The high estimation of the signs of Jesus, as the decisive proofs of His Messiahship, is not in any degree modified by what Jesus said to the king's officer in Capernaum, "If ye do not see signs and wonders, ye will not believe" (iv. 48); and to Thomas, "Blessed are they that have not seen and yet have believed" (xx. 29). The interpretation which takes these words as directed against the seeking for a sign is a distorted one. In each case the context shows that there is no intention to contrast a faith without signs with a faith founded on signs. The whole stress lies on the idea of *seeing*. A faith which depends upon its owner having *seen* a miracle with his own eyes is set over against one which, though it is concerned with miracles, has yet no prurient desire to *see* one, but believes the *word* which testifies to them. Thus the king's officer stood the test of a right faith when "he believed the word that Jesus spake unto him" about the miraculous healing of his sick son (iv. 50). So, on the other hand, Thomas earned the rebuke of the risen Jesus, because he would not believe the word of his fellow-disciples about the resurrection of the Lord until he had himself beheld the miracle. No exposition is needed to show how important the exhortation to believe without seeing was rendered by the very fact that faith in Jesus' Messiahship was founded on His miracles. Only the generation of the first disciples of Jesus had themselves seen them. None who came later could do more than hear the account of them. So the blessing upon those who have not seen and yet have believed is a very important preparation for the final word of the evangelist: "These signs are written that ye may believe that Jesus is the Christ, the Son of God" (xx. 31).

The outcome of our inquiry so far is that in several

important connections the historical narrative of the Fourth Gospel bears the stamp of the secondary tradition, and cannot be taken as true and credible. This fact, however, is decisive against the authorship of the Gospel by the Apostle John. It would, of course, be conceivable that in the later recollection of the apostle many single events and circumstances in the history of the life he had lived with Jesus might have been displaced, many might have appeared during his old age in another light, in a loftier meaning, than before. But with regard to such important general questions as these,—whether the Baptist had recognised and borne witness to Jesus before his ministry began, and whether Jesus Himself had made Himself publicly known from the beginning as Messiah, and accredited Himself by demonstrative miracles,—that the apostle should have lost the true view, and adopted that of the sub-apostolic generation,—a view with but a specious claim to loftiness, which actually destroys the whole significance of the development of Jesus' ministry and of His recognition as Messiah,—this is inconceivable.

C. THE LITERARY DEPENDENCE OF THE FOURTH GOSPEL ON THE SYNOPTICS

1. *The Acquaintance of the Fourth Evangelist with the Synoptic Literature in general*

Our view of the relation of the historical record in the Fourth Gospel to the synoptic tradition is further advanced, and the verdict which we have passed is confirmed, if we take into account the literary dependence of this Gospel on the Synoptics.

In spite of the obvious general contrast between his narrative and the synoptic tradition, the fourth evangelist was nevertheless acquainted with the synoptic literature.

NARRATIVE PLAN OF THE FOURTH GOSPEL 33

He must have known our three synoptic Gospels. This is revealed by his close verbal coincidence with them in those sections in which the same events are related. He also assumes an acquaintance with the synoptic tradition in his readers. In two places at the beginning we may perceive his intention to bring his separate account of the commencement of Jesus' public ministry into agreement with that tradition. When he is telling of the work of baptism by Jesus, which followed His first appearance in Galilee (ii. 1–12) and in Jerusalem (ii. 13–iii. 21), a baptism which went on side by side with that of John (iii. 22–iv. 3), he remarks "for John was not yet cast into prison" (iii. 24). As he has made no mention as yet of the imprisonment of the Baptist, and does not refer to it again, that remark can only be explained by an intention to fix the chronology of his account in connection with the synoptic tradition,—which, as his readers knew, recorded the imprisonment of the Baptist, and made Jesus' Galilean ministry date therefrom (Mark i. 14 sq.; Matt. iv. 1). That baptismal ministry of Jesus in Judæa was earlier, since the Baptist was still at large.—The same is true of the curious remark (iv. 54) that the healing of the son of the king's officer in Capernaum (iv. 46 sqq.) was "the second sign that Jesus did, having come out of Judæa into Galilee"; this remark is surprising, because it passes over the many signs which Jesus wrought at the feast in Jerusalem (ii. 23, iii. 2, iv. 45); it can only be explained as a reference to another record in which the miraculous help given to the king's officer in Capernaum appeared as Jesus' first sign in Galilee. That other record was the Logia, of which both our first and third evangelist made use as a source. In the Logia this episode stood right at the beginning, immediately after the great discourse of Jesus on righteousness; this is settled by the agreement of Matt. viii. 5 sqq. and Luke vii. 2 sqq. in the placing of this piece. The fourth evangelist must have had some

3

further acquaintance with it than is afforded by the derivative account in Matthew and Luke. In them the incident of the king's officer has lost the character of first miracle which it had in the Logia (cf. Matt. iv. 23 sq., viii. 2–4; Luke iv. 33, v. 26, vi. 6–11, 17–19).

The acquaintance of the fourth evangelist with the synoptic literature is now emphasised not only by the assailants of the apostolic authorship of the Gospel,[1] but also by most defenders of that theory.[2] It was also assumed by the ancient ecclesiastical tradition.[3] Indeed, the mere fact of such an acquaintance cannot be used as a disproof of the apostolic authorship. The peculiar value of this Gospel might be made to rest on its providing an apostolic complement to the synoptic literature. Only it must be asked whether the special use which is made of that earlier literature is of a kind that is compatible with the authorship of this Gospel by an apostolic eye-witness.

2. *The detailed Coincidences of the Fourth with the Synoptic Gospels*

In order to answer this question we must go in detail through the cases where the Fourth Gospel and the synoptic narratives coincide.

The first case of this kind occurs in the account of the Baptist's testimony (i. 19–34). We have already shown how the Johannine conception stands related to the primary and secondary synoptic tradition.[4] The parallelism between

---

[1] Cf. especially H. Holtzmann, *Zw. Th.*, 1869, pp. 62 sqq., 155 sqq., 446 sqq.; Jacobsen, *Untersuchungen über das Johannesev.*, 1884, pp. 46 sqq.; O. Holtzmann, *Das Johannesev.* pp. 6 sqq.

[2] Cf. especially Th. Zahn, *Einleitung in das N.T.*, 1899, ii. pp. 498 sqq.; *secus* O. Wuttig, *Das Joh.-Evang.*, 1897, pp. 5–19 and 52–59, who makes the Fourth Gospel precede the synoptic literature.

[3] Clement of Alex. in Euseb. *Hist. Eccl.* vi. 14, 7; cf. Euseb. *H. E.* iii. 24, 11.

[4] Cf. pp. 14 sqq.

NARRATIVE PLAN OF THE FOURTH GOSPEL 35

the Baptist's utterance in John i. 26 sq. and the passages Mark i. 7 sq., Matt. iii. 11, Luke iii. 16 is as follows:—

MARK.	MATTHEW.	LUKE.	JOHN.
ἔρχεται ὁ ἰσχυρότερός μου ὀπίσω μου, οὗ οὐκ εἰμὶ ἱκανὸς κύψας λῦσαι τὸν ἱμάντα τῶν ὑποδημάτων αὐτοῦ· ἐγὼ ἐβάπτισα ὑμᾶς ὕδατι, αὐτὸς δὲ βαπτίσει κ.τ.λ.	ἐγὼ μὲν ὑμᾶς βαπτίζω ἐν ὕδατι εἰς μετάνοιαν· ὁ δὲ ὀπίσω μου ἐρχόμενος ἰσχυρότερός μου ἐστίν, οὗ οὐκ εἰμὶ ἱκανὸς τὰ ὑποδήματα βαστάσαι· αὐτὸς ὑμᾶς βαπτίσει κ.τ.λ.	ἐγὼ μὲν ὕδατι βαπτίζω ὑμᾶς· ἔρχεται δὲ ὁ ἰσχυρότερός μου, οὗ οὐκ εἰμὶ ἱκανὸς λῦσαι τὸν ἱμάντα τῶν ὑποδημάτων αὐτοῦ· αὐτὸς ὑμᾶς βαπτίσει κ.τ.λ.	ἐγὼ βαπτίζω ἐν ὕδατι· μέσος ὑμῶν στήκει, ὃν ὑμεῖς οὐκ οἴδατε, ὁ ὀπίσω μου ἐρχόμενος, οὗ οὐκ εἰμὶ ἐγὼ ἄξιος ἵνα λύσω αὐτοῦ τὸν ἱμάντα τοῦ ὑποδήματος.

Here John agrees with Matthew and Luke against Mark in the placing of the phrase ἐγὼ βαπτίζω ἐν ὕδατι and in the use of the present βαπτίζω. The ἐν before ὕδατι he has in common with Matthew alone, with whom he also agrees in the participial turn ὁ ὀπίσω μου ἐρχόμενος. On the other hand, he is at one with Mark and Luke in the idea of loosing the latchet of Jesus' sandals, instead of which Matthew has that of carrying the sandals.

The words in which the Baptist twice alludes to the wonderful occurrence at Jesus' baptism (John i. 32 and 33*b*) agree substantially with Mark i. 10, Matt. iii. 16, Luke iii. 22.

MARK.	MATTHEW.	LUKE.	JOHN.
εἶδεν σχιζομένους τοὺς οὐρανοὺς καὶ τὸ πνεῦμα ὡς περιστερὰν καταβαῖνον εἰς αὐτόν.	καὶ ἰδοὺ ἀνεῴχθησαν οἱ οὐρανοί, καὶ εἶδεν πνεῦμα θεοῦ καταβαῖνον ὡσεὶ περιστεράν, ἐρχόμενον ἐπ' αὐτόν.	ἐγένετο... ἀνεῳχθῆναι τὸν οὐρανόν, καὶ καταβῆναι τὸ πνεῦμα τὸ ἅγιον σωματικῷ εἴδει ὡς περιστερὰν ἐπ' αὐτόν.	τεθέαμαι τὸ πνεῦμα καταβαῖνον ὡς περιστερὰν ἐξ οὐρανοῦ καὶ ἔμεινεν ἐπ' αὐτόν... ἐκεῖνός μοι εἶπεν· ἐφ' ὃν ἂν ἴδῃς τὸ πνεῦμα καταβαῖνον καὶ μένον ἐπ' αὐτόν κ.τ.λ.

Here John's agreement is closest with Matthew, both in the order of the words τὸ πνεῦμα καταβαῖνον ὡς περιστεράν, and also in the addition, καὶ ἔμεινεν ἐπ' αὐτόν (ver. 33: καὶ μένον ἐπ' αὐτόν), which corresponds with the words ἐρχόμενον ἐπ' αὐτόν, added by Matthew alone.

The account of the cleansing of the Temple (John ii. 12-22) exhibits at the beginning only, in vv. 14-16, certain verbal coincidences with the parallel synoptic records. The ἐκβάλλειν of the πωλοῦντες τὰς περιστεράς and the upsetting (ἀναστρέφειν instead of καταστρέφειν in Mark and Luke) of the τραπέζαι τῶν κολλυβιστῶν are noted as they are in Mark xi. 15, Matt. xxi. 12. Alongside these, however, unique features appear: sellers of oxen and sheep are also mentioned; we are told that Jesus made a scourge of cords, and that He poured out the money of the changers. In particular, Jesus' utterance in ver. 16 has a substantially different form from that found in the Synoptics (Mark xi. 17 and parallels). There He says that they have made the Temple, which ought according to the Scripture to be called a house of prayer, a den of robbers; here, that they should not make of His Father's house a house of merchandise. The report too, which follows in vv. 18-20, of the credential sign given by Jesus, is peculiar to the fourth evangelist. That saying of Jesus, indeed, in ver. 19, λύσατε τὸν ναὸν τοῦτον, καὶ ἐν τρισὶν ἡμέραις ἐγερῶ αὐτόν, agrees substantially with the utterance with which, according to the Synoptics, Jesus was reproached by the false witnesses at His trial before the Sanhedrin. And certainly it coincides more closely with the form in Matthew (xxvi. 61), δύναμαι καταλῦσαι τὸν ναὸν τοῦ θεου καὶ διὰ τριῶν ἡμερῶν αὐτὸν οἰκοδομῆσαι, than with that in Mark (xiv. 58), ἐγὼ καταλύσω τὸν ναὸν τοῦτον τὸν χειροποίητον καὶ διὰ τριῶν ἡμερῶν ἄλλον ἀχειροποίητον οἰκοδομήσω. Moreover, the difference between John and Matthew is that in Matthew, in the utterance cited by the false witnesses, it is of Himself that Jesus speaks as able or willing to destroy the Temple, whereas in the Johannine saying He challenges the Jews to do so. But observe: the synoptic text does not contain the slightest indication that this saying, which was so misunderstood, was spoken at the time of the cleansing of the Temple.

We cannot satisfactorily dispose of this separate Johannine account of the cleansing by simply calling it a secondary form of the synoptic account. Further on we shall reach a special standpoint from which to estimate this section of the Johannine narrative. The saying in John iv. 44 exhibits a mixture of the three synoptic parallels, Mark vi. 4, Matt. xiii. 57, Luke iv. 24.

MARK.	MATTHEW.	LUKE.	JOHN.
οὐκ ἔστιν προφήτης ἄτιμος εἰ μὴ ἐν τῇ πατρίδι ἑαυτοῦ καὶ ἐν τοῖς συγγενεῦσιν αὐτοῦ καὶ ἐν τῇ οἰκίᾳ αὐτοῦ.	οὐκ ἔστιν προφήτης ἄτιμος εἰ μὴ ἐν τῇ ἰδίᾳ πατρίδι καὶ ἐν τῇ οἰκίᾳ αὐτοῦ.	οὐδεὶς προφήτης δεκτός ἐστιν ἐν τῇ πατρίδι ἑαυτοῦ.	προφήτης ἐν τῇ ἰδίᾳ πατρίδι τιμὴν οὐκ ἔχει.

John agrees here with Luke in speaking simply of a prophet's lack of recognition in his native country, whereas Mark and Matthew make this a single exception to the honour which is everywhere else accorded him; and secondly, in naming only πατρίς, while Mark and Matthew both mention his house, and Mark also his kindred. On the other hand, the expression τιμὴν οὐκ ἔχει in John goes back to the ἄτιμος of Matthew and Mark; Luke has δεκτός. And the phrase ἐν τῇ ἰδίᾳ πατρίδι agrees only with Matthew; Mark and Luke have ἐν τῇ πατρίδι ἑαυτοῦ instead.[1]

The incident of the king's officer in Capernaum (John iv. 46–54) is, as we saw above, regarded by the fourth evangelist as identical with that recorded at the beginning of the Logia, and reproduced in Matt. viii. 5–13 and Luke vii. 2–10. Certainly the point of the synoptic story is materially altered in the Johannine version. Both extol the grandeur of a faith which relies on the *word* of Jesus. In the synoptic story, however, this faith attaches itself to the *power* of Jesus' word, and contrasts with one which

[1] For the application of this phrase, in the Fourth Gospel, to Judæa, cf. *sup.* p. 30.

requires His bodily presence and personal activity. But in the Johannine account it attaches itself to the *truth* of the word of Jesus concerning the recovery which He has miraculously effected, and contrasts with a faith which requires actually to *see* the wonders of which He speaks (iv. 48 and 50). This attitude of the fourth evangelist is doubtless induced by a remark at the end of Matthew's account (viii. 13),—perhaps taken from the Logia,—that "in that hour" the boy was healed. The fourth evangelist lays the greatest stress on this coincidence of the time of healing with that of Jesus' announcement of it (vv. 52 sq.). It appeared to him a proof of Jesus' miraculous knowledge. He took it that the especial greatness of the officer's faith was shown in his taking for granted this miraculous knowledge, and so trusting Jesus' word before he had convinced himself by actual eyesight of the truth of the promised miraculous healing. Matthew alone, not Luke, has this final comment, that the boy was healed "in that hour." Another point which John has in common with Matthew as distinguished from Luke is that he makes the man himself come to Jesus from Capernaum, instead of conducting the affair by messengers. But the ἤμελλεν ἀποθνήσκειν of John (iv. 47) corresponds to the ἤμελλεν τελευτᾷν of Luke (vii. 2), and has no parallel in Matthew.

In the story of the healing of the sick at the Pool of Bethesda (John v. 1 sqq.), the bidding of Jesus and its sequel (vv. 8 sq.) are closely connected with Mark ii. 11 sq.

MARK.	JOHN.
ἔγειρε, ἆρον τὸν κράββατόν σου καὶ ὕπαγε εἰς τὸν οἶκόν σου. καὶ ἠγέρθη καὶ εὐθὺς ἄρας τὸν κράββατον ἐξῆλθεν ἔμπροσθεν πάντων.	ἔγειρε, ἆρον τὸν κράββατόν σου καὶ περιπάτει. καὶ ἐγένετο ὑγιὴς ὁ ἄνθρωπος καὶ ἦρεν τὸν κράββατον αὐτοῦ καὶ περιεπάτει.

Mark alone of the Synoptics has here the Latin word κράββατος; Matthew (ix. 6) has κλίνη; Luke (v. 24) κλινίδιον.

A closer connection with Mark vi. 33–43 than with the

NARRATIVE PLAN OF THE FOURTH GOSPEL 39

parallels Matt. xiv. 13–21 and Luke ix. 10–17 is also to be seen in the account of the miraculous feeding (John vi. 1–14). The agreement of the opening words ἠκολούθει δὲ αὐτῷ ὄχλος πολύς, John vi. 2, with the οἱ ὄχλοι ἠκολούθησαν αὐτῷ of Matt. xiv. 13, and the οἱ δὲ ὄχλοι γνόντες ἠκολούθησαν αὐτῷ of Luke ix. 11, rather than with Mark, and of the words θεασάμενος ὅτι πολὺς ὄχλος ἔρχεται πρὸς αὐτόν, John vi. 5, with καὶ ἐξελθὼν εἶδεν πολὺν ὄχλον, Mark vi. 34, Matt. xiv. 14, rather than with Luke, is immaterial. It is, however, material that the definite sum of money which is mentioned, according to John, by Philip,—" two hundred pennyworth of bread is not sufficient for them " (ver. 7)—is also named in Mark, in the question of the disciples (vi. 37)—" shall we go and buy two hundred pennyworth of bread ? "—while in Matthew and Luke there is no mention of such a sum. There is a further agreement with Mark only in the use of ἀναπίπτειν to denote the sitting down of the multitude (John vi. 10; Mark vi. 40). The number of the loaves and fishes (ver. 9), of the people fed (ver. 10), and of the baskets of broken meats (ver. 13), is given by John as well as by all three Synoptics. Otherwise, however, the synoptic account is somewhat materially altered. While in Mark the occasion for the miracle is a need which is brought about by the multitude listening long to Jesus' preaching (vv. 34 sq.), the Fourth Gospel tells us neither that Jesus had been long preaching, nor that the place was desert and the day far spent, but makes Jesus take the first steps towards the miracle as soon as he sees the multitude approaching. While Jesus' object, according to Mark, was to help His disciples in fulfilling the behest He had laid upon them, which they thought could not be fulfilled (ver. 37), so that the whole distribution of the food passes through their hands (ver. 41),—in the Fourth Gospel there is no mention of any injunction being laid on them to care for the multitude, nor of any distribution by them of the food (*vide* ver. 11). While in Mark the people receive as much of the bread as Jesus allots to them, and are satisfied therewith (vi. 41 sq.), in the Fourth Gospel they receive "as much as they would" (ver. 11). Finally, whereas Mark gives no sign of the miraculous nature of the feast becoming known to the multitude, John depicts the impression which the witnessing of the miracle made upon them (ver. 14).

The story which follows, of Jesus' walking on the sea (John vi. 15–21), agrees with the synoptic story in several small particulars which are common to Mark (vi. 45–52) and Matthew (xiv. 22–27): that Jesus withdrew "into the mountain" (ver. 15); that it was evening when the disciples went down to the sea (ver. 16); that the disciples in the boat "behold Jesus walking on the sea," and "were afraid" (ver. 20). There is, however, a remarkable alteration in the close; according to Mark vi. 51 and Matt. xiv. 32, Jesus "went up unto them into the boat, and the wind ceased"; according to John vi. 21, the disciples "were willing to receive him into the boat: and straightway the boat was at the land whither they were going."

The relation in which the account of the anointing in Bethany (John xii. 1–8) stands towards the synoptic texts is very characteristic. Reference has already been made to this event in xi. 1 sq. as to something already known through the synoptic tradition. But the Johannine story not only forms a parallel to the synoptic (Mark xiv. 3–9 and Matt. xxvi. 6–13), but has also certain affinities with two special stories in Luke, which in all probability come from the Logia. First, with the story in Luke x. 38–42. Whereas Mark and Matthew give no name for the woman who anointed Jesus, our evangelist knows that Bethany was "the village of Mary and her sister Martha" (xi. 1; cf. Luke x. 38 sq.). He identifies the woman of the ointment with this Mary; and here again, as in the story in Luke, the διακονεῖν is assigned to Martha (xii. 2; cf. Luke x. 40). At two points, however, our story touches that of the woman, who "was a sinner," in the Pharisee's house (Luke vii. 36 sqq.). This is especially important. Luke has not separately reproduced the account in Mark of the anointing of Jesus in Bethany, because he identified it with the story of the sinner who showed her love to Jesus; and it is his practice, in cases where he finds cognate passages in both his sources, to omit that of Mark in favour of its correlative in the Logia. But as it is also his habit in such cases to insert in the Logia piece some touches from the omitted notice of Mark,[1] so, too, here he not only, following Mark xiv. 3, calls the householder Simon (vv. 40, 43, 44), but notably he has taken the touch that the woman "brought an alabaster cruse with ointment . . . and anointed" Jesus (vv. 37 sq., 46) from Mark xiv. 3. By observing Luke's usual method in combining the material of his sources, we may conclude with great confidence that what he found in the Logia was only this, that "standing behind at his feet, weeping, she began to wet his feet with her tears, and wiped them with the hair of her head, and kissed his feet." Now our fourth evangelist, departing from the account in Mark xiv. 3 and Matt. xxvi. 7, where the woman pours out her ointment on Jesus' *head*, tells us that Mary anointed Jesus' *feet*, and wiped them with her hair (xi. 2, xii. 3). This departure is clearly brought about by reliance on the narrative given in Luke vii. 37 sq.,—not, however, in its original form as it stood in Luke's source, but in the secondary form given it by our third evangelist, who has combined the anointment of Jesus with the washing of His feet with tears. The rest of the narrative as given by the fourth evangelist agrees substantially with Mark and Matthew, and makes use alternately of their respective wording. The ointment is described as follows:—

[1] Cf., *e.g.*, the fusion of Mark vi. 1–5 with Luke iv. 16–30; of Mark x. 41–45 with Luke xxii. 24–28; of Mark xii. 28–34 with Luke x. 25–37.

MARK.	MATTHEW.	JOHN.
ἀλάβαστρον μύρου νάρδου πιστικῆς πολυτελοῦς.	ἀλάβαστρον μύρου πολυτίμου (Β : βαρυτίμου).	λίτραν μύρου νάρδου πιστικῆς πολυτίμου.

Here the verbal dependence of John on Mark is clear; but the word πολυτίμου is derived wholly or in part from Matthew. According to Mark xiv. 4 there were "some" who murmured at the supposed waste; according to Matt. xxvi. 8 these were the "disciples"; according to John xii. 4 there was but one, the traitor Judas. In the statement that the ointment might have been sold for three hundred pence, John (ver. 5) follows Mark (xiv. 5), whereas Matthew (xxvi. 9) makes the expression run that it might have been sold πολλοῦ. The introductory ἄφες αὐτήν, too, in John's version of Jesus' reply (ver. 7) has its parallel only in Mark (xiv. 6). The words of Jesus which follow in John, ἵνα εἰς τὴν ἡμέραν τοῦ ἐνταφιασμοῦ μου τηρήσῃ αὐτό, entirely transform not only the wording, but also the thought of the synoptic saying (Mark xiv. 8; Matt. xxvi. 12). The sense of the synoptic saying is that the woman with her anointment has anticipated the embalming of Jesus' corpse. The sense of the Johannine utterance is that she is to keep the ointment—that is to say, what she still retains and might sell—until the day of Jesus' burying. Then the wording of ver. 8 in the Johannine version agrees again with Mark xiv. 7 and Matt. xxvi. 11; only, as in Matthew, the middle clause of Mark, καὶ ὅταν θέλετε δύνασθε εὖ ποιῆσαι, is omitted.

In the account of the entry into Jerusalem (John xii. 12 sqq.), the beginning of the people's cry, ὡσαννά, εὐλογημένος ὁ ἐρχόμενος ἐν ὀνόματι κυρίου (ver. 13), with its reference to Ps. cxviii. 26, agrees exactly with Mark xi. 9 and Matt. xxi. 9. The continuation in John, καὶ ὁ βασιλεὺς τοῦ Ἰσραήλ, recalls that of Mark, εὐλογημένη ἡ ἐρχομένη βασιλεία τοῦ πατρὸς ἡμῶν Δαυείδ, but also recalls the phrasing in Luke xix. 38, εὐλογημένος ὁ ἐρχόμενος, ὁ βασιλεὺς ἐν ὀνόματι κυρίου. In the explicit notice that the riding of Jesus into Jerusalem on an ass was a fulfilment of the prophecy, Zech. ix. 9, John v. 14 sq., coincides only with Matt. xxi. 4 sq. The most important peculiarity of the Johannine narrative consists in the fact that the homage here paid to Jesus is represented as an effect of the miracle wrought upon Lazarus. The multitude who pay it are people of Jerusalem, who throng to Jesus because they have heard of that sign (John xii. 17-19). On the other hand, according to the synoptic account, it is the crowd of disciples which accompanies Jesus from Jericho that prepares the homage for Him. There is, however, a certain point of contact between the Johannine narrative and that of the third evangelist, who tells how " the whole multitude of the disciples began to rejoice and praise God with a loud voice, for all the mighty works which they had seen " (Luke xix. 37).

Jesus' utterance at the Last Supper about the traitor among the disciples (John xiii. 21), ἀμὴν ἀμὴν λέγω ὑμῖν, ὅτι εἷς ἐξ ὑμῶν παραδώσει με, exactly agrees, except for the doubling of the ἀμήν, with Mark xiv. 18, Matt. xxvi. 21. We have already seen that the remainder of this episode in the Fourth Gospel presents a very characteristic transformation of the older synoptic record.[1]

In the last discourses of Jesus in the Fourth Gospel there are certain further expressions attributed to Him which associate themselves with synoptic reports. Special considerations, to which we shall come later, make it appear questionable whether in these cases also there is any literary dependence on the Synoptics: but they must be mentioned here, in order that a complete survey of the relation of the fourth to the synoptic evangelists may be obtained. In the discourse given in xii. 23 sqq. the expression in ver. 25, " he that loveth his soul loseth it ; and he that hateth his soul in this world shall keep it unto life

[1] Cf. p. 29.

eternal," gives a parallel to Mark viii. 35, Matt. xvi. 25, Luke ix. 24; also to Matt. x. 39, Luke xvii. 33. The saying in John xiii. 16 and xv. 20, "the servant is not greater than his master," is also recorded in Matt. x. 24. The saying in John xiii. 20, " he that receiveth whomsoever I send receiveth me; and he that receiveth me receiveth Him that sent me," agrees substantially with Mark ix. 37 and Matt. x. 40, and also recalls Luke x. 16 and Matt. xxv. 40. In the foretelling of Peter's denial, John xiii. 38, the wording οὐ μὴ ἀλέκτωρ φωνήσῃ ἕως οὗ ἀρνήσῃ με τρίς accords more nearly with the form in Luke xxii. 34 (οὐ φωνήσει σήμερον ἀλέκτωρ ἕως τρὶς ἀπαρνήσῃ μὴ εἰδέναι με) than with that in Mark xiv. 30 (σήμερον ταύτῃ τῇ νυκτὶ πρὶν ἢ δὶς ἀλέκτορα φωνῆσαι τρίς με ἀπαρνήσῃ) and the parallel Matt. xxvi. 34. Finally, the closing words in John xiv. 31, ἐγείρεσθε, ἄγωμεν ἐντεῦθεν, agree with the ἐγείρεσθε, ἄγωμεν of Mark xiv. 42, Matt. xxvi. 46.

In the Johannine account of how, at Jesus' arrest, one of the disciples cut off the ear of the High Priest's servant (xviii. 10 sq.), the mixture of the three synoptic accounts (Mark xiv. 47, Matt. xxvi. 51–54, Luke xxii. 50 sq.) is again characteristic.

MARK.	MATTHEW.	LUKE.	JOHN.
εἷς δέ τις τῶν περιεστηκότων σπασάμενος τὴν μάχαιραν ἔπαισεν τὸν δοῦλον τοῦ ἀρχιερέως καὶ ἀφεῖλεν αὐτοῦ τὸ ὠτάριον.	καὶ ἰδοὺ εἷς τῶν μετὰ Ἰησοῦ ἐκτείνας τὴν χεῖρα ἀπέσπασεν τὴν μάχαιραν αὐτοῦ, καὶ πατάξας τὸν δοῦλον τοῦ ἀρχιερέως ἀφεῖλεν αὐτοῦ τὸ ὠτίον· τότε λέγει αὐτῷ ὁ Ἰησοῦς· ἀπόστρεψον τὴν μάχαιράν σου εἰς τὸν τόπον αὐτῆς· ... πῶς οὖν πληρωθῶσιν αἱ γραφαί, ὅτι οὕτως δεῖ γενέσθαι;	καὶ ἐπάταξεν εἷς τις ἐξ αὐτῶν τοῦ ἀρχιερέως τὸν δοῦλον καὶ ἀφεῖλεν τὸ οὖς αὐτοῦ τὸ δεξιόν· ἀποκριθεὶς δὲ ὁ Ἰησοῦς εἶπεν· ἐᾶτε ἕως τούτου. καὶ ἁψάμενος τοῦ ὠτίου ἰάσατο αὐτόν.	Σίμων οὖν Πέτρος ἔχων μάχαιραν εἵλκυσεν αὐτὴν καὶ ἔπαισεν τὸν τοῦ ἀρχιερέως δοῦλον καὶ ἀπέκοψεν αὐτοῦ τὸ ὠτάριον τὸ δεξιόν· ἦν δὲ ὄνομα τῷ δούλῳ Μάλχος. εἶπεν οὖν ὁ Ἰησοῦς τῷ Πέτρῳ· βάλε τὴν μάχαιραν εἰς τὴν θήκην. τὸ ποτήριον ὃ δέδωκέν μοι ὁ πατήρ, οὐ μὴ πίω αὐτό;

NARRATIVE PLAN OF THE FOURTH GOSPEL 45

John has here the expressions ἔπαισεν and ὠτάριον in common with Mark alone, the notice that it was the right ear in common with Luke alone, and Jesus' command to the disciple to put his sword into its sheath in common with Matthew alone. Jesus' closing utterance agrees in its underlying thought, if not verbally, with that recorded in Matthew. The giving the names both of the striker and the struck is quite peculiar to John.

In the story of Peter's denial John agrees with Mark alone (xiv. 54 and 67) in the notice that Peter was θερμαινόμενος (xviii. 18, 25); and further in reporting one of the three denials merely by the words πάλιν ἠρνήσατο, instead of giving Peter's words (xviii. 27; cf. Mark xiv. 70). Peter's answer, οὐκ εἰμί, however (xviii. 17, 25), is given in common with Luke alone (xxii. 58); and finally the wording in xviii. 27, καὶ εὐθέως ἀλέκτωρ ἐφώνησεν, with Mark xxvi. 74. In giving the occasions for the three denials all the evangelists are at variance. According to Mark xiv. 66 sqq., a maid in the High Priest's court says first to Peter himself that he is of Jesus' company; later again, this same maid repeats her assertion to the bystanders; after a little while the bystanders say to Peter that of a truth he is one of them. Both the other synoptic accounts agree with Mark that it is a maid who first recognises Peter. The second time it is in Matt. xxvi. 71 another maid that speaks, in Luke xxii. 58 a man; the third time according to Matt. xxvi. 73 the bystanders speak, according to Luke xxii. 59 another single man. According to John xviii. 17 sq., 25–27 it is first "the maid that kept the door" who asked Peter as he entered whether he was not one of Jesus' disciples; afterwards this question is repeated by the servants that stand by; lastly, by a single servant, a kinsman of him whom Peter had wounded in Gethsemane. The Johannine account is here as far from one of the Synoptics as another.

In the account of Jesus' sufferings there are several coincidences sometimes with one, sometimes with another of the synoptic Gospels. John agrees with Mark alone (xiv. 65) in the expression ῥάπισμα (xviii. 22); also in the πρωί of xviii. 28 (Mark xv. 1). He gives Pilate's question (xviii. 33) in accord with all three Synoptics: σὺ εἶ ὁ βασιλεὺς τῶν Ἰουδαίων (Mark xv. 2; Matt. xxvii. 11; Luke xxiii. 3). In Pilate's words acknowledging the innocence of Jesus (xviii. 38; cf. xix. 4, 6) he coincides with Luke alone (xxiii. 4); in Pilate's words in xviii. 39, βούλεσθε ὑμῖν ἀπολύσω τὸν βασιλέα τῶν Ἰουδαίων, with Mark alone (xv. 9), but Mark has θέλετε for βούλεσθε. In the mocking scene John's wording (xix. 2), πλέξαντες στέφανον ἐξ ἀκανθῶν ἐπέθηκαν αὐτοῦ τῇ κεφαλῇ, agrees with Matt. xxvii. 29; that of John xix. 3, χαῖρε ὁ βασιλεὺς τῶν Ἰουδαίων, also exactly agrees with Matt. xxvii. 29. On the other hand, the expression ἱμάτιον πορφυροῦν of John xix. 2 corresponds to πορφύραν, which only occurs in Mark xv. 17. In the account of the superscription over the cross John xix. 19 agrees with Mark alone (xv. 26) in omitting the οὗτος (ἐστιν) which is inserted in Matt. xxvii. 37 and Luke xxiii. 38. But Mark has merely the brief ὁ βασιλεὺς τῶν Ἰουδαίων; in Matthew the name Ἰησοῦς is prefixed, and in John the inscription is still fuller, Ἰησοῦς ὁ Ναζωραῖος ὁ βασ. τ. Ἰουδ. In the story of Jesus' burial John (xix. 38) agrees with Matthew alone (xxvii. 57) in the notice that Joseph of Arimathea was a disciple of Jesus, whereas Mark (xv. 43) and Luke (xxiii. 51) only record that he was looking for the kingdom of God. Finally, in the description of Joseph's tomb (John xix. 41), we have once more a mixture of elements from Matt. xxvii. 60 and Luke xxiii. 53. Matthew alone of the Synoptics speaks of the μνημεῖον as καινόν, and only Luke gives the addition οὗ οὐκ ἦν οὐδεὶς οὐδέπω κείμενος. John combines these expressions thus: μνημεῖον καινόν, ἐν ᾧ οὐδέπω οὐδεὶς ἐτέθη.

In the account of the Resurrection in John xx. the story of the two disciples who ran to the empty tomb (vv. 3–9) seems to be an expansion of Luke xxiv. 24. The statement, again, that two angels appeared in the tomb is given, in common with John (xx. 12), only by Luke (xxiv. 4), while Mark (xvi. 5) and Matt. (xxviii. 2) know of only *one* angel. On the other hand, the story that Jesus appeared to Mary Magdalene at the grave (John xx. 11–18) is connected, not with Luke, but with Matt. (xxviii. 9 sq.). In particular, the charge which Jesus lays on Martha to go and tell " His brethren " of His resurrection, coincides with Matt. xxviii. 10. John is singular in making Mary Magdalene alone behold the appearance of the angel and of Jesus Himself: according to Matt. xxviii. 2 sqq., they appeared to two Maries. Finally, the story of the appearance in the evening of the risen Lord amid the disciples gathered together (John xx. 19 sqq.) is paralleled only by Luke xxiv. 36 sqq. There is, especially, a striking coincidence with Luke xxiv. 36 in the touch that Jesus showed them His hands and feet (xx. 20, 27).

3. *Final Inferences*

On a survey of this whole series of coincidences between the Johannine narrative and the Synoptics, we are led to the following conclusions :—

(1) It is evident that the fourth evangelist knew and made use of our three synoptic Gospels. A few isolated coincidences might have been fortuitous, but in view of the great number of such cases, and of the fact that we often find an actual identity of characteristic words or considerable phrases, the appeal to chance is excluded. A literary connection between the Synoptics and John must be acknowledged.

(2) With regard to the use which the fourth evangelist

made of the synoptic literature, it is characteristic that his wording coincides, in steady alternation, first with one, then —and often immediately afterwards—with another of the synoptic Gospels. Definite reasons for these changes are generally unassignable. It is often in minutiæ of expression, or unimportant side-strokes in the narration, that the fourth evangelist makes a sudden change from one synoptic Gospel to another. The explanation of his peculiar procedure seems to be that he had not the actual Gospels before him as he wrote, but knew them only by previous reading or hearing; and that reminiscences of the various synoptic versions pressed upon one another in his mind as he composed his own.

(3) In his use of these synoptic reminiscences the fourth evangelist does not seem to be led by any sure instinct for selecting the most authentic of the parallel Synoptics. In one case, the account of the anointing in Bethany, he takes from the Gospel of Luke one trait which has obviously been produced, in that Gospel, by confusing two distinct stories. This is an especially clear proof that his record of the incident is not based on his own sight of it. And, indeed, the whole nature of his employment of the synoptic literature is symptomatic of the secondary character of his history. An independent witness might, of course, have been acquainted with earlier presentations of the same history: his own might have coincided with them in its main features; but, writing in the light of his own recollection and the impression formed on himself, he must have preserved some originality of detail. The fourth evangelist, on the other hand, is dependent, even in minute details, on the earlier narratives. When, however, we compare the main features of the course of his history, and the chief points of its several incidents, with the *older* synoptic record, we find it in several cases modified, and modified in the direction of the *secondary* synoptic conception.

CHAPTER II

INDICATIONS OF THE USE OF A WRITTEN SOURCE IN THE FOURTH GOSPEL

A. THE QUESTION OF THE SOURCES OF THE GOSPEL

THE discovery that the Fourth Gospel has many elements of a plainly secondary character, and cannot be the work of the Apostle John, is neither a full solution of the problem which the Gospel presents, nor a final determination of its value. It is true also of our First and Third Gospels that they are not by apostles, and that they include many elements of secondary tradition. In the parts where they run parallel to the Gospel of Mark they are a secondary reflection and deflection of their original. Yet they have for us, apart altogether from Mark, a very high value, because they preserve for us a precious store from another tradition, which we have good reason to ascribe, in great part, to a genuine apostolic source. May not something similar be true of our Fourth Gospel? With regard to two points at which the Johannine narrative is at variance with the synoptic,—that Jesus was several times in Jerusalem during the time of His public ministry, and that He was crucified on the 14 Nisan,—I have tried above to show that John is by no means unworthy of credit. Are there not, however, many more notices, peculiar to the fourth evangelist, in reference to which the verdict of an unprejudiced mind will likewise be that they are derived from some credible record?

The comparison with the synoptic Gospels shows not only that the fourth evangelist knew and used them, but, more especially, how comparatively little material he drew from them. There is a connection between them; but the greater and more important part of his record is not derived from them, and cannot be understood as merely a version or perversion of theirs. He possesses a great wealth of independent matter. Our inquiry has hitherto been concerned only with the historical narrative of the Fourth Gospel. This is the part which leads first and most directly to a comparison with the synoptic tradition, and it is herein that a literary dependence on the synoptic Gospels becomes most evident. But this historical narrative really forms no more than the frame for the great discourses and other utterances of Jesus in the Fourth Gospel. From the closing word (xx. 30 sq.) it might be thought that the evangelist had written in his book of nothing but Jesus' wonderful signs. In reality, however, the signs he records only belong to that frame, from which the great discourses of Jesus stand out with an independent significance. Where did the evangelist find the rich material of these passages? Are the discourses and sayings he records substantially original compositions of the evangelist with a doctrinal purpose, or are they founded on actual recollections of real historic discussions and discourses of Jesus? Is it possible that the evangelist has drawn their main substance from an older written source?

So long as the authorship of this Gospel by the Apostle John is accepted, it is clear that the question of its sources cannot enter. It arises, however, as soon as the verdict has been pronounced, that the Gospel is of sub-apostolic origin. The question must then be definitely answered whence the author, who could not draw on his own memory, obtained his material. There is the theoretical possibility that he has created most of it by his own untrammelled imagination;

or that he has received and expanded purely oral traditions of various nature and origin, which had, perhaps, already undergone a somewhat protracted course of evolution. But there is the further possibility, of which we must not lose sight, that he had access to a definite written source, and took from it a great part of his material.

The theory that use has been made in the Fourth Gospel of an older non-synoptic tradition has recently found expression on various sides. H. Holtzmann has laid stress on the fact that certain elements in the narrative cannot be simply derived from the leading religious ideas of the evangelist, but "look like reminiscences without regard to dogma."[1] He has also tried to show that a certain "Johannine" cycle of ideas, which can be recognised in the oldest sub-apostolic literature, is not to be explained as first due to the use of our Fourth Gospel, but rather formed the soil in which our Gospel grew.[2] Ed. von der Goltz has attempted to prove, in particular by means of the Ignatian epistles, that the existence of this "Johannine" cycle of ideas, which he derives from the Apostle John, was independent of our Fourth Gospel.[3] He draws thence the conclusion, with regard to the Fourth Gospel, that "besides Hellenistic and legendary elements, the Gospel contains a unique and precious tradition of the earliest Christian thought, genuine words of the Lord and historic reminiscences, which must go directly back to the Apostle John."[4] Harnack too, in his criticism of the external evidence concerning the Fourth Gospel, reaches the result that "in some way or other John the son of Zebedee stands behind" it, though it was written by John the Presbyter; and refers

---

[1] *Einleitung in das N. T.*, 3rd ed., pp. 445 sq.
[2] *Zw. Th.*, 1871, pp. 336 sqq., 1875, pp. 40 sqq.; *Einleitung in das N. T.*, 3rd ed., p. 469.
[3] "Ignatius von Antiochien als Christ und Theologe" (*T. U.* xii. 3), 1894, pp. 118 sqq., 168 sqq.
[4] P. 177.

the closer investigation of this relationship to an internal criticism of the book.¹ All these inquirers, however, agree in holding that any more exact delimitation of the parts of our Gospel which are derived from the "Johannine" tradition is impossible.² The hypothesis that the fourth evangelist, in his composition of the great discourses, made use of an older *written* source,—memoirs of the Apostle John,—was put forward by Ch. H. Weisse.³ His attempt to carry it out into greater detail was one on which he himself afterwards laid but slight weight. It still "lacked," as he expresses himself, "such a clear perception of the plan and character of the apostle's autograph memoirs as might afford, with sufficient certainty, some special criterion of what did and what did not belong to this original document."⁴ But he still considered the fundamental idea to be quite sound: "that the evangelist's narrative is founded on communications from the hand and lips of the apostle, and that to them the whole doctrinal and reflective part of the Gospel, in the true sense of the words, belongs—this can and will be demonstrated without leaving a doubt, even if the original state of those communications should never be recovered, except approximately and incompletely, from the text before us."⁵ A transient assent to Weisse's hypothesis was

¹ *Chronologie der altchristl. Litteratur*, i. p. 677.
² Cf. H. Holtzmann, *op. cit.* p. 445; Ed v. d. Goltz, *op. cit.* p. 171; Harnack, *op. cit.* p. 700.
³ *Die evangelische Geschichte*, 1838, i. pp. 97 sqq., ii. pp. 183 sqq.; *Die Evangelienfrage in ihrem gegenwärt. Stadium*, 1856, pp. 49 sqq., 111 sqq.
⁴ *Die Evangelienfrage*, pp. 111 sq.
⁵ *Die Evangelienfrage*, p. 118. In this work Weisse indicates as follows what he "believes that he has discovered with certainty" on this question (pp. 112 sqq.). The evangelist had before him, as notes of the apostle: (1) a speculative treatise by the apostle, consisting of the Prologue i. 1-18 (omitting vv. 6-8, 15, 17), and iii. 13-21, 31-36, v. 19-23, 25-27; (2) the discourses of Christ in chaps. xiv.-xvii. (omitting the passages of dialogue, xiv. 5, 8, 9*a* and *c*, 10*a*, 22, 23, 31*c*, xvi. 17-19, 29-32, xvii. 1*a*); (3) v. 30-47 and a substratum of the discourses in chaps. viii. and x.

yielded by D. Schenkel, who saw in the discourses of chaps. i.–xii. and xiii.–xvii. the separated members of two great contexts from one source.[1] But he did not carry this idea any further, and has since entirely given it up.[2] G. A. Freytag also upheld a similar hypothesis.[3] Later, I myself took up Weisse's fundamental idea,[4] but supported it by considerations quite different from his, and worked it out in quite another way.[5]

The indications that a written source was made use of in the Fourth Gospel group themselves into two classes. In the first place there are certain strange differences between

[1] *St. Kr.*, 1840, pp. 763 sqq.
[2] *Das Charakterbild Jesu*, 4th ed. 1873, pp. 24 sq. ; *Das Christusbild der Apostel*, 1879, pp. 188 sqq.
[3] *Die heil. Schriften des N.T. kritisch beleuchtet*, 1861 ; *Symphonie der Evang.*, 1863. I have not been able to consult these works.
[4] *Die Lehre Jesu*, 1886, i. pp. 215–342.—How B. Weiss, *Einleitung in d. N. T.* § 52, n. 6, comes to the conclusion that I founded my hypothesis "on hints from Ritschl" (cf. *St. Kr.*, 1875, 3), I do not know. I myself had no idea that I had obtained any such hints from Ritschl. In the passage cited Ritschl is supporting the hypothesis that in the text of the Prologue there has been a dislocation of the verses. He takes the original order to have been : vv. 1–5, 10, 11–13, 6–8, 9, 14, 16–18, 15. Is there any hint here of my source-hypothesis? Ritschl held that the Fourth Gospel as a whole was the work of the Apostle John. He said in the lecture-room that he regarded certain single passages as interpolated, namely, v. 25, 28 sq., the concluding words in vi. 39, 40, 44, 54, xii. 48 ; and, if I recollect aright, also the explanations in ii. 21, vii. 39, xii. 33, and xviii. 9, 32. On the appearance of my *Lehre Jesu*, pt. i., I confess, he wrote to me, "I am very much disposed to adopt your theory of the Fourth Gospel.
[5] I am astonished that theologians who themselves uphold theories of earlier sources in the case of the Synoptics should prejudge and attack my analogous theory concerning the Fourth Gospel on the ground that it arises from a "very suspicious" desire to save, at least, an apostolic nucleus for the Gospel (Jülicher, *Einleitung in d. N. T.* § 30, 3, p. 246), that it is framed "in accordance with preconceived ideas" (B. Weiss, *loc. cit.*), or even that its "perfectly transparent motive" is prompted by the dogmatic standpoint of the Ritschlian theology (A. Meyer, *Th. R.*, 1899, p. 262). I have brought to bear on the establishment of my hypothesis a considerable array of definite and purely literary data. Why impute desires and motives, instead of going into the reasons which I have clearly set forth?

the attitude of the evangelist and the thoughts in the discourses of Jesus which he records, differences such as would be inconceivable if the evangelist had been the independent author of those discourses. In the second place there is, in many cases, a curious discrepancy between the discourses and their narrative framework. At times the discourses presuppose a different historical situation from that which is indicated in the narrative framework; at other times passages of discourse, whose internal connection shows them to form one context, suffer disruption by the insertion of narrative passages.

In appealing, on behalf of the source-hypothesis, to indications of this kind, we are contravening the traditional opinion, unanimously emphasised by the defenders both of the conservative and the critical position, that the Fourth Gospel exhibits a unitary completeness, a formal and material homogeneity in all its constituents, and that the discourses and narrative episodes in it are indissolubly interconnected.[1] The image first used by D. F. Strauss is continually repeated, that "this Gospel is itself the seamless tunic of which it tells us, for which men may cast lots, but which they cannot rend."[2] But the very question which is being asked is whether this traditional judgment is not a prejudgment. Of course a source-hypothesis does not mean that later patches were sewed on an originally seamless coat.[3] It means that in preparing his new and

---

[1] Cf., e.g., B. Jülicher, loc. cit.; O. Holtzmann, Das Johannes-evangelium, p. 137; H. Holtzmann, Einleitung in d. N. T., 3rd ed., p. 445.
[2] Ulrich von Hutten, iii. 1860, Vorrede, p. xliv.
[3] The distinction must be kept in mind between a source-hypothesis and a hypothesis of interpolation, such as has been projected by A. Schweizer, Das. Evang. Joh. nach seinem innern Werte, etc., 1841, and recently by H. Delff, Das vierte Evang., 1890. The two may of course come into contact here and there; the same symptoms of an internal discrepancy or breach of context may be taken by the one as signs of interpolation, by the other as signs that a source has been made use of. But there is still an important distinction between the view that an

artificial garment the evangelist has taken over and worked up older material, and that in the whole so put together many seams may now be noticed, where that older stuff has been joined to material of another kind. One kind of unity the Gospel undoubtedly possesses: the evangelist has made all his material his own, and used it as his own; and it is therefore perfectly right to seek to understand the whole in the light of his integrating ideas. But it may nevertheless be true that the Gospel includes matter which was not originally the work of the evangelist himself; and we are therefore justified in attempting, with regard to certain of its components, to distinguish between their proper, original sense and that which is imposed by the evangelist's manner of employing them. A source-hypothesis, then, does not necessarily reject outright the internal unity of the Gospel: it only denies that this unity is different in kind, or greater in degree, than that of the First Gospel or the writings of Luke, in which the employment of passages from older sources can be distinguished.

original record has been interlarded with longer or shorter passages of foreign matter which are later additions, by detaching which the original unitary text can be restored, and the view that an author has employed a written source in compiling his record. In this latter view the original order and connection of the passages from the source, which the compiler has dissolved, may in some cases be again discovered; but one cannot of course count on being able to disengage all those elements from the work of the compiler in such a way as to exhibit them in their original connection, or to leave the remainder in the form of a connected narrative. I have been much astonished to find so sagacious a critic as Jülicher, *loc. cit.*, describing my source-theory simply as a theory of interpolation, and as such rejecting it together with that of A. Schweizer. I have been led to regard as interpolations the passages v. 4 and vii. 53–viii. 11; but it has not occurred to me to explain any other section in the Gospel, either of discourse or narrative, as an interpolation in an "original John." My hypothesis as to the relation of our Fourth Gospel to an apostolic source, a collection of discourses, is entirely analogous to that which Jülicher upholds as to the relation of our First Gospel to an apostolic collection of λόγια. Jülicher would hardly be satisfied with a description of this hypothesis as an hypothesis of interpolation.

The contention that there are in the Fourth Gospel indications, of the kind already described, in favour of a source-hypothesis, is not to be confuted by the general remark that "discrepancies and contradictions are characteristic of the Gospel of John," and that "the task of setting forth an idea in the form of a history could not be performed without them."[1] If the concrete instances to which I appeal are examined, it will be seen that we are not dealing, in their case, with incongruities and contradictions of the kind which are incident to the attempt to depict an idea in historical form. Indeed, the discrepancies, inconformities, and interruptions which present themselves are of such a type that a writer, whose aim was to clothe doctrine like narrative, to combine miracles with discourses, and speak with a double reference, would rather have been led to avoid them—and most assuredly so if he had been writing with a free hand, unhampered by any older material. If a critic refuses to explain these concrete phenomena by the theory that the evangelist was making use of a written source, he is called upon to furnish a better explanation. An explanation of some sort is certainly required; it is not enough to invoke the doctrinal aim of the evangelist, and his addiction to ambiguity and obscurity.

Or is a source-hypothesis precluded by the obvious unity of style and language throughout the Gospel? If a source has been made use of, it is quite comprehensible that the passages taken from it may have been revised in point of form, and so assimilated to the language of the redactor, or *vice versâ*. The writings of Luke also exhibit a uniform character in speech and in style. Nevertheless

---

[1] Jülicher, *ad loc. cit.* Cf. the arguments of H. Holtzmann that the fourth evangelist has a special inclination towards ambiguity, obscurity, contradictions, and equivocal expressions: *Einleitung in d. N. T.*, 3rd ed., pp. 442 sq.; *Neut. Theologie*, ii. pp. 375 sqq., 451, 457.

we can say with a high degree of confidence that in them older sources were made use of, and even sometimes exactly reproduced, with very slight modifications of style. It cannot be held that there is any substantial distinction of language between those passages in the Acts which use the first person plural and the rest of the book. Is that a proof that those passages were not taken from an earlier source?

Before I begin to treat in detail the indications that a source was made use of in the Fourth Gospel, especially in the longer speeches, I wish to lay stress on one point. A capital distinction must be drawn at the outset between the questions—whether an older written source was employed, and whether that source was a true apostolic document, of direct historical value. The impression which those discourses leave on some minds, that they accord with the preaching of Jesus in the Synoptics, and may be received as utterances of the historic Jesus, cannot decide the question in favour of the employment of a written source; on the other hand, the conviction which others hold, that neither in form nor content do the speeches bear a historical character, is not decisive against the use of an earlier writing. The only question before us is whether any such signs of the redaction of an earlier written document can be discovered as are taken in other literature to indicate the use of a source: signs of the same kind as those from which we infer that our First and Third Gospels and the Acts of the Apostles are based upon an older literary stratum. If cogent reasons appear for assuming a source behind the Fourth Gospel, then the further and quite independent questions will arise, whether we are to attribute to this source a historical value, and whence it derives,—whether it is of apostolic or sub-apostolic origin. It is possible to agree unreservedly with my arguments for the view that a source was employed, without being able to accept my answer to these further questions.

B. DIFFERENCES BETWEEN THE POINT OF VIEW OF THE EVANGELIST AND THAT OF THE DISCOURSES OF JESUS

1. *The Distinction between the "Signs" and the "Works" of Jesus*

In the first place, the fact deserves attention that the "signs" of Jesus, on which such especial stress is laid in the narrative parts of the Fourth Gospel, do not play the same important part in the discourses: indeed, they play no part at all. With the exception of the one passage, already alluded to (vi. 26, p. 24), which forms the transition from the miracle of the feeding to the discourse of Jesus on the true bread of life (vi. 27 sqq.), the term σημεῖα is not found in these discourses. Now it is by pointing to these signs that the evangelist answers the problem with what credentials Jesus supported His claim to divine Lordship, and to being the Son of God. Is this problem, then, not raised in the discourses? It is, in fact, continually raised, but it receives a different answer from that given in the narrative parts of the Gospel.

When, on the day after the feeding of the multitude, Jesus says that He has meat to give which abideth unto eternal life, and that men must believe on Him as sent by God (vi. 27, 29), the people ask Him what He will do for a sign, like Moses' miracle of the manna, that they may see and believe (vv. 30 sq.). If the discourse which follows had been an original composition of the evangelist, we must have expected, in accordance with his attitude in other cases, that he would make Jesus answer with a strong appeal to His actual signs—either to that of the miraculous feeding which His questioners had witnessed (v. 26), or to greater wonders which they should see in the future. But Jesus answers them quite otherwise. He declares that

He is Himself the bread from heaven, given of God; and that this may be known for the true bread from heaven, in that he that eateth thereof hath eternal life, which the manna could not give (vv. 32-50). Whatever interpretation may be put upon the words that follow, " he that eateth my flesh and drinketh my blood hath eternal life " (see vv. 51-58), in any case the key to the paradox and the explanation of the preceding claims of Jesus are given in the closing words (ver. 63): "it is the spirit that giveth life; the flesh profiteth nothing; the words that I have spoken unto you are spirit, and are life." That is to say, Jesus claims to be the bread from heaven which giveth eternal life, in the sense that His *teaching* contains the Spirit of God and the life eternal, and bestows them upon others (cf. v. 24, viii. 51, xii. 49 sq., xvii. 2 sq.). In agreement with this declaration of Jesus is the confession of Peter: " Lord, to whom shall we go?' Thou hast words of eternal life; and we have believed, and know that thou art the holy one of God " (vv. 68 sq.) What Jesus lays as the foundation of His saving power,—His words of spirit and life,—is acknowledged by Peter as the firm ground of His disciples' faith in His Messiahship. If this continuation of the thought is kept in view it clearly shows the relation in which Jesus' answer in vv. 32 sqq. stands to the demand for a sign in vv. 30 sq. The sign for which they ask is refused, not because Jesus has already done signs enough, but because He Himself, with His words of spirit and life, is a divine gift of so high a kind as to need no miraculous credentials. The gift accredits itself by its own life-giving effect. It might be said: " Jesus puts forward Himself and His teaching as the true and supreme sign of God, because He knows that the real basis and power of His being and of His preaching lies not in this world, but in God." But a sign, in the sense in which the Jews demanded it, this to which Jesus refers assuredly was not: nor is it a sign of the kind to which the fourth evangelist, in the narrative parts of his Gospel, and at its close (xx. 30 sq.), points as credentials for Jesus' Messiahship.

This one passage (vi. 32 sqq.) is confirmed and its effect enhanced by others which show a similar divergence of conception in the discourses from that which prevails in the narrative. Jesus appeals several times in the discourses to His "works" (ἔργα) to accredit His claims. In chap. v. He repudiates the witness of men, even that of the Baptist, to Himself. He has a greater witness: "The *works* which the Father hath given me to accomplish, the very works that I do, bear witness of me, that the Father hath sent me" (ver. 36). Again, in x. 25 He speaks of the witness of His works. In the same context, when the Jews are about to stone Him for saying, "I and my Father are one" (x. 30), He asks, "Many good works (καλὰ ἔργα) have I showed you from the Father; for which of those works do ye stone me? . . . If I do not the works of my Father, believe me not; but if I do them, though ye believe not me, believe the *works*: that ye may know and understand that the Father is in me, and I in the Father" (vv. 32, 37 sq.). This same appeal to the witness of His works recurs in xiv. 11 and xv. 24. What are we to understand by these "works"? It is natural, in reading the Fourth Gospel, where so much is said about the σημεῖα of Jesus, to think first of those miracles; nor can there be any doubt that the evangelist himself understands the expression in this sense. But is this the original and true interpretation? The term ἔργα has a more general sense: it may be used of miracles, but also of works in which there is nothing miraculous. Can it be by a mere accident that the evangelist, when speaking of the miracles of Jesus in the discourses, always uses the more general term, while in the narrative portions he uses only the expression σημεῖα?

There is no lack of clear indications in the Johannine

discourses how this question should be answered. "The works," of which Jesus says in v. 36 that the Father has given them to Him to accomplish, must be understood in the same sense as "the work" of which He says in iv. 34, "My meat is to do the will of Him that sent me, and to accomplish His work," and in xvii. 4, "I glorified Thee on the earth, having accomplished the work which Thou hast given me to do." The "works" spoken of in the plural in v. 36 collectively form the one great "work" which His Father has committed to Him. What Jesus meant by these "works" is clearly shown in both places (iv. 34 and xvii. 4) by what follows. The utterance in iv. 34 is followed by a prophetic forecast by Jesus of the result of the work He is to do: the fields are already ripe for harvest; but it is not He Himself that shall gather it in; His disciples, whom He sends forth to continue His labour, will reap what He has sown (vv. 35–38). It is clear that He is speaking of His work of teaching, through which He gathers "fruit unto life eternal" (ver. 36); a work which His disciples shall carry on in a broader field with a grander result (xiv. 12, xvii. 18). This same work of teaching is meant in xvii. 4, as is shown by the following words, in which He reviews His accomplished task: "I manifested Thy name unto the men whom Thou gavest me out of the world; . . . the words which Thou gavest me I have given unto them" (vv. 6, 8). The conclusion must follow that in v. 36 also, by "the works which the Father hath given me to accomplish," He means, not His thaumaturgy, but His labours as a teacher. He appeals to these to accredit His claims in the same sense which we have already defined as that of vi. 63.

This result is further confirmed by the fact that even in the two places (xiv. 10 sq. and xv. 24), where Jesus appeals to His "works" for a witness, these works are set in the closest conjunction with His "words"—in one of the passages, indeed (xiv. 10 sq.), in such a way that "works" and "words" appear to be equivalent terms. Jesus says to Philip, "Believest thou not that I am in the Father, and the Father in me? The *words* that I say unto you, I speak not from myself: but the Father abiding in me doeth His *works*. Believe me that I am in the Father, and the Father in me: or else believe me for the very *works'* sake." Here He rests His claim to full union with the Father first, in ver. 10, on His words, which He obtains not from Himself or from this world, but from God—that is to say, on the words of spirit and life which He puts forward also in vi. 63 (cf. vi. 68 sq.) as the sign of His divine efficacy unto salvation. Then in ver. 11 He rests a like claim upon His works. By these works, however, He does not mean a second something, apart from His words: this is made clear by the intermediate clause, which consists of two complementary statements, the one negative and the other positive—" I speak not these words from myself," " On the contrary, it is the Father within me that Himself doeth His works." This striking form of expression becomes fully intelligible, if in Jesus' mind the "works" which the Father wrought in Him consisted in His labour of teaching, and so included His "words." If these passages stood alone, we might perhaps avoid taking "words" and "works" as coincident terms, by regarding the phrase quoted above as a compressed expression, and expanding it thus: " On the one hand, I do not speak my words from myself; on the other hand, it is the Father (and not I) that doeth the works, which are, indeed, at root His own."[1] In that way words and works would be co-ordinated. But if we recollect how Jesus, in iv. 34 sqq. and xvii. 4 sqq., reckons among His "works" His work as a teacher, and how in vi. 63 He puts forward His "words" alone as His credentials, we shall retain here also (xiv. 10 sq.) the interpretation, which the wording itself suggests,

[1] Cf. Haupt, *St. Kr.*, 1893, p. 242.

that the teaching of Jesus is looked upon as His work, and therefore instead of the term "words" the term "works" can be used of it. The same striking form of expression, arising out of the same mental attitude, occurs at viii. 28, "I *do* nothing of myself, but as the Father taught me, I *speak* these things." It follows, however, that we must also understand in the same sense Jesus' words in xv. 22, "If I had not come and *spoken* unto them, they had not had sin," and their immediate sequel in xv. 24, "If I had not done among them the *works* which none other did, they had not had sin." Here, too, the "works" of Jesus are not simply a second something, apart from His "speaking"; but when the thought of ver. 22 is taken up and enhanced in ver. 24, instead of the specific term "speaking," we have the generic term "works," which is used of Jesus' labours *as a teacher*.[1] Of course, we must not say that in the discourses of the Fourth Gospel the "works" mean no more than His "words." The term "works" has always a more general meaning. But it cannot be by accident that in all the passages just cited the term "works" never makes way for that of "words," but the term "words," though used first, gives place to the more inclusive term "works." The "work" or the "works" of Jesus are the whole of that practical activity by which He set Himself to fulfil His Messianic call. But it is not enough to say that Jesus' public discourse is to be reckoned in with His healing of the sick and the rest of His practical activity as part of the work of His calling: according to the view assumed in the discourses of the Fourth Gospel, Jesus considered His Messianic work *as a whole* to be directed towards the knowledge of God which avails unto the life eternal (xvii. 2–28)—that is to say, to be a

[1] This interpretation by no means makes ver. 24, as Haupt thinks (*op. cit.* p. 243), a "tautological repetition" of ver. 22. The utterance in ver. 24 contains a real addition to that of ver. 22—first, in the substitution of the more general term "work" for that of "speech"; and, secondly, in the express declaration of the incomparable character of this work.

work of teaching. It is natural, then, when He is thinking of this work, that He should speak first of all of His " words." He did not, however, look upon His words as words merely spoken, in distinction from works actually done; rather, He knew that His whole practical activity subserved His verbal teaching—completed, explained, and made it effective: therefore in place of the term " words " he sets one which includes it and has besides a fuller meaning, that of " works."

There is now no difficulty in clearly perceiving the conceptual relation of the " works " of Jesus in the discourses of the Fourth Gospel to His " signs." His " works " include, among the rest, all His helpful deeds of love. In vii. 21, for instance, He uses the expression " work " in reference to His healing of the sick man at the Pool of Bethesda (v. 1 sqq.).[1] But it is by no means true that by the works His miracles alone, or even chiefly, are meant.[2] It is rather His ministry as a whole that is thought of, and chiefly His work of teaching, which, derived from divine revelation, avails unto eternal life, and to which all else that He does is indirectly subservient. This sense, which comes out clearly in many places, must therefore be assumed also for the sayings in x. 25, 32, 37 sq. When Jesus speaks here of the ἔργα, to which He appeals to accredit His high claims, as καλά (ver. 32), it is not their wonderful character but their moral and religious grandeur that He has in view. He is reasoning here in substantially the same sense as in viii.

[1] The healing spoken of as an ἔργον is not here (vii. 21) considered as a *miraculous* deed, but as a *labour* performed on the Sabbath, and therefore regarded by the Jews as forbidden. Cf. the term ἐργάζεσθαι in v. 17 and Luke xiii. 14.

[2] Even in vii. 3 the ἔργα are not simply synonymous with σημεῖα. The brothers of Jesus are speaking of the works which, in v. 19-27 and in the discourse beginning at vi. 27, He claims to have performed. The brothers, it is true, regard these works, if they really happened, as external miracles. Jesus, however, meant a work of another and a higher kind.

46, "Which of you convicteth me of sin? If I say truth, why do ye not believe me?"

It follows, further, from what we have said, that there is a real difference between the mental attitude of the evangelist in the narrative parts of the Fourth Gospel and that which prevails in the discourses. Two distinct answers are given in the one and in the other to the question, which is fundamental to the teaching of the Gospel, how the Messiahship of Jesus was accredited. In the narrative parts, as in the closing words of the evangelist (xx. 30 sq.), we are directed to Jesus' "signs"; in the discourses we find that the demand for a sign is refused, and we are directed to Jesus' words of spirit and life and to His "works"—that is to say, to His whole ministry of teaching, which attests itself as a thing divine. The existence of this difference constitutes a riddle which can neither be solved by taking the whole Gospel as the work of the Apostle John nor, on the theory of a sub-apostolic authorship, by regarding the discourses as free compositions of the sub-apostolic evangelist. If the apostle had written the whole Gospel, and had recorded, out of his living memory, how Jesus, in the discourses, refused the demand for a sign and continually appealed, in the sense already made clear, to His words and His works,—is it then conceivable that in the narrative parts of the Gospel this same apostle should have forgotten Jesus' own attitude, and put forward His miraculous signs as all-important? Is it conceivable that at the close of his Gospel he should have applied to the signs *alone*,—without even mentioning the words of Jesus recorded by himself, the significance of which he had displayed in passages like vi. 63, 68 sq., vii. 16 sq., viii. 31 sq., 51, xiv. 10, xvii. 2 sq., 6–8,—such language as this: "These are written that ye may believe that Jesus is the Messiah, and that, believing, ye may have life"? On the other theory, if the sub-apostolic evangelist had freely composed the discourses in his Gospel, is it conceivable that he should have laid aside so completely, in writing them, his own estimate of the σημεῖα, which is so clearly made known in the narrative parts, and even repudiated it as not in accordance with Jesus' real meaning? Nor is the riddle cleared up by the theory of a proclivity on the evangelist's part towards a mysterious ambiguity: what is here remarkable is precisely the clearness with which the terms ἔργα and σημεῖα are distinguished, when it would have been so easy to use one or other of them in an equivocal manner, and so to slur over the difference of view. The only hypothesis which reconciles the discrepancy and solves the riddle is this, that the evangelist has reproduced the discourses of Jesus from an older document, whose form was already fixed. It was in this way that he was led to conserve in them a point of view which was foreign to his own consciousness. No doubt he interpreted the sayings of that source in his own sense; but he conserved, nevertheless, wording and context to such an extent that we can clearly recognise the original divergence of its meaning from his own point of view, as independently expressed by himself.

2. *Misinterpretations of Particular Sayings of Jesus*

There is another consideration which constrains us towards the same hypothesis. Certain utterances of Jesus in the Fourth Gospel have appended to them explanatory comments, such as by no means suit their true sense, as the wording and context reveal it.

After the cleansing of the Temple, the Jews ask Jesus by what sign He can vindicate His right to act so. Jesus answers, "Destroy this temple, and in three days I will raise it up" (ii. 19). The evangelist explains this saying by the comment, "He spake of the temple of his body" (ver. 21). This cannot be the original sense of ii. 19. On the one hand, the use of the demonstrative, "*this* temple," in the circumstances recorded, requires that the word should refer to the Temple of Jerusalem. It is also clear that the reference of the Jews in ver. 20 is to the Temple building. On the supposition that Jesus attached His allusion by a gesture to His own body, this answer of the Jews in ver. 20 is incomprehensible. On the other hand, the use of the active voice in ἐγερῶ forbids the application of the word to the body of Jesus. According to the form of expression which runs consistently throughout the New Testament, Jesus *was raised up* by God (cf., *e.g.*, ver. 22, ἠγέρθη). As soon as we ignore the comment of the evangelist, the true meaning of ver. 19 immediately becomes clear. This Temple of Jerusalem, which ought to be the place of the true worship of God, may be destroyed by the hierarchs, as by its degradation to a house of merchandise (ver. 16), which they permit and encourage, it is indeed being destroyed; but Jesus, in the shortest space of time (cf. Hos. vi. 2), will raise in renovated state that worship which they have abased. This is an answer which is related to the demand of the Jews for a sign, exactly as is the answer in the incident of vi. 30 sqq. to the demand there put forward. The deed to which He points is not a σημεῖον in the external sense, not an isolated proof of His miraculous supernatural power: nevertheless, in spite of its being wrought within the normal course of nature, it affords a much loftier warrant of His divine activity than any external σημεῖον whatsoever could give. And this warrant stands in direct and immediate relation towards that which it intends to accredit—the conduct of Jesus, and His right to assume it. Jesus has the right to come forward as a critic of the misordering of the Israelite Temple worship, because He has within Him the divine power to create anew the true worship of God.

After the utterance in vii. 37 sq., "If any man thirst, let him come unto me and drink. He that believeth on me, as the scripture hath said, out of his belly shall flow rivers of living water," the evangelist adds, " But this spake he of the spirit, which they that believed on him were to receive: for the spirit was not yet, because Jesus was not yet glorified" (ver. 39). This exegesis of the thirst-quenching gift of Jesus as the spirit which should come after Jesus had been glorified is too narrow. If we consider the analogous sayings of Jesus in iv. 14 and vi. 27, 35, we shall see that His meaning can only be this: He offers in His teaching, to those who will faithfully accept it, an enduring instrument for gaining and keeping the eternal life, as water is the transient instrument for maintaining the earthly life. But, according to the view which appears everywhere else in the Johannine discourses, this power of the higher, the eternal life, of which Jesus is the mediator, does not remain inoperative until after His death: its operation is instant and immediate in the present, through His teaching (cf. v. 24, vi. 47). In the discourse with Nicodemus the idea of the spirit, wherein lies the requirement for membership of the kingdom of God (iii. 3-8), corresponds to that of the life eternal, which Jesus knew Himself sent to bestow on those that believed (iii. 14-17). Again, at the close of the discourse in chap. vi., Jesus explains His claim to be the mediator here and now of eternal life (vv. 27, 35-40, 47-51) by referring to His spoken words, which are spirit and life (ver. 63). If we keep these instances in mind, we may indeed allow that here, too (vii. 37 sq.), that higher power of life, of which Jesus is speaking, may also, in accordance with the Johannine way of thought, be spoken of as "spirit": but the spirit in this sense, the spirit which those who believe the teaching of Jesus receive, does not become effective for the first time after He is glorified, but operates now, during His lifetime, in His disciples. The Spirit, on the other hand, in the special sense in which during the lifetime of Jesus "it was not yet,"—that is, as the substitute which took Jesus' place among His disciples, as teacher and helper (xiv. 26, xvi. 7 sqq.), and as the bearer of miraculous gifts of grace,—does not fill the whole circumference of the power of eternal life, which is meant to be taken in this place (vii. 37 sq.) as the gift of Jesus Himself.

After xii. 32, where Jesus says, "And I, if I be lifted up from the earth, will draw all men unto myself," the evangelist adds the remark, "this he said, signifying by what manner of death he should die" (ver. 33). This remark corresponds to another in the story of the passion: when the Jews refuse to follow Pilate's behest that they should judge Jesus according to their own law, the evangelist says that this befell "that the word of Jesus might be fulfilled, which he spake, signifying by what manner of death he should die" (xviii. 32). The meaning of the evangelist, therefore, is that by the word ὑψοῦσθαι Jesus referred to the Roman method of capital punishment, crucifixion. The incorrectness of this explanation is shown not only by the context, but also, and especially, by the words ἐκ τῆς γῆς. Jesus cannot have used the expression ὑψοῦσθαι of the external manner of His death, but only of His heavenly exaltation through His death, in a sense which accords with the term previously (ver. 23) used, δοξάζεσθαι.[1]

Jesus' words concerning His disciples in the high-priestly prayer (xvii. 12): "While I was with them, I kept them in Thy name which Thou hast given me: and guarded them, and not one of them perished," are interpreted by the evangelist later, in the scene of the arrest. On Jesus'

---

[1] The terms ὑψοῦσθαι and δοξάζεσθαι are here employed with a reminiscence of Isa. lii. 13 (LXX): ἰδοὺ συνήσει ὁ παῖς μου καὶ ὑψωθήσεται καὶ δοξασθήσεται σφόδρα. There comes into Jesus' mind the thought which is expressed in the prophetic account, introduced by these words, of the sufferings of the servant of Jahweh, that this suffering will issue in His glorification. On the meaning of the term ὑψοῦν in John iii. 14 and viii. 28, see my *Lehre Jesu*, p. 596 (2nd ed., p. 571) (*Teaching of Jesus*, ii. pp. 330 sq. [Edin.: T. & T. Clark, 1901]).

request to the officers to let His disciples go their way, He comments, "that the word might be fulfilled which he spake, Of those whom Thou hast given me, I lost not one." But the perdition spoken of in the original context, where it is contrasted with preservation in the name which God has given to Jesus, must have a meaning which bears relation to that name: it must mean a lapse from the revelation of salvation of which God has made Jesus the bearer. The later comment of the evangelist, however, can only—unless we force the sense—be understood to mean that the disciples would have "perished" if they had met with earthly trouble and death, such as would have befallen them if they had shared Jesus' arrest.

The style of comment in these four cases is substantially the same. Jesus' words in their original sense refer to events which do not happen in the world of external phenomena, but in that of the religious consciousness. The evangelist, however, applies them to incidents of an external kind, which were still in the future when Jesus spoke. In that way they take the character of miraculous predictions. In view of this character it is plain that the evangelist assigned to them a specially high value (cf. ii. 22). Beyond all doubt, however, the deeper meaning is that which the context shows to have been the original one.

How is the remarkable fact of these interpretations to be explained? If we assume that the Apostle John wrote the whole Gospel, we can distinguish between the original sense of the words on the lips of Jesus and the meanings given to them by the apostle who records them.[1] But this explanation is not satisfactory; for it can hardly be thought that while the memory of the apostle retained intact, in proper order, the wording of Jesus' discourses, so that their original sense is clearly apparent, he should nevertheless

[1] Cf., *e.g.*, B. Weiss, in Meyer's *Commentary*, at the places cited; and Haupt, *St. Kr.*, 1893, p. 249.

have mistaken that original sense. He does not even give the prophetic reference of the word to future phenomena as a secondary sense, but proffers it as the sole true meaning. But it is a much less satisfactory explanation to assume a sub-apostolic authorship, and hold that the evangelist made intentional use of equivocal terms.[1] In the first place, an evangelist who had really had such an intention, would have so worded his ambiguous report of Jesus' sayings as to leave room for the sense indicated in the interpretations which he appends. Instead of the ἐγερῶ of ii. 19 he would have used the passive ἐγερθήσεται, and would have assuredly omitted the phrase ἐκ τῆς γῆς in xii. 32. In the second place, in the interpretations themselves, he would not have proposed one meaning alone as the only right one, and thereby wilfully excluded the other sense, which he had himself conceived and intended! What lies before us, in fact, is not an intentional ambiguity, but a *misunderstanding* of the original sense. This fact can only be explained if we distinguish between the original reporter of Jesus' words and the author of the exegetic clauses. If we had only to deal with these individual cases, we might have recourse to the hypothesis that the comments in ii. 21 sq., vii. 39, xii. 33, and xviii. 9, 32 were later interpolations in the Fourth Gospel. But if we take into consideration the fact already demonstrated, that there is, apart from these cases, a significant difference between the point of view of the evangelist and that of the discourses which he records, a difference which can only be reconciled and explained by the hypothesis that he made use of a written source, we shall recognise in these cases a confirmation of our source-hypothesis. While the evangelist reproduced those sayings of Jesus in ii. 19, vii. 38, xii. 32, and xvii. 12 as they appeared in his source, it was open to him to append such interpretations as accorded with his general view of the nature of Jesus'

[1] Cf. H. Holtzmann, *Neutest. Theologie*, ii. p. 457.

miraculous soothsaying power, and also with the atomistic and allegorical treatment of the Scriptures which was in his time in vogue. At the same time, he has so closely followed their wording and arrangement that we can still recognise the meaning which they had in the source.[1]

C. DISTURBANCE OF THE ORIGINAL REFERENCES AND CONTEXTS

A second group of indications that a source was made use of appear in the fact that the original reference and connection of the passages of discourse are destroyed by the narrative framework in which they now stand. I proceed first of all to collect the cases which seem to me especially evident. Afterwards I will show that similar disturbances can be perceived in many other places. But the practical

---

[1] The synoptic analogue to these misinterpretations of Jesus' sayings in the Fourth Gospel, especially to John ii. 21 sq., is to be found in the comment on the utterance about the sign of Jonah, Matt. xii. 40. Here, too, the difficulty is solved by our distinguishing between the constituents derived from a source, and the additions of the evangelist who used it. In view of the parallel in Luke (xi. 29 sqq.) the correctness of this solution can hardly be doubted. In order to understand what Jesus Himself meant by the "sign of the prophet Jonah," the only sign which He would concede to His generation (Matt. xii. 39), the interpretation given in Matt. xii. 40 (which does not occur in Luke), must be altogether ignored. In Luke the reading runs: "For even as Jonah became a sign unto the Ninevites, so shall also the Son of man be to this generation" (xi. 30). Jonah was a sign to the Ninevites, not through his wonderful experience on the sea, but through his preaching of judgment. When Jesus goes on to speak of the preaching of Jonah, at which the Ninevites repented, while the Jews will not listen to Him that is greater than Jonah (Matt. xii. 41), He must have meant that His own preaching of judgment would be the only sign accorded to His contemporaries who clamoured for a sign—truly a sign of quite another kind from that which they desired. But the meaning of our first evangelist was that Jesus' "sign of the prophet Jonah" must have been a portent like that which befell Jonah. The three days which Jonah spent in the sea-monster corresponded to the three days between the death and the resurrection of Jesus. So that the evangelist saw in Jesus' words a significant prediction of His resurrection after three days.

course might seem to be to exhibit at first only those cases which must be relied on as chief evidence for the hypothesis of a source.

1. *Discrepancy between Narrative and Discourse in Chapter v.*

The occasion of the discourse in v. 17 sqq. is that Jesus, according to the conception of the Jews, had broken the Sabbath (ver. 18). Later again, in vii. 19–24, Jesus refers once more to this charge brought against Him of breaking the Sabbath. According to the introductory notice (v. 1–16) what Jesus had done on the Sabbath was this,—He had by a word miraculously healed the sick man at the Pool of Bethesda, and had charged him to take up his bed and walk (vv. 8 sq.). It is not the utterance of the command to be whole, nor yet the miraculous healing, but only the carrying of a burden that can have been considered by the Jews as a labour forbidden on the Sabbath day. Jesus was only charged with having caused the man He healed to perform this labour. This, too, is the account given in vv. 10 sq. But in the discourse (v. 17 sqq.), and again later in vii. 19–24, Jesus does not defend the carrying of a burden by the man healed, but only His own healing of the sick man (vii. 23). He does not treat this as a mere word which had a miraculous effect, but does not fall under the idea of labour; He assigns to it the force of a labour, an ἐργάζεσθαι (v. 17; cf. Luke xiii. 14). But in justification of such work on the Sabbath He appeals to His heavenly Father. Even as His Father, whose rest after the work of creation is the prototype of the human Sabbath, nevertheless still labours, so does He too labour (v. 17). In all His doing He imitates the Father: He does such deeds as He sees the Father do (v. 19 sq.). And the Father will show Him yet greater works than the healing of the sick:

namely, the giving of life unto the dead (v. 20–27). Then in chap. vii. He appeals to the fact that even the law recognises exceptions to the rest of the Sabbath. If circumcision might be performed on the Sabbath, how much more might He make a man every whit whole (vii. 22 sq.). They must not judge according to appearance, but judge righteous judgment — that is, one which estimates things according to their true significance (vii. 24).

This whole defence has no applicability to the bearing of burdens on the Sabbath, or to any incitement to such work. Its contents relate only to Jesus' work of love for the sick, and imply the presumption that this work bore the aspect, "according to appearance," of an actual deed or deeds. But this reference and presumption are rendered meaningless by the introduction (v. 1–16), in which the whole emphasis is laid on the bearing of burdens on the Sabbath. Is it conceivable that an author, who, by reporting the discourses in v. 17 sqq. and vii. 19 sqq., had acquainted himself with this relation and presumption,—and with these he must have been acquainted, whether he wrote down the discourses from memory or prepared them as an independent composition,—should have concealed from the reader in this fashion the real reference of what he reported? If we now go on to reflect that the command to be whole, including the charge to carry the bed and its miraculous sequel, are recorded in v. 8 sq.,[1] we are driven to the conclusion that the evangelist has superadded this incident of the command and its consequences upon an older document. This older document must have stated that the sick man, for whom nobody else cared, received from Jesus some practical help, directed towards his healing, on the Sabbath day. At the godless violation of the Sabbath by such a laying on of hands the Jews who stood by were greatly astonished (cf. θαυμάζετε, v. 20, and πάντες θαυμάζετε, vii.

[1] Cf. *sup.* p. 38.

21). But Jesus appealed to the example of the work of God Himself on His own Sabbath. How the evangelist came to alter his source is obvious. The sub-apostolic generation did not understand that Jesus in His healings had made use of any active gesture or deed, such as we learn from Mark vii. 33 and viii. 23–25 that He did employ. They thought it self-evident that He wrought His healings by a mere word of command. But this preconception made it incomprehensible that the Jews should have taken offence at Jesus' healing on the Sabbath day. In order to supply a motive for such a feeling, which is the occasion of the discourse in v. 17 sqq., the evangelist assumed that Jesus had combined His word of healing with the same command, "take up thy bed and walk," which He used in the healing of the paralytic, recorded by the other evangelist.[1]

2. *Discrepancy between Narrative and Discourse in Chapter vi.*

In chap. vi., again, there is by no means a close connection between the narrative and the passages of discourse which are attached to it: the same kind of discrepancy appears between the two parts of the account as in chap. v. At first sight it certainly appears very fitting that the history of the miraculous bodily feeding is bound up with the discourse on the heavenly food, which

[1] A synoptic analogue to the conduct of the evangelist in this case occurs in Luke xiii. 10–17. Here the healing word and its sequel in vv. 12 and 13 are clearly an addition of the evangelist to the account in his source. In the command in ver. 12 Jesus is made to use the metaphorical expression, "be thou loosed from thine infirmity"; and the motive for this does not appear until ver. 15, where the loosing of beasts from the mangers is spoken of as permitted on the Sabbath. The words of the ruler of the synagogue in ver. 14 presuppose that Jesus made use of some such active deed or gesture as must be looked upon as chirurgical practice ($\theta\epsilon\rho\alpha\pi\epsilon\acute{u}\epsilon\sigma\theta\alpha\iota$), and so brought into the class of forbidden labour ($\epsilon\rho\gamma\acute{a}\zeta\epsilon\sigma\theta\alpha\iota$). A trace of this remains in ver. 13a—$\epsilon\pi\acute{\epsilon}\theta\kappa\mu\epsilon\nu$ αὐτῇ τὰς χεῖρας.

avails unto eternal life. It was undoubtedly of deliberate purpose that the evangelist set the one as an introduction to the other.[1] The strangeness lies in the fact that the actual starting-point of the discourse—the demand by the Jews for a sign, which leads Jesus to speak of Himself as the true bread from heaven—fits as ill as possible into the situation immediately after the great miracle of the feeding. I have shown above (pp. 58 sq.) how extraordinary it is that the Jesus of the Fourth Gospel, who is elsewhere perfectly ready to publish His wonderful signs, does not meet this demand in chap. vi. by appealing to the signs He has already wrought. But it is even more extraordinary that the same Galileans who the day before had witnessed the miracle of the feeding, and been led by it to proclaim Jesus as "the prophet that cometh into the world," and to desire to make Him king (vv. 14 sq.), should now demand of Him a sign, and—strangest of all—a sign of bread-giving, like Moses' miracle of the manna! Their demand does not presuppose the sign which they have seen: it is not for a new, a higher sign. In language as general as it can be, "What doest thou for a sign," they ask, "that we may see and believe thee? What workest thou?" How are we to take the fact that the miraculous feeding is so completely ignored? Is it enough to assume such gross impudence in the people that they would not remind Jesus of the miracle of yesterday, for fear He should retort that they must be satisfied with that?[2] Could they then suppose that Jesus, who, according to the evangelist's account, had just addressed them as the witnesses of that sign (ver. 26), would never think of it again unless He were reminded? And even if they in their impudence had embraced such a notion, is it conceivable that Jesus would actually have done them the favour to avoid all reference,

---

[1] Cf. *sup.* p. 23.
[2] So Haupt, *St. Kr.*, 1893, pp. 231 sq.

on His part, to the fact that they had been spectators of His great sign of yesterday? If we assume that chap. vi. as a whole was not written by the apostle from his own memory, but freely composed by a sub-apostolic author, the enigma of the disregard in vv. 30 sqq. of the sign of the miraculous feeding is not solved, but complicated. How could the evangelist, who desired to bring the discourse on heavenly food into harmonious connection with the feeding sign, have neglected this principle of conformity at the very beginning of the passage? It would have been so easy to shape the demand for a sign in such a way that it referred to the sign already beheld, but represented it as failing to satisfy the Jews. The only hypothesis which solves the enigma is that in an older document, used by the evangelist, the passage in vi. 27 sqq. was given *without* the preceding account of the feeding of the multitude, and generally without the presupposition of earlier miracles publicly wrought by Jesus. It was with the intention of finding a suitable setting for this passage that the evangelist attached it to the miracle of the feeding, which is recorded by the Synoptics. He assumed, in accordance with his general view of Jesus' thaumaturgy, that Jesus had performed this miracle, like the rest, in full publicity, and had thereby made a deep impression on the beholders. But the Jews, to whom Jesus speaks, are represented in the original of this passage as unbelieving: to account for this, and adjust it to his introductory narrative, the evangelist added ver. 26, where Jesus lays down that they sought Him, indeed, because of the miracle, but only through the physical satisfaction of their hunger, not through a true appreciation of its credential value as a sign. But this device does not really effect a true connection between the narrative and the content of the discourse. By taking over, at the beginning of the passage of discourse, the demand of the Jews for a sign, as it was recorded in the older document, he unconsciously preserved an indication that this passage was not originally connected with the story of the feeding.[1]

Another indication to the same effect has been preserved by the evangelist. He records that when Jesus, in reply to those who asked for a sign, pointed to Himself as the true bread from heaven that giveth eternal life (vv. 32–35) He added the words: "but I said unto you, that ye have seen me, and yet believed not" (ver. 36). To what earlier utterance does Jesus here refer? The general assumption is to ver. 26.[2] True, there is no other utterance in the foregoing narrative of chap. vi. that need be considered; but does the reference to ver. 26 suit the sense? It certainly contains the general idea that the Jews did not believe in Jesus in spite of what they had seen. But the special

---

[1] In view of the strained connection between the beginning of the passage of discourse in vi. 27 sqq. and the preceding narrative, Al. Schweizer assumes (*Das Evang. Joh.*, 1841, pp. 80 sqq.) that the "Galilean passage," vi. 1–26 (like the Galilean passages ii. 1–12, iv. 44–54, and xxi. 1 sqq.), was interpolated by a later redactor of the Gospel. So H. Delff, *Geschichte des Rabbi Jesus v. Naz.*, 1889, pp. 109 sqq.; *Das vierte Evang.*, 1890, pp. 11 sqq.; in the same sense, J. Dräseke, *Nk. Z.*, 1898, pp. 184 sqq., 584 sqq. Delff, *Das vierte Evang.* pp. 13 sqq., and Dräseke, *op. cit.* pp. 139 sqq., 584 sqq., conclude from the way in which Celsus, according to Origen, *contra Celsum*, i. 67, speaks of a demand for a sign addressed to Jesus in the Temple, that in the copy of John which Celsus used the section vi. 1–29 was not included. Celsus says that Jesus gave no beautiful and wonderful sign, although He was challenged in the Temple to give some clear token that He was the Son of God. Delff and Dräseke hold that the Temple scene of John ii. 18 cannot be here meant, because there is no special mention in that place of a sign concerning the personal religious significance of Jesus, His Messiahship. The allusion must be to the scene of vi. 30: this, however, is not placed in the Temple; it must be, then, that section vi. 1–19 is interpolated. I cannot agree with this inference: Celsus may very well have had in mind the Temple scene of John ii. 18. A sign which should accredit Jesus' right to cleanse the Temple would have been in the second instance a sign which accredited His personal claims. Moreover, there is not, in vi. 30 either, any direct mention of a sign that Jesus was the Son of God.

[2] So, *e.g.*, Luthardt and B. Weiss *ad. loc.*

object of their sight is here expressly denoted as the *signs*. On the other hand, the sense of ver. 36, to accord with the context, vv. 32–35, must be: although the Jews had seen Jesus *in His ministry of salvation*, which bestows eternal life, nevertheless they would not believe in Him. And this ministry of Jesus, which avails unto eternal life, and attests Him for the true bread from heaven, is expressly *contrasted with those signs* which the Jews demanded to enable them to believe in Him. They needed no signs, because His life-giving ministry attested Him, and this ministry they had seen. So the object of sight, on account of which they were to believe in Jesus, is here, in ver. 36, other than in ver. 26, and obviously could not be explained or extended by any allusion to the signs. To what earlier utterance, then, does ver. 36 relate? Can it refer to any word of Jesus which is not recorded in the Fourth Gospel? Lücke[1] has already rightly perceived that the reference is to the discourse in chap. v.,—in particular, as he assumes, to v. 37–44 : but it will be better to say, to the whole exposition from v. 17 onwards. In that discourse Jesus has declared that He is engaged in a ministry divinely allotted to Him, the purpose of which is to bestow eternal life (vv. 19–30). He has laid it down that the attestation of the truth of this claim lies in His ministry itself (ver. 36). He has also reproached the Jews for refusing to believe in Him in spite of the witness of His works, with the witness of Scripture superadded (vv. 37–47). His "works," to which He here appeals, consist in His ministry of teaching which bestows eternal life (ver. 24).[2] Here again, in chap. vi., it is upon this teaching of His, which contains and confers spirit and life, that Jesus founds His claim to be the heavenly bread of life (cf. vi. 63). The reference, then, of vi. 36 to v. 17–47

---

[1] *Kommentar über d. Evang. Johannes*, Bonn, 1834, 2nd ed., ii. pp. 99 sqq.
[2] Cf. *sup*. pp. 61 sqq.

is in entire accordance with the sense. But the discourse of chap. v. is addressed to the inhabitants of Jerusalem, whereas, according to the account of the Fourth Gospel, the discourse of chap. vi. was addressed much later to multitudes in Galilee. It is for this reason that the reference of vi. 36 to the discourse in chap. v. appears unnatural and impossible. That the historical Jesus should have worded His address to the crowd which pressed about Him by the Lake of Galilee, after the miracle of the feeding, as if they were identical with the inhabitants of Judæa with whom He had once before had a dispute in Jerusalem, is inconceivable. And it is equally inconceivable that a writer who was the sole and original author of the notices and discourses of chaps. v. and vi. should have represented Jesus as alluding in this way, amid the Galilean situation, to the discourse in Jerusalem. It does not, however, follow from the unnatural character of this allusion in the Gospel as we have it that we must discard the view that vi. 36 refers to the discourse of chap. v., and adopt that which refers it to vi. 26, although according to the sense the first view is perfectly apt, and the second impossible. The problem is solved by the explanation that the reference which now appears so unnatural was by no means unnatural in the original document which our fourth evangelist employed, because in that document the discourse in chap. vi. was not introduced by the historical notice of vi. 1–26, but belonged to the situation of chap. v. Our evangelist was *not aware* that vi. 36 referred to the discourse in chap. v. The reference to that utterance which he had put in the mouth of Jesus in vi. 26 seemed to him entirely suitable, because, in his view, it was precisely by the seeing of signs that faith in Jesus was to be aroused. A meaning which the original author of the sequence of thought in vi. 30–36 could not possibly have conceived is quite conceivable to one who merely reproduces that sequence of thought at second hand.[1]

The correctness of the hypothesis that, in the intention

[1] Haupt, *St. Kr.*, 1893, pp. 226 sqq., regards as a decisive objection to my view of this passage the fact that in other places in the Gospel, especially in x. 25 sq., reference appears to have been made to a discourse which belongs to another situation—in this case x. 1–18. This argument (cf. the similar one of H. Holtzmann, *Neut. Theol.* ii. p. 457, n. 1, with reference to my explanation of xii. 32 sq.) I cannot understand. The fact that there are several cases which exhibit the same difficulty seems to me to be a substantial confirmation of my hypothesis, which gives an appropriate explanation of the difficulty in those other cases as well as in this. Haupt offers the following explanation. It belongs to the special character of this Gospel not to give detached historical pictures, in which the individuals continually change; but the individuals recede behind larger classes of men. We have depicted a common fight with a common enemy. Since to the eyes of the evangelist the concrete was obscured by the universal, and it is always with "Judaism" that he is concerned, we may understand how he fails to distinguish between what belonged to one set of individuals and what belonged to another. Under the impression that *his readers* knew what had preceded, the idea intruded itself into his mind that *the actual hearers* knew all that had preceded. This may be called a literary inadvertence.—This explanation seems to me by no means satisfactory. As a matter of fact, it is not true that the evangelist depicts no detailed historical pictures with different concrete individuals. A more definite historical picture, with a clearer account of the change of scene and of persons, than is given in vi. 1 sqq. could not well be given at all. The strange thing is that, *in spite of* the concrete outline which is given to this new picture, the wording of the discourse that follows presupposes the same opponents as in an earlier concrete situation. Therein lies an internal discrepancy such as an author whose matter was all his own could hardly have allowed to intrude. The assumption that the author was led into these peculiarities of narrative style by thinking of his readers, who knew what had gone before, does not in any way relieve the difficulty. The most senile and negligent of writers must have felt that his readers could only look for the reference of vi. 35 within the limits of the concrete situation of chap. vi., and were expressly withheld, by the form of the utterance, from looking for its reference in chap. v. H. Holtzmann, in his *Hand-Commentar* on vi. 36, explains that εἶπον ὑμῖν "refers back to ver. 26, and in a certain degree to v. 37–40." This explanation agrees accidentally with my own, except that I have defined the "certain degree." In the mind of the evangelist the reference is to ver. 26, in the original sense of the source to the discourse in chap. v.

of the source from which it came into our Gospel, the discourse of vi. 27 sqq. belonged to the situation of chap. v. is further confirmed by the consideration that, if it be adopted, vv. 27–29 gain substantially in meaning. Is it a mere accident that here, at the beginning of the exhortation in chap. vi., the subject matter is the same ἐργάζεσθαι and ἔργα τοῦ θεοῦ as at the beginning of that in chap. v.? Jesus says in ver. 27, "Work not for (ἐργάζεσθε μή) the meat which perisheth, but for the meat which abideth unto eternal life, which the Son of man shall give unto you": if these words were connected with the miraculous feeding, the term ἐργάζεσθαι is very surprising. No motive for it is supplied by the conduct of those who were addressed, as ascribed to them in ver. 26. They sought to obtain the meat that perisheth, not by labouring for it, but by the help of a miracle. Nor is it called for by what Jesus enjoins, that they should aspire after the meat which the Son of man offered them, which abideth unto eternal life. For this—which is spoken of in ver. 29 as belief in Him whom God hath sent—presents itself rather as the acceptance of a proffered gift, than as the earning of anything by labour. We must then assume that the term, in this passage as it stands, bears the attenuated meaning "to seek to obtain," without reference to the manner of acquiring, whether by labour or not. But in that case why is ἐργάζεσθε used, instead of the much more suitable term ζητεῖτε? If, however, the discourse of vi. 27 sqq. belongs to the situation of chap. v., the term ἐργάζεσθε is fully explained and admirably pregnant. Jesus has just been defending Himself for labouring on the Sabbath. He has declared that He labours after the example of His heavenly Father, and that He carries out the works which His Father shows Him, and lays upon Him (v. 17, 19 sqq.). Now He proceeds in vi. 27 to exhort the Jews that they too, in similar wise, should labour, not for the meat which perisheth, but for the bread of eternal life. As His own work, divinely laid upon Him, consists in offering mankind a doctrine which avails for eternal life (v. 24), so the work which God would have them do consists in the faithful acceptance of His teaching.

There is, finally, another trace by which we may perceive the original connection of the discourse in chap. vi. with the narrative of chap. v., whose scene is in Jerusalem; in vi. 41 and 52 the listeners to Jesus' discourse, who according to the account of the evangelist were Galileans, are spoken of as οἱ 'Ιουδαῖοι, like the Judæan opponents of Jesus in v. 18 and elsewhere in the notices relating to Jerusalem. At first sight the use of these words is not remarkable, because the term οἱ 'Ιουδαῖοι in the Fourth Gospel, as elsewhere in the New Testament, is clearly used to denote the Jews in general, as distinguished, by race or religion, from the Samaritans or from the Gentiles. In this sense the term, of course, includes the Jews of Galilee (as well as those of the dispersion). This sense comes out in John iv. 9, 22, xviii. 33, 35, and in all the places where mention is made of the feasts and legal customs of the 'Ιουδαῖοι (ii. 6. 13, v. 1, vi. 4, vii. 2, xi. 55, xix. 40, 42). But the term οἱ 'Ιουδαῖοι may also denote the Judæans in distinction from the Galileans: as it clearly does in vii. 1, xi. 8, 54. This distinction was by no means merely geographical. In contrast with the despised Galileans, who had only recently become Judaised,[1] the people of Judæa regarded themselves as the real kernel of the people of Israel, as the genuine sons of Abraham, the possessors of the old Jewish traditions, as the inhabitants of the Holy City and the Holy Temple, with all the holy ordinances that belonged to it, as the rightful inheritors of the promises that had been delivered to Israel (cf. John i. 47, vii. 41, 52). Now

[1] Cf. Schürer, *Geschichte des jüdischen Volkes im Zeitalter Jesu Christi*, 3rd ed., ii. pp. 5 sqq. (*History of the Jewish People in the Time of Jesus Christ*, Div. II., vol. i. pp. 2 sqq. [Clark's Foreign Theological Library, 1885]).

in the Fourth Gospel it is brought out very strongly that the real foes unto death of Jesus of Nazareth were the men of Judæa. Whenever the 'Ιουδαῖοι appear as His opponents, these Judæans, and especially their religious chiefs, are meant (ii. 18, 20, vii. 15, 35, viii. 22 and *passim*). The only exception lies in those two places, vi. 41 and 52, where according to the account of the evangelist Galileans must be meant. Hitherto, in the narrative part of chap. vi., these Galileans with whom Jesus has to do have been spoken of as ὁ ὄχλος (vv. 5, 22, 24) or οἱ ἄνθρωποι (vv. 10, 14). It is only in the discourse-section proper that the expression οἱ 'Ιουδαῖοι occurs. Is this change of expression merely accidental? Or is it occasioned by the desire to bring into notice the Jewish unbelief of the Galileans?[1] It is also possible that the use of this expression in these verses depends on the fact that a passage from an earlier source is here reproduced, in which Judæan opponents of Jesus were really meant.[2] It must be conceded that if no other traces were to be found of an original connection between the discourse of chap. vi. and chap. v., the mere employment of this expression οἱ 'Ιουδαῖοι in these two places would not be enough to demonstrate such a connection. In consideration, however, of the indications of different kinds which have already been pointed out, this

[1] Cf. B. Weiss in Meyer's *Komm.* on vi. 41.

[2] Wuttig also, *Das Johanneische Evangelium*, whose exhaustive inquiry into the 'Ιουδαῖοι of the Fourth Gospel (pp. 38–52) is worthy of consideration, recognises that in accordance with the usual terminology of the Gospel the 'Ιουδαῖοι in vi. 41 and 52 must be regarded as Judæans. He assumes that certain isolated Pharisees and scribes from Jerusalem (cf. Matt. xv. 1; Mark vii. 1) are meant, who had listened in the throng (vi. 2, 5), and afterwards in the synagogue at Capernaum (vi. 59), were the leaders of the discussion (pp. 43 sq.). But if the evangelist had meant isolated Jews amid an otherwise Galilean multitude he must have expressed this differently, just as it is differently expressed in Matt. xv. 1 and Mark vii. 1. This use of οἱ 'Ιουδαῖοι, without prelude or modification, can only have referred, in the mind of the evangelist, to the Galileans in general about whom he has been writing.

USE OF A SOURCE IN THE FOURTH GOSPEL 85

peculiar use of οἱ 'Ιουδαῖοι must be recognised as an additional trace that such a connection exists.

3. *The Detachment of vii. 15–24 from Chapter v.*

In vii. 15–24 we are once more placed in the situation of chap. v. In the second part of this passage, vv. 19–24, Jesus justifies the work on the Sabbath which is recorded in v. 1 sqq. We have already seen (pp. 73 sq.) that here, as in v. 17 sqq., this work on the Sabbath is regarded as consisting in Jesus' ministry itself, not, as we should expect from the notice in v. 7–16, the carrying of a bed by the man who was healed. If we must conclude from this discrepancy with the narrative introduction, as we have it, that the evangelist was not the independent author of the discourse in v. 17 sqq., but gave it in reliance on an older document, the same conclusion must hold good for this section, vii. 19–24. This conclusion is now confirmed by the observation that the section, as it stands in our Gospel, is singularly misplaced; and that in point of time, as well as of thought, it is immediately connected with chap. v.

According to the account of our evangelist the incident of v. 1 sqq., which happens at a "feast of the Jews" (v. 1) before the Passover (vi. 4),—that is, at latest, the Feast of Purim in March of the same year,—is separated from the discourse of vii. 15 sqq., delivered during the Feast of Tabernacles (vii. 2), by an interval of at least seven months. In the mere fact that Jesus, after so long a period, alludes to that earlier incident there is no cause for surprise, but the nature and manner of His allusion is very remarkable. After the words of Jesus in vv. 16–18, which speak of His teaching as coming from God, He breaks abruptly into the reproach, "Did not Moses give you the law? and none of you doeth the law" (ver. 19*a*); and then, with equal abruptness, He adds the question, "Why seek ye to kill me?"

(ver. 19*b*). It is clear that Jesus had in mind the earlier design on His life recorded in v. 18, for He goes on to give a further justification of the healing on the Sabbath, on account of which that design had been conceived. But how can Jesus treat the people who now surround Him at the Feast of Tabernacles as simply identical with the Judæans of v. 18? Just as He speaks of the design on His life (that of v. 18) as of something existing in the present, so He goes on to speak of His healing on the Sabbath as of an act that had just been performed before those bystanders (cf. the present tense in θαυμάζετε, ver. 21, and χολᾶτε, ver. 23). It is the "one work" which the bystanders have seen to their astonishment (ver. 21), although according to our evangelist's account Jesus had, earlier in Jerusalem, wrought many wonderful deeds in the sight of the people (ii. 23, iii. 2, iv. 45). This style of allusion to the earlier event is, in the much later scene which the evangelist sets out, most unnatural. The historical Jesus cannot have spoken in that sudden way of an incident so far removed.[1] Nor would any writer who had composed the words of Jesus in vii. 19–24 with a free hand have made Him allude to that incident in that way. He would in any case have attempted some introductory transition, and undoubtedly He would have spoken of the conduct of the Jews on that occasion in the past tense. The style of the allusion becomes clear and intelligible only on one hypothesis,—that originally, that is to say in the source whence the passage is taken, these words of Jesus (vii. 19–24), were really connected in point of time with the story of healing in v. 1 sqq.

---

[1] B. Weiss on vii. 20 (cf. *Leben Jesu*, ii. pp. 386 sq.) explains that while it is true that the evangelist is referring to the incident of chap. v., the discourse must originally have been rather on the whole category of Jesus' works of healing on the Sabbath than on the single one which had so far given Him occasion to defend a breach of the law. This implies an acknowledgment that the allusion to the incident of chap. v., at any rate as it now appears in the Gospel, is historically inconceivable.

It must now be observed that the section vii. 15–18, which precedes that of which we have been speaking, but has no obvious connection with its content, forms the aptest continuation possible of the discourse in chap. v. If we assign to the whole passage, vii. 15–24, an original place immediately after v. 47, we have before us a clear and homogeneous sequence of thought. In the discourse of v. 17 sqq. Jesus justifies His activity on the Sabbath day by appealing in the first place to that of His Father (ver. 17). The Jews take offence at this saying: and in reply to them Jesus asserts with all the greater force that in all that He does He is but performing the ministry which the Father has assigned to Him, whose purpose is to call the dead to life (vv. 18–30). To attest this claim He appeals first to the witness of His ministry itself, next to the earlier revelation of God (vv. 31–37*a*). But He upbraids His opponents that in spite of all their study of the Scriptures they have no understanding of that earlier revelation; for although the Scriptures bear direct witness to Him, yet they will not believe in Him (vv. 37*b*–40). This is because they have no love for God, and take no thought of what He recognises, but only of what is recognised by mankind (vv. 41–44). Even Moses, therefore, on whom they have set their hope, accuseth them; for if they believe not the writings of Moses, how shall they believe Jesus' words (vv. 45–47)? What an apt sequel to this is afforded by the question which the Jews ask in scornful astonishment (vii. 15): "How knoweth this man letters, having never learned?" Where it now stands in chap. vii. this question can only rest on the general ground that Jesus had taught in the Temple (vii. 14), but at the close of chap. v. it is prompted in a much more urgent way by the reproach which Jesus has addressed (v. 37–47) to His learned opponents that they do not understand the Holy Scriptures, and the implied claim that He understands them better than they. The word γράμματα, without the article (vii. 15), does not indeed refer directly to the Holy Scriptures, but to learning in general. But the learning of the Jews was concerned with nothing besides the Scriptures. In this place, however, it was not a simple acquaintance with the Scriptures, such as even the laity might possess, that was in question, but a *learned* knowledge of them, which could not be expected of the uneducated. Jesus' reply to this scoffing protest is a reiteration of the claim which was the special theme of His discourse in chap. v.—that His teaching is not from Himself, but from God (vii. 17; cf. v. 19 sq. and 30). In attestation of this claim He takes up, first of all, the thought with which He had closed His preceding justification, and appeals to the testimony of those who really seek to do the will of God (vv. 16 sq.; cf. v. 41 sqq.); then, in contrast to the aspiration after human glory, with which He had upbraided His opponents as the sign that they lacked a true desire to do God's will (v. 44), He appeals to His own aspiration, not after glory for Himself, but the glory of God (ver. 18). In this sequence of thought the words that follow, " Did not Moses give you the law, and none of you doeth the law ? " are no longer abrupt and unintelligible. They connect themselves with the preceding discussion, and especially with v. 45–47. Jesus reiterates what He has already maintained, that His opponents do not possess that which would enable them to recognise the divine origin of His teaching, since they have no real anxiety, of any moral or religious kind, to fulfil God's revelation in the Old Testament.[1] In the same way the sudden transition to the

---

[1] Haupt's remark in *St. Kr.*, 1893, p. 237, is incorrect. He says that Moses is approached from two different points of view in v. 45–47 and in vii. 19. The first reference is to his promise, which must be believed, the second to his law, which must be obeyed. But in appealing to the testimony of Moses in v. 45–47 Jesus cannot have been thinking of the promise in Deut. xviii. 15 of a prophet that should be raised up. That this promise referred to the coming Messiah was a con-

question, "Why seek ye to kill me?" (ver. 19*b*), and the following reference to the work of healing of v. 1 sqq. now lose their startling abruptness. For this event did not belong to the past, but had just happened. The disquisition of Jesus concerning the origin and significance of His work in general (v. 19 sqq.) had been occasioned by the word in v. 17, by which Jesus had justified His action on the Sabbath day. It is therefore quite natural that He should make this parenthetical discussion, which draws to a close in vii. 16–18, issue in a further justification of His activity on the Sabbath.

The hypothesis, then, the ground of which I have indicated, that the passage vii. 15–24 was originally attached to the discourse in chap. v., is one which materially helps the intelligibility of that passage; is it to be defeated by the consideration that if so excellent a context had really stood part of his original, we cannot conceive how any redactor could have broken it up?[1] Or, if the fact that it did so stand originally cannot be disputed, are we to explain the separation of the section which now stands in chap. vii. by an accident, through which a page of our Gospel was misplaced?[2] In reality, if two postulates be conceded,

viction common to Jesus' contemporaries. The question was whether Jesus Himself was or was not this divine messenger, and this question could not be answered by a mere appeal to the word of promise. Moreover, Jesus does not speak only of an utterance of Moses, but of Moses and his writings in general. His meaning must be that the revelation of the Old Testament Scriptures in general (ver. 39), including therefore the law of Moses, do not, when rightly understood, bear witness against Him, as His Jewish opponents thought, rather they bear witness to him. This saying is based on the assurance, which He proclaims elsewhere, that the new revelation, of which he knows Himself to be the bearer, is in perfect harmony with the prevailing, inner conception of the Old Testament revelation. Cf. *Lehre Jesu*, ii. pp. 365 sq. (2nd ed., pp. 206 sq.) (*Teaching of Jesus*, ii. pp. 44 sqq. [Edin.: T. & T. Clark, 1901]).

[1] So Haupt, *St. Kr.*, 1893, p. 226.

[2] This hypothesis has been applied by Bertling, *St. Kr.*, 1880, pp. 351 sqq., to vii. 19–24, whose original place he takes to have been before v. 17 (*secus* Waitz, *St. Kr.*, 1881, pp. 145 sqq.), and by Spitta, *Zur*

then in this case, as well as in others which we shall have to notice, the disruption of the sequence of thought which was to be found in the source is very far from inconceivable. These postulates are, first, that as a general rule the source did not contain narrative notices, but only discourses—Logia of Jesus, like the Logia which are combined in our First and Third Gospels with matter from the Gospel of Mark; second, that while working upon this source the redactor had no written copy before him, but had only at some former time read or heard it, and used it memoriter, just as the Synoptics made a memoriter use of one another and of other writings, and as the New Testament writers used to quote from the Old Testament. On the basis of these two postulates it may very easily have come about that the redactor-evangelist confused the outlines of the several discourses. A question or remark of the Jews, which led Jesus to further comment, may have given him the impression that a new discourse was beginning, in a new situation, whereas, in the true sense of the original, the remark or question was merely parenthetical. Again, the chance occurrence in the source of such a phrase as εἶπεν οὖν πάλιν αὐτοῖς, before any of Jesus' words, might lead him to treat these words as a separate utterance, though in the source the phrase only marked an extension of the preceding discourse. There are many examples of such a disruption of original contexts in the Synoptics, all open to the objection that no such context can ever have existed, because its wanton destruction by a redactor is inconceivable, were it not that the synoptic parallel exhibits that context beyond dispute.[1] In the case with which we are dealing in

Geschichte und Litteratur des Urchristentums, i. pp. 199 sqq., to vii. 15-24, to which, in substantial agreement with my reasoning, he assigns a place after v. 47.

[1] An especially significant example, analogous to this in John, is provided by the Woes over the Galilean cities (Matt. xi. 20-24), which in their present place stand outside the context. A connection in point

the Fourth Gospel, the words of the source (vii. 15) must have led the evangelist to suppose that a new discourse was beginning. He did not perceive the ironical character of the Jews' question, nor how it was prompted by Jesus' words in v. 37–47. Nor did he reach a perception of the thought-connection between Jesus' words in vii. 16–18 and the discourse in chap. v. He understood the utterance of the Jews in vii. 15 as an expression of real wonder at the learning of Jesus, and supposed Jesus' answer to be concerned with a fresh theme, suggested by their astonishment. Regarding this therefore as a new discourse, he assumed for

of time with the following words, Matt. xi. 25–30, is indicated by the phrase ἐν ἐκείνῳ τῷ καιρῷ in ver. 25 : but in what way the ταῦτα of this verse can refer to them is not perceptible. The affinity of ver. 22 (cf. ver. 24) with Matt. x. 15 suggests that the original place of these "Woes" was in the charge to those whom Jesus sent out (Matt. x.). The idea of the punishment of those who despise their preaching (Matt. x. 14 sq.) leads Jesus to speak of that which will come upon those who despise His own work. The proof that this really is the original setting is supplied by the parallel account in Luke x. 10–16. It further appears from the following verses in Luke (x. 17–22) that the passage given in Matthew as xi. 25–30 really pertains to a much later situation, namely, to a discourse which Jesus delivered on the return of those He had sent ; and that the mysterious ταῦτα of Matt. xi. 25 originally referred to the charmed security which His disciples enjoyed against all hostile, harmful powers (Luke x. 18–20). Compare, further, the separation of Luke xiv. 25–35 from Luke xii. 49–53. Luke xiv. 26 affords, in point of meaning, an immediate sequel to Luke xii. 52 sq. The parallel in Matt. x. 34–39 shows that the two passages really form one context. How disconnected and uncalled for, again, are the words of Luke xvi. 16, 17, 18! Even if we did not possess the parallels of Matthew, we could not but suppose that they stand outside of their proper place. They interrupt and destroy the connection between the words in ver. 15*b* and the incident of vv. 19 sqq., which is intended to illustrate those words. The parallels in Matthew show that they do actually belong to other contexts : ver. 16 to the discourse about the Baptist (Matt. xi. 12 sq.), vv. 17 and 18 to the Sermon on the Mount (Matt. v. 18, 32). On the other hand, there are good reasons for holding that the Parable of the Pharisee and the Publican (Luke xviii. 10–14) was originally connected with the discourse of xvi. 14 sqq., and stood between the two parts of ver. 15. It illustrates the thought of ver. 15*a*, that justification in God's sight does not always accord with the self-justification of men (cf. the term δικαιοῦν in xvi. 15 and xviii. 14).

it a new situation in Jerusalem, a situation in which Jesus is dealing, not with opponents, but with seeming well-wishers. It is true that later in the discourse Jesus addresses these people as His enemies, even unto death, but the evangelist did not find any greater difficulty in this than in the subsequent passage, viii. 30 sqq. Rather this seemed to him a specially significant sign that Jesus was not deceived by the friendly appearance of the men of Jerusalem, but discerned them from the first as the foes who should slay Him (cf. ii. 24).[1] According to the view of the evangelist Jesus' question in vii. 19b did not relate to the previous design on His life (v. 18), but to the effort to destroy Him which these men were yet to make; as this was still latent in the future, the multitude denied its existence (vii. 20);[2] but Jesus prophetically foresaw it. It is true that the following words, vii. 21–24, clearly refer to the preceding incident of v. 1 sqq., but the abrupt character of such a reference amid a new set of circumstances is overlooked by the evangelist, simply because he was not the original narrator, but was reproducing an earlier narrative.

4. *Severance of Connected Passages in Chapters vii. and viii.*

In the further course of chap. vii. certain sayings of Jesus appear (vv. 28 sq., 33 sq., 37 sq.), which according to the evangelist were uttered in three distinct sets of circumstances. They appear also to deal with quite different themes. In the first Jesus is replying to the objection that His earthly origin is notorious (ver. 27): His real origin, as known to Himself, He says, is quite other than that which is known to men (vv. 28 sq.). The second occasion is the attempt of the chief priests to arrest Him (ver. 32), on which

---

[1] *Vide sup.* pp. 29 sq.
[2] Ver. 20 and the opening words of ver. 21 are certainly an addition by the evangelist to the matter of his source.

Jesus says that in a little while He will depart, and be sought in vain (vv. 33 sq.). On a later day of the Feast of Tabernacles He calls to Him all those who thirst, and promises to them an ever flowing spring of water (vv. 37 sq.). After a report of what the populace said about Jesus (vv. 40–44) comes a sketch of the discussion in the Sanhedrin, when the officers who were to have arrested Jesus announce the failure of their mission (vv. 45–52). This is immediately followed, without any definite indication of a change of scene, by a new discourse of Jesus (viii. 12 sqq.).[1] The introductory formula is merely πάλιν οὖν αὐτοῖς ἐλάλησεν ὁ Ἰησοῦς. It is quite clear that this word αὐτοῖς cannot mean either the members or the servants of the Sanhedrin, with whom the preceding notice is concerned. It can only refer to the Jewish multitude which Jesus had addressed before. In other words, the introductory phrase in viii. 12 is worded as if the narrative in vii. 45–52 did not exist, and therefore no special reference were needed to the circumstances of the preceding passage, vii. 37–44. At first we may be tempted to call this a piece of literary slovenliness on the part of the evangelist, but we must take into account the very significant fact that the thought of the discourse which begins in viii. 12 is connected as closely as possible with the isolated utterances of Jesus in vii. 28 sq., 33 sq., 37 sq. The ideas of these sayings in chap. vii. are not only taken up again in viii. 12 sqq., but definitely explained and set in relation to one another.

These words in viii. 12, "I am the light of the world; he that followeth me shall not walk in darkness, but shall have the light of life," is a reiteration of vii. 37 sq., "If any man thirst, let him come unto me, and drink. He that

---

[1] The incident of the woman taken in adultery (vii. 53–viii. 11) may be left out of account, as it is not an original portion of the Gospel. If it were taken into consideration the difficulty to which attention is called would be in no wise diminished.

believeth on me, as the scripture hath said, out of his belly shall flow rivers of water." Jesus expresses under two different figures the same thought,—that He offers to those who come to Him in faith a life which is life indeed. This idea is expounded in the further course of the speech in chap. viii.: while those that will not believe in Jesus shall remain, He says, in their sins, and die, those who receive His teaching shall obtain the ἀλήθεια which maketh free, and the eternal life (viii. 31b–36, 51). Similarly, these words in viii. 14, "I know whence I came, and whither I go; but ye know not whence I come, or whither I go," are a repetition of vii. 28 sq. In contrast to the arrogant assumption of the Jews, who judge after the flesh (viii. 15), that they "know whence he came," He sets His own true knowledge of His origin,—of His Father who sent Him, and to whom He returns. Then in viii. 23, 42 sqq. He goes on to declare what is the unknown origin, and who the unknown Father, to which He lays claim: His opponents are from beneath, but He is from above; their father is the devil, but His Father is God. Finally, the words (viii. 21), "I go away, and ye shall seek me, and shall die in your sin: whither I go, ye cannot come" repeat what has been said in vii. 33 sq. These thoughts, taken from chap. vii., are here in chap. viii. set in mutual relation. Jesus' knowledge of His origin is the foundation of His claim to saving power (viii. 12–14); but since He is soon to depart, and will be sought in vain, it follows that they who will not now believe in Him shall then die in their sins (viii. 21, 24). The announcement, therefore, that He is soon to depart, gives reason for the exhortation that men should lay hold now, while He is still here, on that salvation which His divine origin enables Him to offer.

When we consider this mutual connection of the thoughts in vii. 28 sq., 33 sq., 37 sq., and the discourse in viii. 12 sqq., we cannot regard the present state of our

Gospel, in which those sayings are separated from one another and from that discourse, as natural or original. In the mind of the original author those utterances must from the first have held that relation to one another which is now made evident by the discourse in viii. 12 sqq. But there never was any speaker or writer who, having certain thoughts which he intended to support and elucidate each other, artificially separated them and distributed them among different scenes. That would be to obscure exactly what he wished to make clear. The severance must be ascribed to some secondary worker, who was not alive to the original sequence of thought. We have here, then, another indication that our evangelist made use of an older document. In that document the sayings in vii. 28 sq., 33 sq., 37 sq., and the discourse in viii. 12 sqq., belonged to one and the same situation. The scene described in vii. 45–52, to which vii. 32 serves as introduction, cannot have been found in the source. It follows that the abrupt reversion in viii. 12a to the circumstances of vii. 37 sqq., without reference to the change of scene that had happened in the meantime, is not merely literary slovenliness on the part of the evangelist, but arises out of his use of a source. We have already seen (pp. 67 *fin.* sq.) that a further indication of the employment of a source appears in vii. 39.

How, then, did the evangelist come to break up the connected whole which this discourse exhibited in his source? Exactly in the same way in which he was led to separate vii. 15–24 from the discourse in v. 17–47. The insertion in the source of the popular judgment concerning Jesus, vii. 40–43, led him to assume that the following words, viii. 12 sqq., were the beginning of a new and independent discourse. The fact that a new figure, that of the light, is here begun, confirmed him in this assumption. But when the introductory clauses of the original discourse, the sayings in vii. 28 sq., 33 sq., 37 sq., no longer stood in their proper contextual relation with its continuation in viii. 12 sqq., their mutual connection was no longer apparent, for it is only in the process of the discourse that it clearly comes out. It seemed therefore justifiable to take these clauses, which may in the original have been separated by interjectory remarks of the Jews, as independent of one another.[1]

5. *Severance of xii. 44–50 from xii. 35 and 36a.*

Another peculiar case occurs at the close of chap. xii. The discourse of Jesus, which extends to ver. 36a, is closed in ver. 36b with a remark that Jesus departed and hid Himself. There follows in vv. 37–43 a reflection of the evangelist concerning the unbelief of the Jews in Jesus, in spite of His many miracles. This is succeeded by a further utterance of Jesus,—introduced only by the formula, "And Jesus cried and said,"—in which He speaks of Himself as the light of the world, and of the importance of belief in Him as a divinely commissioned teacher (vv. 44–50). This concluding speech of Jesus, which is assigned to no definite situation, has an odd, supplementary appearance, coming as it does after a notice of the close of Jesus' public preaching

---

[1] A synoptic analogue is afforded by the way in which Luke provides a new setting (*i.e.* a dinner, xi. 37 sq.) for the discourse against the Pharisees in xi. 39 sqq., whereas in the source it certainly followed immediately after the speech in xi. 17–36, which is prompted by the taunt in xi. 15. The metaphor (vv. 34–36) of the eye as the light of the whole body, which cannot itself be dark, must have served in the source as an introduction to what Jesus went on to say, as Matthew's parallel shows, about the spiritual blindness of the Pharisees (Matt. xxiii. 16, 17, 19, 24, 26). Compare also the way in which, after the discourse on the second advent (Luke xvii. 22–37), a new passage appears to begin in xviii. 1, with a new theme, "pray without ceasing"; though it appears from xviii. 7 sq. that the injunction is especially to pray for the salvation that shall dawn at the second advent, and therefore that in the source this section, xviii. 1–8, formed the continuation of the discourse upon that theme.

(in ver. 36*b*), and a summary of the result of His ministry. Commentators usually make a close connection between these words of Jesus and the reflection of the evangelist in vv. 37–43. It is not, they say, another single discourse of Jesus' that is here recorded, but "a compendium of Christ's preaching in general."[1] This may, in fact, have been the way in which our evangelist conceived it. Still, if this be a summary of the leading ideas of Jesus' earlier discourses, the manner in which it is introduced is very remarkable. The words in 44*a* do not suggest the beginning of a recapitulation of former speeches, but of a new and separate utterance. But we are left with the question under what circumstances it was given, and who are to be thought of as its hearers.

This strange state of things takes a new aspect when we observe that the words of Jesus in vv. 44 sqq. stand in the closest internal relation to the close of the preceding speech. It is not merely that xii. 44 can be intelligibly read immediately after xii. 36: we have in xii. 44 sqq. the natural, and it may even be said the necessary, sequel to the thought of vv. 35 sq. In vv. 35 and 36*a* Jesus exhorts His hearers, in figurative language, to use the light, while it is yet for a little time among them, to walk with, lest darkness overtake them. The figure has not received as yet any definite interpretation. That follows in ver. 46: "*I* am come a light into the world, that whosoever believeth on me may not abide in the darkness." The connection between this interpretation and the figure which precedes is as close as that between vi. 35 and the figure in vi. 32 sq., or between x. 7–9 and the parable in x. 1–5. But while Jesus proclaims Himself to be the light, and demands faith in Himself, it is nevertheless incumbent on Him emphatically to declare that the real object of such faith is not Himself,

[1] O. Holtzmann, *Das Johannes-evang.* p. 105. Cf. B. Weiss and H. Holtzmann, *ad loc.*, and Haupt, *St. Kr.*, 1893, pp. 235 sq.

but God. The claim which He makes on their faith is only that of God's agent, the bearer of a divine commission. This thought is therefore given in vv. 44 sq. as a preface to the interpretation in ver. 46 of the figure in vv. 35 sq., and is further expounded in vv. 47–50. When this internal affinity between vv. 44 sqq. and 35 sq. is perceived, the discourse in 44 sqq. no longer conveys the impression of a detached, supplementary piece; the remarks of the evangelist in vv. 36*b*–43 stand revealed as an intrusive interpolation, which breaks into two parts what was, in his source, a homogeneous unit. This at once removes the perplexity caused by the omission in ver. 44 of any definite note of time and place. In the source there was no change of scene: and our evangelist, although by the remark in 36*b* he has brought the former scene to an end, nevertheless contents himself in 44*a* with the formula he found in the source.

But the objection is made that it "is inexplicable that the redactor should have inserted the heterogeneous piece, vv. 36*b*–43, in the middle of Jesus' speech as he had it before him, when he was perfectly free to place it at the end of the entire discourse."[1] The reply to this objection is that the reason which prompted the evangelist to interrupt the original context of the discourse was certainly analogous to that which led him to sever viii. 12 sqq. from vii. 37 sq. After xii. 36*a* in the source there was doubtless a remark about the demeanour of the Jews towards the words of Jesus. This remark gave the evangelist the impression that the discourse was closed; for, glancing at the words immediately following, vv. 44 sq., he overlooked the close connection between ver. 46 and the figurative words in vv. 35 and 36*a*. We can make a somewhat more exact conjecture as to the context of that remark. It must have been of a similar type to that which is inserted after the metaphor of the door to the sheepfold in x. 6: "but they understood not what things

[1] Haupt., *op. cit.* p. 235.

they were which he spake unto them." It must in some terms have expressed that the sense of Jesus' metaphor—or, in other words, that Jesus Himself, who was meant by it—was *hidden* from the Jews who heard it. It was that fact, according to the source, which prompted Jesus to proclaim clearly, with uplifted voice ($\xi\kappa\rho\alpha\xi\epsilon\nu$, ver. 44), that He was Himself the light of which He spake. The evangelist, however, mistook the meaning of the remark, and thought that Jesus had literally hidden Himself from the Jews (ver. 36*b*). And he extended the observation in the source—which speaks of the failure of the Jews to understand these special words of Jesus—to cover their lack of faith towards His work in general, that is, in the sense of the evangelist, His work of thaumaturgy.

6. *Disruption of the Context in xiii.* 12–20

A specially clear case of departure from the source is exhibited by the evangelist's addition in xiii. 17–19. After washing the disciples' feet Jesus charges them to imitate Him, and to do to one another what He has done to them (vv. 12–15). A servant is not greater than his master. If He, their Master, has performed for them this menial office, they must not think themselves too high to condescend to such a service (ver. 16). If they know this, which He has but now made known to them by word and example, blessed are they if they do it (ver. 17). To this blessing the following words are now attached: "I speak not of you all; I know whom I have chosen: but the scripture must be fulfilled: He that eateth his bread with me has lifted up his heel against me. From henceforth, I tell you before it come to pass, that, when it is come to pass, ye may believe that I am he" (vv. 18 sq.). These words clearly convey that this blessing, which was addressed to the disciples in general, did not hold good for the traitor.

Finally comes the clause: "Verily, verily, I say unto you, he that receiveth whomsoever I send receiveth me; and he that receiveth me receiveth Him that sent me" (ver. 20). The perfect isolation of this clause is obvious and striking. It cannot be brought into connection with the words about the traitor. Some commentators would dismiss it as a gloss: but this only removes one difficulty to discover another, for the insertion of such a gloss in such a place is itself inexplicable. Others have supposed that ver. 20 must be taken *per saltum* with ver. 17, vv. 18 and 19 being disregarded.[1] This does, in fact, give a clear connection of thought between the discourse in vv. 12–17 and the words of ver. 20. Jesus follows up His example of service by a charge to His disciples that they shall serve one another, adds thereto a blessing on those who obey that charge, and enhances the blessing by proclaiming the supereminent worth of such conduct as He enjoins. But could an author who was awake to this sequence of thought rend it asunder, by the insertion of an utterly foreign passage, so that on a mere reading or hearing of the passage it is impossible to perceive the original connection between the last member of the sequence and those that precede?

Not only, however, do the inserted verses (18 sq.) cut off ver. 20 from its natural place after ver. 17; they are not themselves in keeping with the position they occupy. Jesus' saying that He well knows the traitor among His disciples is occasioned by the blessing on those disciples in ver. 17, and is intended to limit its scope: "I speak not of you all." But the blessing is only conditional upon their following Jesus' exhortation to mutual service. The attachment of this condition excludes any natural reason for expressly excepting the traitor. It cannot appear to be called for unless the condition is overlooked. The occasion,

[1] Cf. B. Weiss, *ad loc.*

then, for those words concerning the traitor in vv. 18 sq. is an imperfect apprehension of the thought in ver. 17. This, however, cannot be attributed to Jesus Himself, or to the author who originally conceived ver. 17, but to a later writer who reproduced the thought without entering fully into it. In the original ver. 20 must have followed immediately after ver. 17. The redactor-evangelist intended to add to the blessing on the disciples such another limitation with regard to the traitor as stands at the end of ver. 10. It was precisely because he was only a secondary worker that he failed to perceive both that the conditional blessing needed no limitation and that the insertion of the words about the traitor leaves ver. 20 disconnected and unintelligible.[1]

7. *Displacement in the Farewell Discourse, Chapters xiii.–xvi.*

In the further course of the farewell discourse of chaps. xiii.–xvi. there are certain clear signs that the shape of this discourse as we have it is not the original one.[2] Here, again, the displacement can be explained very simply on the hypothesis that the long discourses in the fourth Gospel depend upon an older document.

The form of the concluding part of chap. xiv. suggests that this was the close of Jesus' address to His

[1] I fail to follow Haupt's objection, *op cit.* p. 24, that a later redactor would not have inserted the words of vv. 18 sq. exactly in this place, where they interrupt the connection of ver. 20 with ver. 17, when they might as easily have stood after ver. 20. Vv. 18 sq. are concerned specially with a presumed limitation to be set on the blessing of the Twelve in ver. 17, because it could not apply to the traitor. How could this limitation have stood after ver. 20, in which Jesus no longer addresses the Twelve in the second person?

[2] For these indications I must acknowledge an obligation to Fr. Spitta, *Zur Geschichte und Litteratur des Urchristentums*, i. pp. 168 sqq., and B. W. Bacon, "The Displacement of John xiv.," in the *Journal of the Society for Biblical Literature*, 1894, pp. 64 sqq.

disciples. This is not merely implied in the final clause (xiv. 31), "Arise, let us go hence." As early as ver. 25 the words take the special tone of a last farewell. Jesus recalls what He has spoken to His disciples while yet abiding with them (ver. 25). Henceforth it is not He, but the Spirit sent from the Father in His place, that shall teach them (ver. 26). The salutation of peace with which He bids them farewell betokens His bequest to them: He leaves with them the peace which is His own (ver. 27a). He bid them not despair at His departure, but rather to rejoice, because He goes unto the Father (vv. 27b–29). He will no more speak much with them, for the prince of the world cometh, to put His obedience to the Father to the last proof (vv. 30 and 31a). He will Himself go forth to meet the struggle which lies immediately before Him, and He gives His disciples the word for departure (ver. 31b). The intention seems to be that with these words the direct address to His disciples should close, and be followed only by the standing prayer in chap. xvii. In the record as we have it, however, the discourse of Jesus simply proceeds, without even any kind of transitional phrase, such as πάλιν οὖν αὐτοῖς ἐλάλησεν (cf. viii. 12, 21). The apparent close of the discourse stands in the middle of it.

This is very remarkable: but this is not all. In xvi. 5 Jesus says to His disciples, "Now I go unto Him that sent me; and none of you asketh me, Whither goest thou?" Their sorrow at His word that He is leaving them has so overcome them that they have given Him no opportunity to tell them whither He is departing: not to any place where He will be separated from them to their hurt, but into eternal life and heavenly Lordship, whence He will send them the Holy Spirit to be their aid, and in a little will Himself again be with them (vv. 7–16). But in an earlier passage (xiii. 36) Peter has already asked the definite question: "Master, whither goest thou?" and Jesus, in His reply, has spoken of the many abiding-places in His Father's house; thither He goes, and there He will receive His disciples unto Himself (xiv. 1-4). Once more, Thomas has used the words, "Master, we know not whither thou goest, how know we the way?" (xiv. 5). Jesus in His reply has proclaimed Himself the way by which they come to the Father (xiv. 6). This whole discussion concerning the goal of Jesus' departure is now, in xvi. 5, ignored: and such disregard of what precedes is not natural.

We are forced by both these cases to the conclusion that there has been a displacement of the original order of the farewell discourse: that xiv. 25-31 originally formed its concluding section, and stood immediately before the prayer in chap. xvii., and that chaps. xv. and xvi. originally stood before the discussion on the goal of Jesus' departure—that is, before Peter's question in xiii. 36. But where, in the earlier part of chap. xiii., is its former place to be determined? Spitta and Bacon both look for it in the principal breach which the evangelist has yet made,— in that of the episode in xiii. 21-30. Spitta places chaps. xv. and xvi. after xiii. 30, Bacon after xiii. 20. But this does not seem to me a correct decision. If not the episode in xiii. 21-20, at any rate the exhortation to the disciples at the washing of feet, to serve one another as their Master has served them (vv. 13-20), is continued in vv. 31-35. The inception of a new theme in ver. 31 is only apparent. In reality, what Jesus says in vv. 31-33 about His own glory and his immediate departure is quite subordinate to the theme of that exhortation, which clearly comes out again in vv. 34 sq. Up to this point, in vv. 12-20, Jesus had not yet spoken of His departure. By doing so now He gives to His commandment of love the force of a farewell charge, an ordinance by which His disciples are to regulate their lives in the coming time when they shall be alone. This connection between xiii. 31-35 and xiii. 1-20 must be preserved. There remains, then, only the possibility that chaps. xv. and xvi. stood between the commandment of love in xiii. 34 sq. and the question of Peter in xiii. 36. The assumption that this was in reality their original place is confirmed by the closer articulation which it gives to the members of the discourse, and the clearer and simpler movement of the thought.

The section xv. 1–17 links itself perfectly to the commandment in xiii. 34 sq. It leads up to an enforcement and extension of that commandment (xv. 12–17). The figure of the vine, with which it begins (xv. 1 sqq.), is not intended, in a merely general sense, to represent the inner communion of the disciples with their Master as something already subsisting and still to endure: its special object is to exhibit the mutual relation between their share in that communion and their power to bear fruit. The duration of that communion depends on their bearing fruit (ver. 2), and is itself needful that they may continue to bear fruit (vv. 4–6). And what is meant by bearing fruit in such communion with the Master is the keeping of His words, His commandments (vv. 7–10). And His commandment is the commandment of love (vv. 12–17). That love which Jesus has hitherto demanded from His disciples only in a brief and general form—love one another, as I have loved you, —that love of which His own is the example, He now sets forth more exactly in its quality and nature, its sacrificing, sharing, helping character (vv. 13–16). Herein lies the most perfect exposition of that demand to which the washing of feet was a prelude. Is not the sequence of thought in xv. 1–17 the natural continuation of the thought in xiii. 1–20, 31–35? With what a significant climax, after giving the commandment of love in vv. 31–35 as the farewell charge before His approaching departure, Jesus now declares in xv. 1 sqq. that the fulfilment of that commandment is the condition and assurance of permanent communion with himself! His disciples are to practise love, not only in remembrance of what He has already shown them, but in accordance with their abiding and vital communion with their Master. If the section xv. 1–7 be taken in its present place in our Gospel, we must suppose that Jesus here, in a second article of His speech, reverts to the commandment which He had given at the beginning of the first article, and from which He had already proceeded to discourse on other themes. Such a reversion is no doubt possible. But the process of the thought is much simpler and clearer if we take xv. 1–17 not as a reversion to that earlier theme, but as its original and direct continuation. Then the brief, compendious utterance in xv. 17 gives us the close of the first, the hortatory part of the address. Thereupon the words which follow, upon the hate and persecution which the disciples shall experience at the hands of the world (xv. 18–xvi. 4), form the very fitting exordium of the second part, which is devoted to comfort and promise.

Moreover, the colloquy with Peter, xiii. 36–38, with the further discourse that follows in xiv. 1 sqq., join on admirably to the close of chap. xvi. The disciples are so uplifted by their Master's comforting promises in xvi. 7–28 that they affirm that they already clearly understand His words as a divine revelation (vv. 29 sq.). But in reality they have no foreboding of the terrible form which Jesus' departure was to take. Jesus therefore calls in doubt the permanence of their faith, and predicts that in an hour, which was even then at hand, they should all flee, and leave Him alone (vv. 31 sq.). What He has said to them is intended to give them peace and courage amid the tribulation of the world (ver. 33). To these words, and especially to the prediction that they shall all forsake Jesus, Peter rejoins: he would know whither Jesus is going, that he for his part at least may follow Him, even though it be to lay down his life for Him (xiii. 36 sq.). Then Jesus foretells Peter's denial (ver. 38). But it is not His purpose to terrify His disciples, but to strengthen and comfort them. Therefore He follows up the prediction of xvi. 32 by the exhortation to courage of xiv. 1. The demand He makes in xiv. 1*b* is closely related to the assurance His disciples had given in xvi. 30. Even though He has called in question the permanence of their faith (xvi. 31 sq.), yet it is indeed His desire that they should have such faith, and hold it fast. And as He said in xvi. 33 that even when they foresake Him He will not be alone, because the Father is with Him, so now He exhorts them to have faith and trust in *both*—in God and in Himself. What He goes on to say about His Father's house (xiv. 2–4), whither He goes before and will receive His disciples to Him, is, on the one hand, a further answer to Peter's question in xiii. 36*a*, and, on the other hand, likewise a continuation of the comforting promise in xvi. 7–28. To comfort them for His departure He has spoken to them of what, even when departed from them, He will yet do for them. He will send them the Holy Spirit as their advocate and guide (xvi. 7–15). And after a short time of severance and sorrow they shall see Him present among them once more, and then they shall obtain lasting joy and the fulfilment of all their prayers (xvi. 16–28). To this promise He now adds, after the episodic colloquies in xvi. 29–33 and xiii. 36–38, the further prediction that He will, in time to come, receive them to Himself in the heavenly abodes (xiv. 2–4). It is in the natural order of thought that He speaks first of their life on earth after His departure, and then of that which shall form the close of their earthly life.

Finally, this hypothesis that in the source the section comprising chaps. xv. and xvi. stood before xiii. 36 makes perfectly intelligible how the displacement of this original order came to pass. Spitta, who does not accept my source-hypothesis, explains the disturbance by assuming that the loose sheets of the original manuscript were accidentally transposed.[1] It is, of course, as easily possible for such an accident to have befallen the manuscript of the source which the evangelist was employing, as a manuscript of the Gospel in the hands of a later scribe. Much more probable, however, is the following explanation, which Spitta, who inserts chaps. xv. and xvi. after xiii. 20, thereby excludes, though it becomes obvious as soon as the place for this section is fixed after xiii. 35. The evangelist, who, as I have already observed, did not work upon a written copy of his source, but used it memoriter, took Jesus' saying in xiii. 33, "Whither I go, ye cannot come," for the occasion on which to add Peter's question, "Whither goest thou?" He recognised, indeed, the connection of the commandment of love (vv. 34 sq.,) with the charge that followed the washing of feet (vv. 12-20). On that account he allowed this commandment to follow next after ver. 33. But he was not awake to the internal relation between the utterances introduced by the figure of the vine (xv. 1-17), on the one hand, and that charge (xiii. 12-20) and the commandment of love (vv. 34 sq.) on the other hand. To him it appeared that with this figure of the vine a new article of the discourse was begun. But it seemed to him very suitable that Peter's question should follow close upon the first mention of Jesus' departure. With Peter's question, however, was bound up the disquisition in xiii. 36*b*-38 and xiv. 1 sqq. The evangelist has therefore attached to it the whole section of the discourse which followed it in his source. Lastly he added the omitted passage, beginning with the apparently new theme in xv. 1 sqq., as a second article of the discourse.

---

[1] *Op. cit.* pp. 182 sqq.

CHAPTER III

Inquiry into the Composition of the Source

A. GENERAL PRINCIPLES IN THE DETERMINATION OF PASSAGES FROM THE SOURCE

IN the previous pages it has been shown that there are many indications of the employment of an older document in the Fourth Gospel, and especially in the long discourses. Glaring difficulties are met with of various sorts, the natural solution of which lies in the source-hypothesis.

When the correctness of the hypothesis has been recognised in several single cases, we have before us the further task of examining the whole Gospel with respect to this Source. The questions arise, What is the extent of the pieces taken from the Source, and how far can they be distinguished from the additions of the redactor-evangelist?

In answering these questions we have not to rely merely on vague conjectures. From those sections of the Gospel which have already been considered as exhibiting traces of the use of the Source we are able to gather an acquaintance with the general character and point of view, on the one hand, of the Source itself, on the other, of the independent additions of the evangelist. In the light of this knowledge we have now to ask, concerning other sections of the Gospel, whether they bear the stamp of the Source or of the evangelist. There are, moreover, in this Gospel many further instances of discrepancy in the narrative, and derangement of the true context, such as have already come into view. These cases, while they serve to confirm the source-hypothesis, are the most important signs of the extent to which the Source was employed.

In deciding whether any particular passage is to be assigned to the Source or to the evangelist we cannot take as a standard the credibility or intrinsic value of the passage in question. Of course, the record in the Source must be allowed, if only as the more ancient document, to have the greater value. Another fact, too, which has already been established, tells in favour of the Source: the high estimate formed by the evangelist of Jesus' "signs" as a most important credential of His Messiahship,— an estimate which, characteristic as it is of this writer, is certainly out of harmony with Jesus' own view,—is not to be found in the passages taken from the Source. But it certainly does not follow that everything of historical value in the Gospel is derived from the Source, and every incredible statement is an addition of the evangelist. We cannot give a verdict on the historical value, and the apostolic or sub-apostolic origin, of the record in the Source, until we have first established, by considerations of another kind, which passages were probably taken over from that document. Besides the chief source from which he took the main matter of his discourses, and besides our synoptic Gospels, the fourth evangelist may have had other oral or written originals at his command. He may therefore at times have made use of good material, even in his additions to his main source.

From the nature of the question, in attempting to mark off the original components of the Gospel, supplied by the Source, from the additions of the evangelist, we cannot always reach certainty in our conclusions. It is not as if the evangelist had merely made interpolations here and there in the older writing. His use of it was distinctively the employment and redaction of a source. At many points we shall be obliged to leave indeterminate the dividing line between the source-components and his editorial matter. We must always remember, even where we have the best ground for deriving a passage from the Source, that it has possibly been reproduced with considerable modifications. Passages, on the other hand, which bear in their broad aspect the unmistakable stamp of the evangelist may yet have an infusion of elements from the Source. Uncertainty of this kind is incident to all similar source-hypotheses. This is shown by the criticism of the sources of the Synoptics and the Acts of the Apostles. But to take the ground that because our efforts to discriminate the source-components cannot be carried, in many cases, beyond a certain degree of probability, therefore the whole attempt must be renounced, would be mere perversity. The task before us, scientifically stated, is to point out the source-components *so far as the evidence at hand will permit*. It is a part of this task to indicate as probable, and no more, that what can be perceived as probable, and no more. And it would be equally perverse to refuse to acknowledge, because of the necessary limit of certainty in this inquiry, that there are some cases in which a perfectly sure distinction can be drawn, by means of definite signs, between the Source and redactory additions.

B. THE PASSAGES FROM THE SOURCE IN DETAIL

1. *Source-components in the Prologue, i. 1–18*

The prologue to the Gospel, i. 1–18, must have belonged in substance to the Source. This is shown, in the first place, by its internal affinity with the discourses which were taken from that document. The concepts *life, light and darkness, being born of God*, are as prominent here as they are later in the discourses of Jesus. Jesus Christ is here denoted as He who has made fully known what God is, just as He Himself in chap. xvii. speaks of His completed work on earth as a manifestation of God (xvii. 1–8). There is a significant absence of any reference to the "signs" of Jesus. In ver. 14 we are told wherein His disciples beheld the glory of His divine Sonship: not, as we should have expected if the evangelist had been writing with a free hand, in the abundance and grandeur of His signs (cf. ii. 11, xi. 4, 40, xx. 30 sq.), but His fulness of χάρις καὶ ἀλήθεια.

The derivation of the prologue from the Source may also be recognised by the manner in which the clauses relating to the Baptist, vv. 6–8 and 15, interrupt the sequence and flow of thought. This indicates that the evangelist who wrote them was not the independent author of the rest of the prologue. These sayings are closely related to what is said about the Baptist in the later historical portion of the Gospel (i. 19–36, iii. 25–36, x. 40 sq.). Here already occurs the emphatic enunciation of a point to which the evangelist evidently attaches a peculiar value,—that the Baptist was not co-ordinate with Jesus, but was a witness on God's behalf to the Messiahship of Jesus. In the intention of the evangelist, therefore, they are not by any means mere parenthetical notes in the prologue, but substantial and important portions of it.[1] But it is equally true that they do not stand in any close or organic connection with the remainder of the prologue, and that, in order to understand aright the true sequence of thought,

[1] This is the sound fundamental idea of Baldensperger, *Der Prolog des vierten Evangeliums*, 1898, pp. 1–57. From the evangelist's point of view the antithesis between Jesus Christ, the Logos made flesh, and the Baptist, is an important object, if not the chief object, of the prologue. The question remains whether, when this has been established as the evangelist's point of view, we have acquainted ourselves with the full, original meaning of the prologue.

we are obliged to treat them as parenthetical interpolations.[1]

This is especially clear in ver. 15. Ver. 14 tells of the experience which Jesus Christ's disciples had of the filial glory of the Logos made flesh, and includes the writer among them: "We beheld his glory, ... full of χάρις καὶ ἀλήθεια." In vv. 16 sq. the account of their experience is continued: "For of his fulness we all received, yea, χάρις upon χάρις. For the law was given through Moses, the χάρις καὶ ἀλήθεια came through Jesus Christ." Ver. 14 gives to the *object* of the experience of which it speaks, the filial glory of the Logos made flesh, the concrete character of a fulness of χάρις καὶ ἀλήθεια: then ver. 16 adds that this very fulness was experienced by the disciples, and that thereby was effected a revelation beyond that which was given through Moses. A similar increase of emphasis attaches itself to the *subject* of that experience; in ver. 14 it is only indirectly implied in the accidence, but in ver. 16 it is expressly denoted as ἡμεῖς πάντες; and instead of the term "beheld," which might be used of mere onlookers who did not partake, we are told that they "received" of that good thing which they saw; finally, the words καὶ χάριν ἀντὶ χάριτος show that they received not once nor sparingly, but permanently and richly, so that one gift of grace was not displaced save by another.

But between these two passages, so closely connected in thought, we have introduced in ver. 15 the witness of the Baptist concerning Jesus. We are told that John bore witness to that person of whom ver. 14 speaks, saying that it was He whom he had meant by his earlier declaration that there was one coming who, because He had been before John, was exalted above him. That is to say, John bore witness to that person as the Messiah, and as a pre-existent being. How does this witness fit in with the thoughts of

[1] Cf. Harnack, *Z. Th. K.*, 1892, pp. 221 sq.

INQUIRY INTO COMPOSITION OF THE SOURCE 113

vv. 14 and 16? It joins on very well to ver. 14. The disciples' own experience of the glory of the Logos made flesh is first declared: then follows an appeal to the witness of the Baptist, which gives a second proof, if of another kind, of the Messiahship of the same person. But how does the next clause, ver. 16, which is introduced by a causal particle, fit on to this witness of the Baptist's words? for the thought of ver. 14 is carried on too clearly in ver. 16 for the ἡμεῖς πάντες in ver. 16 not to be identified with the ἡμῖν and the subject of ἐθεασάμεθα in ver. 14. The chief person included in ἡμεῖς πάντες, on whose account the first person of the verb is used, cannot in ver. 16 be the Baptist, but must, as in ver. 14, be the writer. So we must seek to understand ver. 16 as an explanation of the fact that the Baptist bore witness: John was able to bear witness to Jesus as the primeval being because we all (and now the Baptist is included) received of his fulness grace for grace.[1] This interpretation may be the most formally correct, but it does not accord with the sense, because that which is spoken of in ver. 16 as having been received stands in no apparent relation towards the burden of the Baptist's testimony. That to which he testifies in ver. 15 is not the special point with which ver. 14 culminates, which ver. 16 elucidates,—Jesus Christ's fulness of χάρις καὶ ἀλήθεια, as a sign of His divine glory,—but the loftier rank of the Messiah as evinced by His priority in time, His pre-existence. This it is which marks the internal disparity between ver. 15 and its context. In view of this disparity the attempt to bind vv. 15 and 16 together is artificial.[2]

[1] Cf. B. Weiss in Meyer's *Commentary*, *ad. loc.*, and Baldensperger, *op. cit.* pp. 44 sq.

[2] Baldensperger, *op. cit.* pp. 44 sqq. evades this disparity by interpreting πλήρωμα αὐτοῦ in ver. 16 not in accordance with πλήρης χάριτος κ. ἀληθ. in ver. 14, but as used of the absolute supremacy of the eternal Christ over all historical, created power and greatness. It was this expression, the Pleroma, which led the evangelist to mention the pre-

The only natural placing for ver. 16 is immediately after ver. 14. There the causal particle at the beginning of ver. 16 is entirely in place. For, as appears from the above exposition of the relation of ver. 16 to ver. 14, the experience of which ver. 16 speaks is not another, merely co-ordinate to that of ver. 14, and set side by side with it, but it is the same, only set forth more strongly and clearly in a fuller and more emphatic clause.

But if we recognise, as most commentators now do, that ver. 16 links on to ver. 14, overleaping ver. 15, we cannot but perceive that the composition of this piece, vv. 14–16, is very remarkable. In the midst of words in which the writer testifies to his own experience of the filial glory of Jesus Christ, which consists in χάρις καὶ ἀλήθεια, is inserted an appeal to the Baptist's testimony, which has no relation to Jesus' fulness of χάρις καὶ ἀλήθεια. After this insertion the writer's own testimony is continued exactly as if the witness of the Baptist had not intervened. Can the author who regarded vv. 16 sq. as a continuation of ver. 14, and intended so to write, have interrupted this sequence of thought by the heterogeneous thought of ver. 15? I consider it psychologically impossible. None but a later mind, which had not independently conceived that testimony from experience, could have allowed such an insertion in such a place. This later mind was, as our earlier inquiry has shown, not that of an interpolator making insertions in our Gospel after its completion, but the evangelist himself, in his redaction of an older written source. Attaching, as he

existence in the Baptist's words of ver. 15. Upon this fulness all have drawn, the Baptist among the rest; from it the Mosaic as well as the Christian dispensation emanated (ver. 17).—But in view of the evidence for the relation of πλήρωμα αὐτοῦ in ver. 16 to πλήρης χάριτος κ. ἀληθ in ver. 14 this is an impossible interpretation. In vv. 16 sq. mention occurs again of χάρις and χάρις κ. ἀληθ. The term πλήρωμα cannot take in that place an altogether different sense from the πλήρης, defined by χάριτος κ. ἀληθ of ver. 14.

did, a peculiar importance to the witness of the Baptist to Jesus' Messiahship, he wished to bring it forward at once, in the prologue which he took from his source, alongside the testimony from experience. The place which he chooses for it, immediately after ver. 14, instead of at the end of the appeal to the witness from experience, after ver. 17 or 18, is to be explained by the very fact that he had not independently conceived and formulated that appeal, and so failed to perceive its close internal chain of meaning. Such a failure is possible in the mind of a later reproducer of the text, but in that of the original conceiver it is unthinkable.[1]

If ver. 15 is an addition to the Source by the evangelist, the same must be said about vv. 6-8, which have so close an affinity with it. It is true that they do not interrupt the context so destructively as ver. 15; but they do not form, any more than that verse, an integral link in the chain of thought. The sum and substance of the prologue is that the eternal and divine Logos has appeared historically among mankind as Jesus Christ. The principle on which the expression of this thought proceeds is to announce that historical manifestation, first of all, in general and indefinite terms, and then to give it a more and more definite and concrete form.[2] In ver. 5a it is indefinitely denoted by the figure of the light shining in darkness. The present tense of φαίνει shows that the manifestation is conceived as still continuously operative in the time of the writer: but the reference is not merely or chiefly to its operation in the present, but rather to its past, historical appearance in Jesus Christ, as is shown by the use of the preterite in ver. 5b: "The darkness comprehended it not." This indefinite, figurative utterance about the *shining* of the light in the darkness is followed in vv. 9-13 by others of a more

---

[1] Cf. the perfectly analogous case of an insertion in xiii. 17-20 (pp. 99 sqq.).
[2] Cf. Harnack, Z. Th. K., 1892, pp. 218 sqq.

definite kind: the light *came* into the *world*, the Logos came to *His own*, His own knew Him not and received Him not, on those that did receive Him He bestowed the divine Sonship; then in vv. 14 and 16 we have the more concrete conception of the *Logos become flesh*, and the manifestation in this form *to the writer himself* of His divine χάρις καὶ ἀλήθεια; until, finally, in ver. 17 the definite historical person, who as God's singly-begotten Son has made known the Father (ver. 18), is denoted *by His historical name as Jesus Christ*. In the middle of this catena of ideas come the words (vv. 6–8) about the Baptist as the man sent to bear witness of the light. The place for them is very appropriately chosen, immediately before the coming of the Logos-light into the world is spoken of. Still it is remarkable that before the naming of the historical Logos, before even the gradual process which leads up to it has begun, the witness to the light should be introduced by his concrete, historical name. This gives to the words referring to the Baptist so different a character from that of the contextual words about the Logos. Moreover, the words which follow, regarding the lack of recognition and the reception in general which befell the Logos in the world, are not brought into any internal relation towards the Baptist's testimony. Luthardt tries to connect the context thus: in spite of the witness of the Baptist the Logos was not received when He came into the world. But this is not the connection of thought which is expressed. Rather it is this: although the world was made by Him, yet when He came into the world He was not known (ver. 10). That is to say, there is a connection of thought between vv. 9 sqq. and ver. 3, which overleaps vv. 6–8; but no analogous connection with vv. 6–8 is to be found. On that ground alone we might regard vv. 6–8 as episodic and parenthetical; their omission does not obscure in any degree the meaning of the rest; rather, it makes the connection more cogent.[1]

2. *Source-components in i. 19–iv. 54*

In the first part of the Gospel (i. 19–iv. 54) is recounted the overpowering testimony to the Messiahship of Jesus at His first appearance. First is described how the Baptist pointed Jesus out as the Messiah (i. 19–34), and how Jesus thereupon made Himself known as such to His disciples by astonishing proofs of His knowledge concerning them (i. 35–51), by the miraculous sign at the marriage in Cana (ii. 1–12), and by an oracular saying, whose fulfilment they afterwards witnessed (ii. 12–22). Then the reception which Jesus met with in His Messianic work in the various parts of Palestine is described: in Jerusalem (ii. 23–iii. 21), in the land of Judæa (iii. 22–iv. 3), in Samaria (iv. 4–42), and in Galilee (iv. 43–54). The composition of this part of the Gospel is clearly dominated by the intention which the

[1] This does not preclude the possibility that the evangelist has made certain alterations in the wording, where he takes it up again in ver. 9. The τὸ ἀληθινόν, which seems to be contrasted with the οὐκ ἦν ἐκεῖνος τὸ φῶς of ver. 8, may have been inserted by him, though without that contrast it is still not inappropriate. Similarly, the participial turn, ἦν . . . ἐρχόμενον, may be due to him. He makes use elsewhere of this construction (cf. i. 28, iii. 23, xi. 1, xviii. 18, 25), in which the copula always precedes the participle (as also in numerous places in the synoptic Gospels: Matt. vii. 29, xix. 22, Mark ii. 18, Luke i. 21, 22, ii. 33 and *passim*). It certainly is not absolutely necessary, in this place either, to assume any alteration in the words of the Source. In the sense of the original the stress in ver. 9 lies on the idea of coming, as distinguished from that of shining (ver. 5). The participial periphrasis does, in fact, bring out precisely the emphasis required. In any case I fail to see how the assumption that slight redactional alterations have been made, in ver. 9, in the wording of the Source, involves my theory in "the development of new difficulties" (Haupt, *op. cit.* p. 220). In every source-hypothesis we must take into account the possibility that the matter taken from the source may have been altered in particular phrases. Such modifications merely show that a source-hypothesis, and not a hypothesis of interpolation, is called for.

evangelist avows in xx. 30 sq. In carrying it out he makes use at times of synoptic material, especially in the account of the Baptist's words and of Jesus' baptism (i. 19-34), and in the story of the healing of the son of the king's officer in Capernaum (iv. 46-54). By its side appears material of different origin. We may perceive in several places that it includes pieces taken from that collection of discourses which we denote "the Source."

No signs of the employment of this source are to be found in the first few sections, i. 19-51 and ii. 1-11. In the following section, ii. 12-22, the saying of Jesus in ii. 19 must, as we have already perceived (pp. 66 sq.), have been derived from the Source. The evangelist regarded this saying as an oracular prediction of Jesus' resurrection after three days (vv. 21 sq.), and for its sake inserted the whole account of the cleansing of the Temple in this place. But the original sense of Jesus' saying must have been other than this. If the saying itself was preserved in the Source, the situation which gave rise to it must also have been noticed there. We may, therefore, derive the main substance of vv. 13-20 from the Source. That does not exclude the suggestion that the evangelist, in reproducing this constituent of the Source, inserted certain reminiscences of the synoptic account of the incident.[1] Ver. 17 is certainly an addition. This is shown by the affinity between vv. 17 and 22: the use of the similar formula ἐμνήσθησαν οἱ μαθηταὶ αὐτοῦ in both places, and the reference to ver. 17 in the ἐπίστευσαν τῇ γραφῇ of ver. 22. The evangelist desired to make clear that Jesus' disciples not only saw in His resurrection the fulfilment of His oracle at the cleansing of the Temple, but also recognised that deed itself as the fulfilment of the Old Testament Scripture.

Then, again, the conversation between Jesus and Nicodemus in iii. 1-21 must be derived from the Source.

[1] Cf. *sup*. pp. 36 sq.

In ii. 23–25 the evangelist relates that while many believed on Jesus, at His public appearance in Jerusalem, because of His signs, Jesus, for His part, did not trust Himself unto them, for He was able to see into the inner part of man. The evangelist attaches great importance to this point, that Jesus was at no time deceived in those who were to become His deadly foes.[1] And so here, in support of what he says in ii. 24 sq., he introduces the conversation with Nicodemus, because in it Jesus speaks to a man of Jerusalem about the lack of acceptance which befalls His witness, His light-giving revelation (iii. 11 sq., 18–20). To the mind of the evangelist these words, spoken at the beginning of Jesus' public ministry, and in spite of the degree of acceptance which is recorded in ii. 23, are in Jesus' mouth an oracular prediction of His future rejection by the inhabitants of Jerusalem. The thought that the light is hated by those that work evil (iii. 19 sq.) is not, however, the dominating thought in Jesus' discourse with Nicodemus. The whole conversation, therefore, cannot be regarded as a free composition by the evangelist, actuated by the ideas we have assigned to him. But it is quite intelligible that, finding in his source a discourse delivered at Jerusalem, in the second part of which that thought was expressed, he attached the whole discourse, for the sake of that thought, to ii. 23–25. The conversation with Nicodemus bears throughout the character of the other large sections of discourse from the Source.

Ver. iii. 2*b* ($οὐδεὶς\ γὰρ\ κ.τ.λ.$)—Nicodemus' reference to the signs of Jesus as a token that He was sent from God— must be an addition by the evangelist to the adopted material. He it is who lays such a continual and overpowering stress on the signs of Jesus. Here, in ver. 2*b*, he makes Nicodemus speak as the representative of the inhabitants of Jerusalem, who according to ii. 23 believed in

---
[1] Cf. *sup.* pp. 28 sqq.

Jesus for the sake of the signs. In Jesus' discourse to Nicodemus this point in his address to Jesus is not considered, though the whole discourse forms a reply to that address. Against his acknowledgment that Jesus was a *teacher* come from God, Jesus sets the higher claim that He was sent by God to confer *eternal life* (v. 16 sq.) This it is to which the assurance at the beginning is intended to lead, that assurance that "except a man be born again, he cannot see the kingdom of God." The view often asserted, because required by ver. 2*b*, that the discourse of Jesus exposes the insufficiency of a faith based on signs,[1] cannot be made good by the discourse itself. The question what are Jesus' credentials, as the object of a faith which leads to eternal life, as the mediator of the eternal life, does not there arise.

Probably the words ὕδατος καὶ in iii. 5 are also an addition by the redactor to the Source. In what follows there is no further mention of being born of water. It is the birth of the spirit only that is spoken of (vv. 6 and 8). This birth of the spirit of God, which initiates a life, not of the flesh, but divine, comes to pass, in the meaning of the Source, when man receives with faith the words of Jesus, which are spirit and life (v. 24, vi. 63; cf. also i. 12 sq.). It was, however, very natural to the redactor to think of the new birth to life eternal as happening specifically in baptism (cf. Mark xvi. 16), and, in order to make this relation to baptism clear, to denote it as a being born of water.

In the section, iii. 22–iv. 3, on Jesus' appearance in the land of Judæa, no source-components can well be discovered. We are told that Jesus with His disciples came forth baptizing at the same time as John, and obtained a larger following than he. To John's disciples this did not seem well, but John himself acknowledged it as necessary, in correspondence with the supremacy of one who had

[1] Cf., *e.g.*, Luthardt, but also O. Holtzmann, pp. 206 sq.

come from heaven over one born of earth. The whole narrative brings out very clearly the view which the evangelist reveals elsewhere, that the Baptist had no separate importance, apart from Jesus, but pointed only to Jesus as the Messiah.

The words of the Baptist in iii. 31–36 seem at first, indeed, so closely akin in thought and style to the discourse with Nicodemus, that we are tempted to suppose they must emanate from the same source. But the similarity rests only on the reproduction of single clauses from that discourse. And at the crucial point we perceive, alongside a great likeness of expression with that and other discourses of Jesus, a substantial difference of conception. In iii. 31 Jesus, as ὁ ἄνωθεν ἐρχόμενος and ὁ ἐκ τοῦ οὐρανοῦ ἐρχόμενος, is contrasted with the Baptist as ὢν ἐκ τῆς γῆς. This contrast at once recalls that which is set up in the discourse with Nicodemus between the ἄνωθεν γεννηθείς, the γεγεννημένον ἐκ τοῦ πνεύματος, and the γεγεννημένον ἐκ τῆς σαρκός (iii. 3, 5, 6); and that in the later discourse (chap. viii.) between εἶναι ἐκ τῶν ἄνω and εἶναι ἐκ τῶν κάτω, ἐκ τοῦ κόσμου τούτου (viii. 23). But in the discourse of the Baptist the contrast has a purely physical meaning: he is of the earth, because he has had no such pre-existence as the Messiah come from heaven. On the other hand, in the discourse with Nicodemus, and in that of chap. viii., the contrast has an ethical and religious sense, such as may hold good between men who have the same physical origin. He is from above, he is from heaven, who has within him an inner life born of God; he is from beneath, of this world, of the flesh, who has within him only the earthly life and desires. In this last sense it not only holds good of Jesus Himself that in spite of His well-known earthly origin, He is yet not of the earth, but from God (vii. 28 sq., viii. 42), but it is said also of all His disciples that they are not of this world, nor of the flesh, but born of

God (i. 13, xv. 19, xvii. 14, 16). In this sense, again, it could not be said of the Baptist that he was of the earth, at the very moment when his acknowledgment and witness of Jesus as Messiah is being emphasised. Much rather, as the first disciple who believed in Jesus, he must be reckoned among those that are of God (cf. i. 12 sq., vi. 65, viii. 47). This fact, that in the discourse of the Baptist the terms are used not in this ethical and religious sense, but in a physical sense, is a clear sign that, in spite of a certain formal likeness which it bears to passages from the Source, this piece is not derived from that document. Our evangelist has collected together in it thoughts taken from the discourse with Nicodemus in such a sort that it looks like a doublet of that preceding discourse of Jesus. He was no doubt guided by the intention of making clear that what the Baptist said about Jesus' divine mission, and the saving power of belief in Him, differed in no wise from what Jesus said Himself.

What is the relation in which the section on Jesus' appearance in Samaria (iv. 4-42) stands to the Source? We gain at first a general impression that Jesus' words to the Samaritan woman (vv. 13 sq. and 21-24) and to His disciples (vv. 32-38) bear the same character in style and standpoint as those longer discourses of the Gospel which we have already recognised as belonging to the Source. On the other hand, the narrative relates that Jesus evoked the faith of the Samaritan woman by a proof of His supernatural knowledge; that He made Himself directly known to her as the Messiah; that after a brief space He was acknowledged as the Saviour of the world by many Samaritans (vv. 15-18, 26, 28-30, 39-42); and all this reveals the characteristic attitude of the fourth evangelist towards Jesus' proclamation of Himself as Messiah, and its result. Must we be content with the indefinite conclusion that the evangelist has introduced some words of Jesus, taken from the

Source, into his delineation of this Samaritan episode? Or can we find more definite grounds for this conclusion, and trace the outline of what has been borrowed from the Source?

In investigating this question we may set out with the certainty that Jesus' words to the woman in vv. 13 sq., that He can give her water that shall quench her thirst for ever, and spring up unto eternal life, must, in the light of its clear analogy to vi. 27, 35, 51, vii. 37 sq., be derived from the Source. But the introductory account of Jesus' meeting with the woman at the well, and the beginning of His conversation with her, is closely bound up with these words. This also, then, in its general sum, must have belonged to the Source. This is confirmed by the observation that at one place in the introduction the original context has been interrupted. When Jesus tells the woman that if she knew the gift of God, she would have asked and received from Him who spoke with her living water, she gives a reply (vv. 11 and 12) whose two members are very different from one another. In saying first, "Thou hast nothing to draw with, and the well is deep," she expresses the idea that Jesus' words must really mean that He would give her water from Jacob's well, by which they stood: her only difficulty is that Jesus has nothing to draw with. But such a misconception can hardly be attributed to her, for Jesus had not promised her simply water, but "living water,"— that is, spring-water. Such water could never be drawn from Jacob's cistern. In fact, the second part of the woman's answer goes on to show that she had perfectly well understood Jesus to mean that He could give her better water than that from Jacob's well. She proceeds, "Whence hast thou that living water? art thou greater than our father Jacob, who gave us the well, and drank thereof himself, and his sons, and his cattle?" She could not have attributed to Jesus a claim to be greater than Jacob unless she had correctly taken the sense of His words that He would give her better water than that of Jacob's well. The two parts of her answer rest, therefore, on two different interpretations of the foregoing words of Jesus. We must explain the first part as a supplementary, and not very appropriate, addition. It was intended to bring clearly out the fact that the woman misunderstood Jesus' words; but it leaves out of account the exact relation in which the reply of ver. 12 stands towards Jesus' words in ver. 10. The fact that this insertion has presumably been made by the evangelist seems to show that the main matter of the conversation has been taken from the Source. It seems to me probable that the words of ver. 10, καὶ τίς ἐστιν ὁ λέγων σοι· δός μοι πεῖν, are also an addition of the evangelist. They are not needed to give point to the woman's question, "Art thou greater than our father Jacob?" Even if Jesus had not already called attention to the higher significance of His person, the wonder in her question is perfectly natural and appropriate. Here is an ordinary man offering to supply better water, spring-water, in the place where the patriarch Jacob had been obliged to content himself with building a cistern and drinking cistern-water. These words in ver. 10 seem intended to prepare the way for Jesus' proclamation of Himself to the woman as Messiah (vv. 25 sq.), and together with that self-proclamation they must belong to the evangelist. In the Source, at the end of ver. 10, the pronoun must, of course, have been με instead of αὐτὸν, and ἔδωκα must have stood where we have ἔδωκεν.

In the further course of the conversation as we have it there are two sudden and surprising changes of theme. The transition from Jesus' words about the water of life which He offers to give (vv. 13 sq.) to the discussion of the woman's experience in marriage (vv. 16–18) is as abrupt as the next transition to the question which is the right place to worship God (vv. 19 sqq.). The usual explanation is that Jesus, perceiving the woman's failure to understand His words about the water of life, next seeks to arouse in her a sense of guilt, and in this way to awaken a desire for His gift of salvation. But this intention of Jesus' words is not revealed by anything in the text. If it were, we should be forced to own that the woman knew how, by a well-timed question about the place of worship, to lead Jesus away from that dangerous theme, and bring His intention to naught. For in what follows Jesus says nothing about the relation of the coming day of Messianic salvation to the sin of mankind, and the necessity that the true worshippers of God should turn in repentance from their sins. Yet how easily He could have given this turn to the conversation about the worship of God! But an earnest consciousness of guilt was not at all required to lead the woman to believe in His Messiahship. She herself bases her belief simply on the fact that Jesus has told her all that she ever did (vv. 28 sq., 39); in other words, that He has given her a proof of His miraculous knowledge. In this foundation of her belief the significance of His words on the place and the true manner of worshipping God has no part. To us, indeed, these words seem the very pivot of the conversation with the Samaritan woman: we see in them a magnificent declaration of Jesus' consciousness of the epoch-making advance which He was to inaugurate in the evolution of true religion. But in the narrative scheme of our evangelist these words are merely incidental. According to ver. 29 it is not they, but the words of vv. 17 sq. which make the decisive impression on the woman. The further account, too, in vv. 28-30 and 39-42 might be attached immediately to vv. 16-18, the talk about the worship of God being omitted. On the other hand, we should miss nothing relevant to this talk, if the conversation on the woman's married life (vv. 16-18) were lacking. The several points of the whole incident, as we have it, have no close organic connection with each other. This is a sign that they did not originally belong to one another. The evangelist must have taken the conversation on the worship of God from the Source. He must have added, for his own part, all that relates to Jesus' miraculous knowledge of the woman's former life, and the belief in Himself which it evoked.

Apparently the woman's remark in ver. 19, "Sir, I perceive that thou art a prophet," was in the Source the answer which followed immediately on Jesus' words in vv. 13 sq.[1] Jesus has here made it clear that He does not mean natural, earthly water. Now, therefore, the woman understands Him. She perceives that He speaks, with holy enthusiasm, of things celestial and divine, and feels Himself the bearer of good gifts from heaven. And so she recognises Him as a prophet, and as such she asks Him to solve a difficult problem of piety. At the same time she solves that which He had propounded to her in vv. 10 and 13 sq.: she begs of Him some of His "living water." If the woman's recognition of Jesus as a prophet is based on her perception of the religious meaning and purpose of His words in vv. 13 sq., the transition to the question where men ought to worship is no longer abrupt. But it is also perfectly clear how the evangelist came to interpolate vv. 16–18 into this portion of the account in the Source. The woman's acknowledgment of Jesus as a prophet did not seem to him sufficiently accounted for by the figurative words of Jesus in vv. 10 and 13 sq. He took it that this recognition naturally presupposed some such proof of Jesus' wonderful knowledge as might compare with those in i. 43 and 48 sq. Before inserting this token of miraculous knowledge he had brought the conversation about the water to a close in ver. 15. It seems to me possible that one of the constituents even of ver. 15 belonged to the

---

[1] Cf. the way in which, after the closely analogous sayings of Jesus in vii. 37 sq., there follows the judgment of the people, "This is of a truth the prophet" (vii. 40).

Source, namely, the request, "give me this water." But if so, this request must, in the meaning of the Source, have arisen out of a suspicion of the higher meaning of Jesus' words, and have formed the transition to the question in ver. 20. As ver. 15 now stands it only expresses a further misconception of the woman, who still thought that Jesus was speaking of water in the physical sense. But when the conversation about the water closes with such a definite misconception on the woman's part, the question where men ought to worship can no longer be understood as a sequel to this introductory conversation. That is how the question took its present inconsequent appearance.

In the Source the conversation on the worship of God must have closed with the woman's words in ver. 25. The answer of Jesus, that He was Himself the Messiah (ver. 26), is certainly an addition by the evangelist, with whose characteristic attitude it accords to make Jesus declare His Messiahship in this unreserved fashion. The continuation of the account in the Source lies in Jesus' conversation with His disciples in vv. 31–38, to which perhaps the original of ver. 27 formed the transition. Jesus' words in vv. 32 and 34–38 are a sequel to His utterances about the worship of God in vv. 19–25. They express the deep, spiritual emotion which that conversation has awakened in Him. That here, in Samaria, where He could not expect it and had not sought it, the opportunity had come to Him to sow the seed of the word, and so be active in the ministry which God had committed to Him, was to Him a feast in which He had forgotten all earthly food (vv. 32, 34). The religious interest which the woman revealed by her question in ver. 20, and the faith with which she looked forward to the coming and preaching of the Messiah (ver. 25), were to Him signs of the receptive soil which was to be found in Samaria for the Messianic preaching of the kingdom of God, and gave promise of the rich harvest which His disciples should one day gather here (vv. 35–38). The evangelist was led to conclude, from the words in ver. 35*b*, "Lift your eyes and look on the fields, that they are white unto harvest," and from the present tense in ver. 36, that Jesus and His disciples had even at that time a great harvesting among the Samaritans. That suggested to him the form in which he closes the story (vv. 39–42). But ver. 37*b* shows that Jesus' words in vv. 35 sq. did not originally refer to an immediate harvest, but to one which should come at a later time, when He was no longer on earth, and His disciples had entered into His work. It is in vivid, prophetic anticipation of that future that Jesus speaks in vv. 38 sq. Here once more the account of the Source and the narrative framework of the evangelist are only superficially connected. When we scrutinise their inner meaning, they are seen to gape asunder.

In the section, then, which deals with the appearance of Jesus in Samaria (iv. 4–42) the following pieces are to be derived from the Source: in the main the introduction to Jesus' conversation with the Samaritan woman, vv. 4–14, with the exception of the words in ver. 10, καὶ τίς ἐστιν ὁ λέγων σοι· δός μοι πεῖν, and the words in ver. 11, οὔτε ἄντλημα ἔχεις καὶ τὸ φρέαρ ἐστὶν βαθύ; perhaps the foundation of ver. 15; the conversation on the worship of God, vv. 19–25; perhaps the foundation of ver. 27; finally, the conversation with the disciples, vv. 31–38.

In the section on Jesus' reception in Galilee (iv. 43–54) there are no traces of the employment of the Source.

3. *Source-components in Chapter v. and Chapter vi.*

In the second part of the Gospel (chaps. v.–xii.) are set forth certain contests which Jesus had with the Jews, who remained unbelieving in spite of the overpowering testimony to His Messiahship. We have already decided, from a series of clear indications, that the evangelist must have taken from the Source the groundwork of several passages of discourse in this part.¹ Something remains to be added to what we have established. In the sections which have been recognised as mainly derived from the Source, the source-components have still to be marked out, as far as possible, from the additions of the evangelist. And we have further to show that there are other sections in this part which betray signs of the employment of a source.

As we saw above,² the groundwork of chap. v. must be derived from the Source. The original introduction to v. 17 sqq. must have been an account of a healing wrought by Jesus on the Sabbath, such as seemed to the Jews an illicit ἐργάζεσθαι. This account has been so transformed by the redactor-evangelist that the healing does not appear as a laying on of hands, but only as a miraculous command: and the labour on the Sabbath which the Jews assail only consists in the carrying of the bed, an act to which Jesus, on the analogy of Mark ii. 11 sq., has instigated the healed man. We are no longer able to determine exactly how much of the account as we have it, vv. 1–16, stood in the Source. The beginning, vv. 1–7, may have belonged to it. Most of the rest, vv. 8–15, must be assigned to the evangelist.

In the following discourse, v. 17 sqq., there are certain additions of the evangelist which stand out from the material of the Source.

First of all, in ver. 27 the word ἀνθρώπου attached to υἱός is to be recognised as one such addition. The context from ver. 17 onwards shows that originally there stood here, as in vv. 21–26, simply the term υἱός. In ver. 17, in justifying His own work on the Sabbath by an appeal to that of God, Jesus speaks of God as His Father. As the Jews saw in this an impious claim to Godhead on

¹ Cf. *sup.* pp. 58–101. ² Cf. *sup.* pp. 73 sqq.

His own part, Jesus lays down with all the more emphasis that He, as the Son, does nothing but what He sees the Father doing, and that the Father shows Him all His work (vv. 19 sq.). The Father, He tells them, has committed to the Son all His own work of quickening and of judgment (vv. 21–27). At the close of this utterance the only appropriate assertion is that the Father has given Him this authority because He is the Son, that is to say, the Son *of God*. However we understand the words υἱὸς ἀνθρώπου,—whether we take it that God has committed judgment to Him as "a son of mankind," in that He must preach the word as a man to men, or must judge men as a man; or, again, that His authority to judge is that of "the Son of Man," that is to say, the Messiah promised in the Apocalypse of Daniel,—in either case we have introduced into the context a strange element, which is neither accounted for nor followed out. It is, however, quite conceivable that the evangelist, finding in the Source at this place the simple term υἱός, thought it appropriate to introduce the term υἱὸς ἀνθρώπου. In reproducing this sequence of thought at second hand he did not catch, in its full force, the necessity in this place for the simple υἱός. He remembered, however, that according to Dan. vii. 13 sqq. all power and authority were committed to One who appeared ὡς υἱὸς ἀνθρώπου, and that, according to the synoptic tradition, Jesus always assumed that title, "Son of Man," when He spoke of His future advent unto judgment (cf. Mark viii. 38 and parallels; Mark xiv. 62 and parallels; Luke xii. 40, xvii. 22, 24, 26, 30, xviii. 8, xxi. 36; Matthew xxv. 31); and so he thought it right that in this place, too, where Jesus speaks of His authority to judge, He should have applied to Himself that title from Daniel.[1]

[1] The absence of the article before υἱός in this place is explained by the fact that υἱός is predicate (cf. x. 36). The use of the genitive ἀνθρώπου without the article is in accordance with the use in LXX, Dan. vii. 13.

INQUIRY INTO COMPOSITION OF THE SOURCE 131

Vv. 28 and 29 form a further addition of the evangelist. As regards their external form these words on the future resurrection of the dead seem to stand in close connection with what precedes. The introductory phrase, μὴ θαυμάζετε, implies that they explain the words just spoken, and deprive them of their astonishing character. Jesus has been saying, in vv. 21–27, that after the example and by the commission of God He quickens the dead and performs judgment. He has expressly and emphatically declared that He fulfils these divine functions, not in the future, but now in the present hour (ver. 25). But since the life which He bestows is *eternal* life, His work has an import which transcends the earthly existence of men. That is the ground of His declaration that He is fulfilling the divine judgment. He who through Him wins eternal life has not to wait for the decision of his fate by some future judgment-seat, but has even now passed out of death into life (ver. 24). In view of the eternal consequence of Jesus' quickening work in the present, it seems at first perfectly appropriate that we should have a reference, in ver. 28, to the future Messianic resurrection of the dead unto judgment. For this can be considered as a result of Jesus' work of to-day, by which He proves the truth of what He tells concerning that present-day work. But in reality the future event in ver. 28 is not conceived as a result of that work. In ver. 24—just as in vi. 63, xii. 49 sq., xvii. 2 sq.—Jesus denoted His *teaching* as the means by which eternal life is bestowed, and—as in viii. 31–36, 51—the *hearing His word with faith* as the requirement of its attainment. In the same sense He added in ver. 25 that the dead that hear the word of the Son of God shall live. The dead here meant are the spiritually dead (cf. Matt. xi. 5 ; Luke ix. 60, xv. 24, 32), and by hearing is not meant a merely external, passive experience, but a faithful acceptance of what is spoken (cf. vi. 45). Here, then, in ver. 25, under a figurative wording which seems to speak of an actual miraculous raising of the dead (cf. xi. 43 sq.), we have described a spiritual event which the teaching of Jesus is even now (καὶ νῦν ἐστίν) bringing to pass. Now if in ver. 28 sq. the future eschatological event were regarded as a consequence of this spiritual event, the same requirement for the gaining of eternal life would be denoted: the criterion in the final judgment would be *the attitude which men have adopted towards the teaching of Jesus*. The wording might run, that of them that come forth at that time from the tomb those who have heard the words of Jesus and kept them shall pass into life; while they who have not received His words, but have loved the darkness more than the light, shall fall into judgment. Such a thought, so expressed, would accord with the context in our discourse, and with the view generally assumed in the Johannine discourses.[1] Instead of this, however, we are told that the resurrection which Messiah shall bring about shall be a resurrection of life or of judgment according as men have *practised good or ill*. This expresses another, a much more general principle for the division of mankind at the final judgment: a principle which prevails for all humanity, even for those who have never come into contact with the teaching of Messiah. On the other hand, vv. 24 sq. were concerned with the decisive, the eternal importance of the teaching of Jesus, to those men to whom it came. The idea of the general resurrection, and the moral criterion in the subsequent judgment of the world, does not naturally arise out of the original context from ver. 19 onwards. It is, however, quite conceivable that the evangelist who reproduced the discourse from the Source felt called upon to explain, by this allusion to the universal judgment which Christ was some day to perform, when men should be recompensed

---

[1] Cf. also the synoptic saying, Mark viii. 38 and parallels.

for their good or evil deeds, the words which Jesus had used about the judgment committed to Him by His Father.[1]

This conclusion, that vv. 28 and 29 did not belong to the discourse in its original state, is confirmed by the fact that, through the intrusion of these words, the utterance of Jesus which follows is left entirely disconnected, whereas it forms a perfectly natural continuation of vv. 26 and 27. In ver. 30 the thought of vv. 28 sq. is not maintained. Jesus is not speaking of the final judgment in the future, but of the judgment which He is performing in the present by means of His work of teaching. In that work He does nothing of Himself,—that is to say, of His own motive and desire,—but acts wholly in accordance with His knowledge of the will of God. This thought corresponds to that of ver. 19. And ver. 30 is connected as closely with vv. 26 sq. as ver. 20 with ver. 19. When the Jews took offence at Jesus' saying in ver. 17, that in His work on the Sabbath He is acting like His Father, Jesus

[1] Even H. Holtzmann, *Hand-Comm.*, 2nd ed., iv. pp. 92 sq. (on v. 21), recognises that "here, if in any place, recourse may be had to a critical hypothesis which permits us to look on vv. 28 and 29, which alone have a definitely eschatological meaning, as an insertion of the redactor, belonging to another and a different stratum of thought concerning the resurrection." But to this hypothesis of mine he prefers the more radical theory of Delff (*Neue Beiträge zur Kritik und Erklärung des vierten Evang.*, 1890, p. 24), that the whole section, vv. 19-29, has been interpolated by a later hand in the original text of the Gospel. But Delff's contention that this whole section, in which Jesus represents Himself as a judge of the world, is out of keeping with the situation, cannot be approved. Jesus' assertion in vv. 21 sqq., that as the Son of God, and by His Father's commission, He quickens the dead, is fully accounted for in the situation described: it is a more emphatic sequel to His assertion that after the example of His Father He has performed the labour of healing the sick on the Sabbath day (ver. 17). But we must distinguish between the sayings in vv. 19-27, which refer to the present, and that which refers to the future in vv. 28 sq. The difficulty of the passage lies in the internal discrepancy between these two sections. And Delff's hypothesis leaves this difficulty unsolved.

only asserted the more explicitly the community between His own work and that of God. This community is complete: on the one hand, He does nothing but what He sees His Father doing (ver. 19); on the other hand, the Father shows and commits to the Son all His own activity (ver. 20). He cites, as work of this kind divinely committed to Him, the quickening of the dead and the execution of judgment (vv. 21–25). And then He declares once more that in the doing of this work He stands in that twofold communion with the Father which He has described in vv. 19 and 20. On the one hand, the Father has given Him to have life and to execute judgment (vv. 26 sq.); on the other hand, He, the Son, in His function as a judge, does nothing but what He hears from the Father (ver. 30). Ver. 30, then, is complementary to ver. 26, and serves to show here also the complete mutual character of the community of work between Father and Son. This close connection, however, between vv. 26 sq. and ver. 30 is obscured by the reference, inserted between them, to the future resurrection of all the dead unto a judgment of the world. Ver. 30 takes the aspect of a belated and detached supplement to the thought of ver. 19. The same conclusion to which we came with reference to the inserted clauses i. 15 and xiii. 18 sq. holds good in this case also, that only a secondary worker could have broken up the original sequence of thought in so destructive a way.

Finally, in the section that follows, the discourse in which Jesus speaks of the witness to truth of His words (vv. 31 sqq.), the words which refer to the witness of the Baptist (vv. 33, 34*b*, 35, 36*a*), are to be regarded as additions of the evangelist. The decisive indications are the reference in ver. 33 to the narrative in i. 19 sqq., which belongs to the evangelist, and the affinity between these verses and the section of the prologue, which also owes its origin to the evangelist, i. 6–8. The real progress of ideas in vv. 31 sqq. is this: Jesus will not bear witness for Himself (ver. 31), but will call in another witness to Himself (ver. 32), who, however, will not be another man (ver. 34*a*), but the Father Himself (vv. 36*b*, 37 sqq.). Our evangelist was called upon to reconcile ver. 34*a*, "but the witness I receive is not from man," with his own citation of the witness of the Baptist, at the beginning of the Gospel, as an important attestation of Jesus' Messiahship. To that end he makes Jesus Himself actually appeal to the witness of the Baptist, and recognise it as a witness unto the truth (ver. 33). His repudiation of human witness (ver. 33*a*) means, then, no more than that He needed no such witness Himself, but nevertheless He refers other men, for their salvation, to this witness of the Baptist (ver. 33*b*). For the Baptist should bring other men, by means of his witness, to believe in the Messiah, and thereby to salvation (i. 7). As, however, the evangelist has already emphatically declared, in i. 6–8, 19–34, that the Baptist, as a witness to the light, was not himself "the light," so now he makes Jesus immediately add that while the Baptist was certainly a lamp that revealed the way, yet they were wrong who found a transient contentment through regarding him as the light (ver. 35). Of course, the proviso holds good in this place also that, in adding the words relating to the Baptist, the evangelist may have altered in some details the source-components with which he fitted his additions. But this cannot be more exactly determined.

In the discourse of v. 17 sqq., then, the following passages are to be assigned to the Source: vv. 17–27 (except the word ἀνθρώπου in ver. 27), 30, 31, 32, 34*a*, 36*b*–47. I have already (pp. 86–92) attempted to show that in the Source the section vii. 15–24 (except vv. 20 and 21*a*) formed the direct continuation of this discourse.

We have also already recognised above that the discourse of vi. 27 sqq. must have belonged to the Source, but cannot then have contained the historical introduction, vi. 1–26, which is given by our evangelist. According to the Source it must have pertained to the same situation in Jerusalem as the discourse in v. 17 sqq.[1] It follows that ver. 59 also, in which the situation in Galilee is again alluded to, is an addition of the evangelist.

Further, in this same passage of discourse, the refrain of vv. 39, 40, 44, and 54, ἀλλὰ (or καὶ) ἀναστήσω αὐτὸ(ν) ἐν τῇ ἐσχάτῃ ἡμέρᾳ, is an addition by the evangelist to the Source, analogous to his addition in v. 28 sq. Jesus here contrasts Himself with the bread from heaven which Moses gave, to which the Jews refer (vv. 30 sq.); and proclaims Himself the true bread from heaven, because He gives to them that eat thereof a true, an eternal, life, such as the manna of Moses could not bestow (vv. 32 sqq.). Here, as in v. 21 sqq., He speaks of this effect of His ministry, to give life, to stay all hunger and thirst, as an effect in the present: he that believeth on Him *hath* eternal life (vi. 40, 47). In this thought, of course, the assurance is indirectly implied that the believer shall also, at the Last Day, arise unto life. In that sense a reference in the context of our discourse to the future event is not impossible. But this reference, in these stereotyped words, is linked on by an external link only to the main thoughts of the discourse, which relate to the salvation which Jesus is bringing to pass in the present. The purely external character of the link is especially clear in ver. 44, where the refrain, with its reference to the future resurrection, is impounded between Jesus' declaration that none can come unto Him except the Father draw him (ver. 44*a*), and the explanation of these words, "except the Father draw him," which Jesus gives (ver. 45) in a quotation from the Scripture (Isa. liv. 13).

[1] Cf. pp. 75–85.

But if the phrase is here, in ver. 44*b*, evidently foreign to the original context, we cannot doubt that in the other places also where it appears in this discourse it has been inserted by the evangelist in the Source.

Spitta[1] has set up the hypothesis that in the discourse of chap. vi. the section in vv. 51–59 is a later addition. Since the previous words of Jesus, in which He speaks of Himself as the bread from heaven and as the bread of life (vv. 32–50), have no relation to the Supper, the obvious reference to it in vv. 51–58 appears, he argues, in an inconsequent fashion, such as must have been unintelligible to the hearers. He regards vv. 51–59 as a doublet of the discourse on the bread of life, in which the simple thought of the original is transformed to suit the ecclesiastical practice of the Supper.—I cannot agree with this hypothesis, which seems to me to rest upon an unsound presumption. It is by no means certain that this section, vv. 51–58, *in its original sense* referred to the Supper at all. Against the opinion that such a reference is here intended we have not only the fact that the section, so interpreted, is out of keeping with the rest of the discourse, but more especially the fact that the expression σῶμα καὶ αἷμα, which is used everywhere else in the New Testament when the Supper is referred to, is not here employed; the expression σὰρξ καὶ αἷμα, which in the New Testament regularly bears a definite —and different—sense, is used instead. A writer who had composed this section with the previously formed intention of making it refer to the Supper would assuredly have made use of the usual word σῶμα. Everywhere else in the New Testament σὰρξ καὶ αἷμα, used conjointly, signify the same idea for which the single term σὰρξ can also be used (and, indeed, this occurs first by itself in our section, ver. 51): created man, or the created part of man's being, as distinguished from God or the divine Spirit (cf. Matt. xvi. 17;

[1] *Geschichte und Litteratur des Urchristentums*, i. pp. 216 sqq.

1 Cor. xv. 50; Gal. i. 16; Eph. vi. 12; Heb. ii. 14). If we assume this meaning here too, in vv. 51 sqq., we obtain a perfectly appropriate thought, which accords admirably with the previous words of Jesus in vv. 32-50, and owes its own special form to the interjectory speech of the Jews in vv. 41 sq. Against Jesus' claim that He is Himself the true bread from heaven which gives life to those that eat of it (vv. 32-40), the remonstrance is urged by the Jews that one whose earthly parentage is known to them ought not to give himself out as having come from heaven. Jesus is induced by this remonstrance not only to reassert His claim to be the true bread from heaven (vv. 47-51*a*), but to add something with reference to His nature as a human creature, His σάρξ and His αἷμα (vv. 51*b*-58). It is precisely this, His nature as a human creature, which seems to the Jews to contradict His lofty and divine claims—this it is that men must consume to obtain eternal life. The idea of eating and drinking is, of course, intended here in a figurative sense, in sequel to the foregoing figure of the bread (vv. 27, 32 sqq.). It means an acceptance with faith (vv. 35, 40). There remains, however, a great paradox in the assertion that the bestowal of eternal life, which Jesus has hitherto ascribed to Himself as one come from heaven, proceeds from His created human existence. This paradox is solved by the words in ver. 63: "It is the spirit that giveth life; the flesh profiteth nothing; the words which I have spoken unto you are spirit, and are life." This seems at first to be only a new contradiction: Jesus has called His flesh, His flesh and blood, the food that avails unto eternal life, and now He says that the flesh profiteth nothing, it is the Spirit that quickeneth. But the contradiction disappears, and the whole riddle is solved, when the last clause comes into play,—it is the *words* of Jesus that contain eternal life, and bestow it on others. It is now clear that while Jesus' flesh, His being as a creature, is

in itself of no avail, because it is only the divine, the Spirit of God, that can bestow life, yet there is a sense in which His flesh and blood may be a necessary condition for the attainment of the life eternal: His human nature is the *instrument* of His words, full of the Spirit of God, which bring eternal life.—If the section in vv. 51–58 can be understood in this sense in the context, there is no reason for regarding it as a later insertion in the original state of the discourse.

The contention that this section *in its original sense* did not refer to the Supper, does not preclude the possibility that the evangelist, in his work upon the Source, took it as bearing such a reference. This is indeed probable: for the evangelist, in commenting on the miraculous feeding which he gives as an introduction and preparation for the discourse on eating the flesh and blood of Christ, calls it a "Eucharist" (vi. 11, 23). The chronological note, too, in ver. 4, that the Passover of the Jews was at hand, seems intended to suggest that the succeeding miracle and discourse of Jesus have reference to the Christian Passover. If, however, we are right in supposing that vv. 51–58, which in the Source had no bearing upon the Supper, were taken by the evangelist to refer to it, we must conclude that in ver. 51 he has turned a present tense, as it stood in the Source, into the future δώσω. This future is the only point in the wording of this passage which seems rather to favour the interpretation of the section with reference to the Supper than that which I place upon it.

The words in ver. 62, "What, then, if ye should behold the Son of man ascending where he was before?" are to be taken for an addition by the evangelist to the source-material. The disciples murmur at His "hard saying"; Jesus asks them, "Does this perplex you?" (ver. 61); the question which follows in ver. 62 must be taken as pointing to some fact which will remove the perplexity from "this," the hard saying which seemed so perplexing.[1] Jesus' ascension from earth to heaven is therefore pointed to as a reason for recognising the truth of His strange words, that through partaking of His flesh and blood men may obtain eternal life. This reason is followed by the saying in ver. 63, in which we have, beyond doubt, an explanation of the riddle inherent in those words. But it must be admitted that the reason given in ver. 62 is very different from the solution given in ver. 63. The only ground which can be derived from the marvel of Jesus' heavenly exaltation for belief in that other marvel, which lies in Jesus' assertion, is the general ground that He was altogether a being of a mysterious, supernal, heavenly kind. It cannot explain *in what respect* His strange saying is true, that His "flesh and blood," His created, human nature, confers eternal life on mankind. That is explained, as we saw above, by the saying in ver. 63. And this saying is certainly enough in itself, without the extension given in ver. 62, to obviate what is perplexing in the discourse of vv. 51–58. This is shown below by the reply of Peter, vv. 68 sq. In obvious allusion to ver. 63 Peter points to the *words of eternal life* which Jesus has as the decisive reason, for the sake of which the disciples believe on Him as the Holy One of God, and refuse to leave Him. When they knew by their own experience that Jesus had the words of eternal life, the disciples had no

---

[1] The question in ver. 62 cannot be regarded as pointing to an intensification of the cause of stumbling, so that it might be completed thus, "How much more will that perplex you?" (Winer, *Gramm.* § 62, ii. [*Grammar of N. T. Greek*, translated by Moulton, T. & T. Clark, 1882, p. 750]; Meyer-Weiss, *ad loc.*). Jesus' death might have been conceived as a greater stumbling-block, but if this were meant the idea of the death of the Son of Man would be denoted, instead of His ascension where He was before,—that is, into heaven. Elsewhere, whenever Jesus' ascension into heaven is contemplated, it is precisely to obviate the stumbling-block caused by His death.

need to wait for the sight of His departure into heaven to attest His claim to be the heavenly bread that gives eternal life to mankind, and brings that eternal life to them in His "flesh and blood." It seems to me inconceivable that the original author, who comprehended the full significance of ver. 63 as the key for the understanding of vv. 51–58, should have set before it the utterly different criterion of belief contained in ver. 62. It is, however, quite intelligible that the redactor-evangelist, seeing as he did in Jesus' miraculous signs the most important attestation of His Messianic claims, should have felt bound to allude in this place to the final miracle of the ascension. And this certainly becomes entirely conceivable if the evangelist interpreted the sayings in vv. 51–58 as referring to the Supper. He could not in that case understand how the saying in ver. 63, which points to Jesus as the bearer of spirit and life, could furnish any solution to the riddle in vv. 51–58. But he did see in the heavenly exaltation of the Lord a necessary precondition for the eating and drinking of His flesh and blood in the Eucharist by the Christian community.

Finally, both the clauses which refer to the traitor, vv. 64*b* and 70 sq., are to be assigned to the redactor-evangelist. His reason for inserting them was the same as for his addition at xiii. 18 sq. He wished to preclude the objection, against his emphatic assertion of Jesus' miraculous knowledge and power, that Jesus had been mistaken in the traitor.[1] For this reason he appends to the words of Jesus about "some who believe not" (ver. 64*a*), the remark that Jesus detected unbelievers in general, and the traitor in particular (cf. ii. 24 sq.). For the same reason, after the acknowledgment of belief which Peter expresses in the name of the Twelve (vv. 68 sq.), he makes Jesus reply at once that one of them, as he well knows, is a devil.

[1] Cf. *sup*. pp. 28 sq.

4. *Source-components in Chapters vii. and viii.*

The initial section of chap. vii., the conversation of Jesus with His brethren, must also be founded on a passage from the Source. This may be inferred from the discrepancy between the words of the brethren in vv. 3 sq. and the earlier narrative of the Gospel, and their complete accordance with the discourses of Jesus in chaps. v. and vi. which are derived from the Source. The "works," to the more public performance of which the brethren incite Jesus, can in their mind be nothing except visible miracles. But in what sense can his brethren say that Jesus should go to Judæa in order that "His disciples also" might see these works of His? According to the account in our Gospel it is precisely in Judæa that Jesus has hitherto worked many marvellous signs, and thereby aroused belief in many (ii. 23, iii. 2, iv. 45). And, if anybody, His disciples had been the witnesses of His miracles in Judæa, as in Galilee. The request of the brethren only becomes intelligible when we put out of sight the earlier historical notices of the evangelist. They refer to the works of which Jesus has spoken in the discourses of chaps. v. and vi. He has asserted that God shows all His works to Him, and will show Him yet greater works than heretofore,— namely, to give life to the dead (v. 19-21). In enigmatical terms He has maintained that He is a bread from heaven, which bestows eternal life, and that man must eat and drink His flesh and blood to obtain eternal life (vi. 27-38). To these assertions the brethren refer in the conditional phrase, "If thou doest these things, manifest thyself to the world" (ver. 4*b*). In view of the reason given in ver. 5 for this request—that even His brethren did not believe in Him—the words in vv. 3 sq. cannot mean that Jesus had already actually performed such works, and must now continue to perform them, no longer on the remote Galilean stage, but on the more public one of Judæa. The sense must be that Jesus has hitherto, in a mysterious, secretive fashion, only *asserted* that He did such works; now He should bring them to pass once more visibly and publicly before His disciples in Judæa. The unbelief of the brethren rests on their external habits of thought, in accordance with which they conceive the divine works of which Jesus speaks merely as visible, external miracles; but of the reality of the divine Spirit which does its quickening work in His teaching, and of the eternal life which those that believe in that teaching attain, they are void of understanding. By the disciples, to whom Jesus is to show His works in Judæa, the brethren certainly understand, first and chiefly, the "many disciples" who, according to vi. 60, 66, had deserted Jesus in consequence of "His hard saying." This utterance of the brethren expresses the mind, unintelligent and unbelieving, of these apostate disciples. It stands in contrast with the acknowledgment of belief by Peter (vi. 68 sq.). If the words of the brethren in vii. 3 sq., together with ver. 5, are derived from the Source,—to which ver. 1, and perhaps also ver. 2, doubtless belonged as introduction,— there must also have been preserved in the Source an answer of Jesus. But it is clear that our evangelist has here expanded his source-material. We find in ver. 8*b* an indication that the record in vv. 6–10 is not the outcome of one unitary conception. The phrase ὁ ἐμὸς καιρὸς οὔπω πεπλήρωται, which is clearly an intensified reiteration of the words in ver. 6, ὁ καιρὸς ὁ ἐμὸς οὔπω πάρεστιν, nevertheless, in its present context, between ver. 8*a* and the historical notice in ver. 9 sq., has a substantially different sense from that which the earlier form of the phrase in ver. 6 takes from its context there. The special meaning which the word καιρὸς has in ver. 6 is determined by the consideration that it must bear some relation to the demand of Jesus' brethren, and that Jesus contrasts His own καιρός with that of the brethren (ver. 6b); and, finally, by the reason which Jesus gives for His καιρός being not yet come, while that of the brethren is always ready,— namely, the different way in which the world receives Him and them (ver. 7). The καιρός of Jesus must be the due season in which he attains effect and the public realisation of His powers. We, too, say in this sense about a man who undertakes, or a work which is undertaken, that its " time " has come, or is not yet come, but is coming. The brethren have urged Jesus to accomplish publicly in Judæa the sublime works which He asserts that He does, and so to make Himself known to the world and realise His claims. Jesus Himself knows that He has already, continually, been accomplishing the divine work of which He speaks. But He has not yet found recognition from the world, nor will He now find it, because His work, His lifegiving work of teacher, involves a condemnation of the sinful works of the world (cf. iii. 19–21). The work of His brethren, which is accomplished in an earthly sense and directed towards an earthly goal, can be fully realised in the sight of the world at any time. But for His divine work the time when, in spite of the hate of the world, it will be brought by God to glorious and public effect is not yet come.

In ver. 8b the word has another sense. If Jesus says to the brothers that He is not going to this feast because His καιρός is not yet fulfilled (ver. 8), then at first remains at Galilee (ver. 9), but soon afterwards goes up to the feast (ver. 10), His καιρός must be here understood to be the suitable moment to which He looked forward for His journey to Jerusalem, which when the brethren addressed their demand to Him had not yet come, but came soon afterwards. And assuredly this suitable moment for a journey must have been conceived quite independently of the right time for the open promulgation of Jesus' ministry, or for the attainment of its effect and public recognition. For there was no change, in regard to this point, within a few days. The phrase, then, in ver. 8*b*, " my time is not yet fulfilled," has the same sense as the words spoken by Jesus to His mother in the story of the marriage at Cana, " my hour is not yet come" (ii. 4). There, too, the moment quickly arrives in which Jesus does what is desired. That on which He lays stress, there as here, is only that He does not allow the moment for His action to be determined by other men, but awaits the moment which He has Himself set before Him. Are we now, applying as a standard to ver. 6 the meaning in ver. 8, to find in " my καιρός is not yet come" merely a statement that the moment for His journey to Judæa had not yet arrived? If so, the utterance is emptied of the characteristic significance which its own proper context indicates. The sound course is to distinguish between the original sense which ver. 6 had in the context of the piece from the Source, and the sense which the redactor-evangelist assumed for it and carried on from ver. 8 onwards. Jesus' words in vv. 6 and 7 must have belonged to the Source. Doubtless it also recounted that Jesus went up later to Jerusalem for the feast. This journey in no wise contradicted the words of ver. 6*a* as the Source intended them. But the evangelist understood ver. 6*a* to say that the right moment for Jesus' journey to Judæa had not arrived. The circumstance that Jesus nevertheless made the journey shortly afterwards did not withhold him from this belief: this very fact seemed to him significant that Jesus, when He had decided on any action, would not allow Himself to be determined by other men to an earlier accomplishment of it than He had Himself contemplated.—Whether and how far the clauses in vv. 11–14 are founded on source-components cannot be decided.

The fact that vii. 15–24 (except vv. 20 and 21a) formed part of the Source, and the original connection of this passage with the discourse in chap. v., have been already discussed.[1]

Similarly we have already reached the conclusion that the isolated sayings of Jesus, vii. 28 sq., 33 sq., 37 sq., are derived from the Source, and these formed a continuous context with the discourse in viii. 12–59.[2] The introduction in the Source to Jesus' words in vii. 28 sq. concerning His divine origin must have been some utterance of the Jews referring to His notorious earthly origin, which discredited His lofty claims. Some foundation, therefore, for vii. 25–27 must have been found in the Source. This cannot be more exactly determined. The identical remarks in vii. 30, 44, viii. 20b, that they sought to lay hold on Jesus, but did not succeed, because " His hour " was not yet come, reveal themselves as additions of the evangelist. " His hour," as in ii. 4, and like His καιρός in vii. 8, must signify the moment which He had fixed for Himself,—that is to say, here, according to the context, which He had fixed for His passion. The evangelist desired to emphasise the thought that the enemies of Jesus had no power over Him so long as He did not of His own accord deliver Himself up to suffering.[3] The account, too, of the futile order to arrest Him issued by the chief priests, vii. 31 sq. and 45–52, an account which so destructively severs the connected words of Jesus, was an addition by the evangelist, intended to illustrate the overpowering impression which Jesus made upon men, and the powerlessness of His foes against Him. The question whether the remarks also in vii. 35 sq. and viii. 22, on the misapprehension which befell Jesus' words about His approaching departure, are additions due to the evangelist, must be left undecided. The substance of the notice in vii. 37a may have stood in the Source, but not in

[1] Cf. pp. 85–92.   [2] Cf. pp. 92–96.   [3] Cf. pp. 29 sqq.

such a sense or form that it denoted a change of situation from that of vv. 28 sq. and 33 sq. We have already seen [1] that the interpretation which is given in ver. 39 to the words of Jesus in vv. 37 sq. is a gloss of the evangelist. The utterances of the multitude in vv. 40–43 certainly stood in the Source. They were what led the evangelist to miss the connection of Jesus' discourse in viii. 12 sqq. with the words in vii. 28 sq., 33 sq., and 37 sq.

The little remark in viii. 30 and 31*a* is beyond doubt an insertion of the evangelist: it says that as Jesus spake many believed on Him, and what He said further was addressed to these believing Jews. This addition is especially worthy of remark, because it yields a clear proof how easily the evangelist discovered, in the sayings of Jesus as he received them, suggestions of historical fact, which he then tried to denote more explicitly. That which prompted him to this statement in ver. 30 is clearly the saying of Jesus in ver. 31*b*, "If ye *abide* in my word, then are ye truly my disciples." The notion of abiding seems to him to presuppose that those who are addressed have already reached a state of belief, the continuance in which is declared by Jesus to be a condition of true discipleship. But the idea that those whom Jesus was addressing had attained belief in Him stands in striking contradiction to certain clauses in the further course of the address. He declares that His word can find no entrance into them (vv. 37, 43), that their very reason for refusing to believe Him is that He teaches the $\dot{a}\lambda\dot{\eta}\theta\epsilon\iota a$ (vv. 45 sqq.), that their whole conduct reveals them as the children of the devil (vv. 38–44). Originally—that is to say, in the Source—the term "abide" in ver. 31 cannot have been used to imply a state of belief already existing in those addressed, one which must be made permanent; it can only have meant that the new faith which Jesus urges them to adopt must be no trans-

[1] Cf. pp. 67 sqq.

itory phase, but an enduring state, if it is to be the foundation of a true discipleship. The real mainspring of the evangelist's readiness to conclude, from μείνητε in ver. 31, that those addressed already believed, in spite of the clear and emphatic declaration of their unbelief in the later course of the speech, is that the term πιστεύειν had in his mind a substantially different significance from that which it had in Jesus' discourses in the Source. In the discourses it means that practical recognition of the divine import of Jesus unto salvation which is performed by receiving and following His teaching. It is used interchangeably with the expression "keeping Jesus' words" (cf. viii. 45–51, xii. 46 sq., xiv. 21–24). Here also, in viii. 31, μένειν ἐν τῷ λόγῳ τῷ ἐμῷ does not denote a state in which πιστεύειν is presupposed, but is rather a periphrasis for πιστεύειν itself. To the evangelist, on the other hand, πιστεύειν signifies a theoretical conviction of the divine nature and power of Jesus, such as was attained chiefly through the impression of His miracles and proofs of supernatural knowledge. He therefore sees no incompatibility between πιστεύειν and a practical attitude of indifference or even hostility to Jesus, or the love of the glory of men rather than the glory of God (ii. 23 sq., xii. 42 sq.). And so he finds no difficulty in this place in the assumption of a πιστεύειν, which consists only in the most fleeting and momentary recognition of Jesus.

5. *Source-components in Chapters ix. and x.*

The story of the healing of a man born blind, in chap. ix., bears as a whole the stamp of the historical conception proper to the evangelist. Its leading idea is that by means of this extraordinary miracle and sign Jesus manifested His divinity in a special degree. This idea comes out at the very beginning in the words of Jesus that the man was born blind, " that the works of God should be made manifest in him" (ver. 3),—that is to say, that he might give occasion for the manifestation of Jesus' divine thaumaturgy (cf. xi. 4). Then the full account of the examination of the man healed (vv. 8–34) serves to set in a strong light the inability of Jesus' adversaries to throw doubt on His miraculous deed, and the consequences which must logically be deduced from it (cf. vii. 31 sq., 45–52). Finally, the adoring acknowledgment of faith in Jesus' Messiahship, to which Jesus Himself prompts the man He has healed (vv. 35–38), shows the positive result which Jesus desired and attained by means of His thaumaturgy.

But this account of the evangelist has attached to it an utterance of Jesus (ix. 39–x. 18) which bears again exactly the character of the other passages of discourse taken from the Source. The general impression that it comes from the Source is confirmed by its original connection with other sayings of Jesus, a connection which can still be traced, though in the record before us they are severed from it.

In the first place, the words in ix. 4, 5 present themselves as the beginning of the discourse in ix. 39 sqq. In their present place,—where, following the words of Jesus in ver. 3, that the man was born blind in order that the works of God might be made manifest in him, they introduce the actual healing in vv. 6 sq.,—it seems at first as though their function was to express the motive of Jesus' miracle. But they have in reality a much broader sense. "The works of Him that sent Him," which Jesus must work while it is day (ver. 4), are identical with His work as the "light of the world," which He performs so long as He is in the world (ver. 5). But the work which Jesus does as the "light of the world" is performed by means of His teaching, which makes God manifest, and leads to eternal life (cf. iii. 19–21, viii. 12). This is the work that His Father has committed to Him (iv. 34, xvii. 2–8). His miraculous gift of the light of common day to the man born blind appears but as a symbol of that higher, inner enlightenment which He brings into the world. So, too, the thought that work can only be done while it is " day,"—that is to say, during His earthly span of life, before the " night " cometh, when no man can work (ver. 4),—does not merely express the ground of Jesus' duty to grant His miraculous aid in this single case, but rather of His duty to devote Himself with unremitting fidelity to the great work of enlightenment which God has committed to Him. This great work of enlightenment is now, however, again the subject of ver. 39, and, under another figure, of x. 1–9 ; and His self-sacrificing fidelity in the work of His calling is the subject of x. 10–18. The theme, then, which was projected in vv. 4 sq. finds its further exposition in ix. 39–x. 18. The only reason why this connection is not plainly evident arises out of the intrusion of that narrative passage.

This discourse, which begins in ix. 4 sq., and is continued in ix. 39–41 and x. 1–18, was probably introduced in the Source by the notice that Jesus, as He passed by, saw a man blind from his birth (ix. 1). The sight of this man, plunged in perpetual night, incapable of any kind of work, prompted Jesus first of all to speak of the night of death which puts an end to all earthly toil, and of the need to work while the day lasts. But the same sight prompted Him yet further to speak figuratively of His own work in the world as the giving of light, whereby those who see not are made to see, though, indeed, those who see are made blind (ver. 39). The evangelist, working on the Source, thought it self-evident that if Jesus met such a man, blind from his birth, He had also miraculously healed him. A miraculous gift of sight to the physically blind seemed to him the most appropriate introduction to Jesus' words concerning His gift of sight to the spiritually blind, just as he regarded the miraculous feeding as a fit proem for the discourse in which Jesus speaks of Himself as the bread from heaven. It also appeared to him that this event, unheard of since the world began (ix. 32), the opening of the eyes of a man born blind, was such a sign for the arousing of faith that in sight of it the unbelief and hostility of the Jewish hierarchs towards Jesus stood revealed as a senseless blindness and hardness of heart. So thinking, he produced the narrative of the healing of the blind man, his subsequent examination, and his meeting with Jesus. Whether the Source contained any sort of historical intimations of which he has made use in this narrative we cannot say.

Next, the encounter between Jesus and the Jews (x. 24–38), which according to the account in our Gospel took place in Jerusalem on a later occasion (ver. 22), must in the Source have been the continuation of the discourse in ix. 39–x. 28. This is shown by the fact that the figure of the sheep intrusted to Him, which Jesus began in x. 10–18, is carried on in x. 26–28. The manner of this continuation is not appropriate or natural unless the same hearers are addressed in the same circumstances as before. If there were no other grounds for supposing a source to have been employed in the Fourth Gospel, we should have to content ourselves in this place with the explanation that certain words of Jesus, which the evangelist assigns to different situations, appear, through the awkward form of his report, as if they belonged to one and the same. But since the use of a source in other parts of the Gospel is clearly and abundantly indicated, and we have often to note that its original context has been severed by the evangelist, we must assume with reference to this case also that these passages which show an internal affinity really belonged, in the Source, to the same situation.[1] The objection may be raised that no reason appears why the evangelist should have interrupted the context of the discourse if it

---

[1] Cf. *sup.* p. 81 n.

had come down to him unbroken, and that the difference in the situations must therefore have been definitely communicated to him, or remembered by him;[1] but this objection is not decisive. That which led the evangelist to break up the context of the discourse was doubtless, here as in the earlier cases we have cited, the presence in the Source of some parenthetical remark, a new departure in Jesus' speech, or a new question of His opponents, which looked like the outset of a new and independent discourse, under different circumstances. The reason why the evangelist was led astray by such a superficial appearance is precisely the fact that it was not he who originally conceived the connected ideas, and so he was not awake to the fact that what followed could only be understood in direct sequence to what preceded.

The occasion which misled him into such a severance was probably, in this case, some clause in the original document which formed the groundwork of the remarks in vv. 19-23. How far it has been modified by the evangelist we cannot say; only vv. 21b and 22 may be definitely marked as his additions. Ver. 21b is related to the narrative in ix. 6 sqq., and is not necessary to explain the judgment expressed in ver. 21a; which, indeed, takes a different sense according as we join on ver. 21b to it or not. In the first case, it means that the words of Jesus are revealed by their own nature and content as the utterance of no demoniac or madman. In the second case, on the other hand, the sense is that His words cannot be regarded as those of a demoniac, because Jesus has proved, by His healing of the blind, that He is not a demoniac. The statement in ver. 22 that the ensuing encounter of Jesus with the Jews happened in the winter at the Feast of the Dedication was actuated by the evangelist's idea that this encounter certainly belonged to a later situation than the

[1] Cf. Haupt, *St. Kr.*, 1893, pp. 227 sqq.; also B. Weiss on x. 23.

preceding passage of discourse, which was dated in the Feast of Tabernacles (vii. 2). He assumed that the next feast in the Jewish calendar to the Feast of Tabernacles was the occasion of a new visit of Jesus to Jerusalem.

At the close of chap. x. ver. 39 is an addition by the evangelist to the Source, on the analogy of his additions in vii. 30, 44, viii. 20*b*.[1] The notice in ver. 40 that Jesus went at that time to Peræa, to the neighbourhood in which John had at an earlier time been baptizing, may be derived in substance from the Source. This may have prompted the evangelist to add, for his own part, the remarks in vv. 41 sq. He expresses yet again in these verses, as in i. 6–8, 19–37, iii. 22–36, v. 33–35, the twofold estimate of the Baptist which he so much affects: the Baptist was not to be compared with Jesus; but he was the witness who truly directed mankind to Jesus as to one greater than himself.

6. *Source-components in Chapter xi.*

A question now arises which claims a peculiar interest, whether there were any elements furnished by the Source for the story of the raising of Lazarus (xi. 1–53). This story as a whole, at any rate, belongs strictly to the narrative scheme of our evangelist. He depicts in it the most sublime of Jesus' miraculous signs, one which transcends even the healing of a man blind from his birth. He tells how Jesus, immediately on receiving news of Lazarus' sickness, announced that this sickness was designed to minister to His own glory (cf. ix. 3), and then deferred the journey to Bethany, in order that He might have occasion for the greater miracle (xi. 4–6, 15). He then depicts how Jesus performed, in full publicity, the unheard-of miracle of raising Lazarus after he had lain four days in the grave (xi. 31–44). And he expressly sets forth the effects that followed

[1] Cf. *sup.* p. 30.

this sign: that it aroused in the spectators and those who heard of it a belief in the Messiahship of Jesus (xi. 45, 48, xii. 9, 11), and was the direct occasion of the homage rendered to Him as Messiah by the multitude at His entry into Jerusalem (xii. 17 sq.), and that it threw His enemies into such confusion that their only door of escape was to plot His death (xi. 46-53, 57, xii. 10, 19). This whole presentment is characteristic throughout of the historical attitude of the evangelist.

Nevertheless, the story has not been struck out at one stroke of the die. It embodies certain elements which do not accord with the evangelist's general conception of the event. He has taken them up into his narrative as elements of a secure tradition. But he has not apprehended them in their original meaning.

After Jesus has ordered the opening of the grave, and Martha has objected that the corpse, being four days dead, had already begun to decay (ver. 39), Jesus replies in ver. 40, "Said I not unto thee, that, if thou believedst, thou shouldest see the glory of God?" This can only be understood as referring to the sole words which Jesus has, so far as the account has gone, addressed to Martha, that is to His promise in ver. 23, "Thy brother shall rise again," and to the supplementary words in vv. 25 sq., that those who believe in Him shall live in spite of death. Now, since the words of ver. 40 are spoken in anticipation of the miraculous raising of Lazarus, which was immediately to follow, whereby Jesus would manifest His divine glory (ver. 4; cf. ii. 11), the reference of ver. 40 to vv. 23 and 25 sq. evidently presupposes that these words signified an assurance of the miraculous resurrection of Lazarus to a continued earthly life. But, in fact, the words referred to (vv. 23 and 25 sq.) have another, a much loftier sense. Jesus is speaking in them of a life which He assures and grants to *all* who believe, of a life for which they have not to wait until the resurrection at the Last Day, for they remain possessed of it even when they die, and possess it for *eternity*. By this cannot be meant the earthly life to which Lazarus was raised again from the grave. For neither does such a miraculous resurrection fall to the lot of all who believe in Jesus, nor did His new earthly life remain to Lazarus for eternity. What is meant can only be that higher eternal life which Jesus, in other places besides (v. 21–27, vi. 35–40, 47–50, viii. 51), claims to bestow on all who believe, a life which dwells in them even now, and, because it is a life eternal and divine, survives the temporal death and gives certain assurance of resurrection to a heavenly life of salvation. There can be no doubt that this is the sense of vv. 23 and 25 sq. These words contain, in reality, no reference on Jesus' part to His subsequent miracle. But, since ver. 40 presupposes that they do contain such a reference, we have here a misapprehension, and one of the same kind which we have already perceived in the interpretations of the evangelist in ii. 21, vii. 39, xii. 33, xviii. 9.[1] It also follows, however, that the evangelist cannot have been free to give what form he would to vv. 23 and 25 sq.: they must have come down to him in a fixed, established shape. Otherwise he would have modified the phrasing in such a way that a reference to the miraculous raising of Lazarus to the earthly life was possible, at least as a secondary meaning. He must have taken Jesus' conversation with Martha, vv. 23–26, probably also ver. 27, from the Source.

[1] Because vv. 23 and 25 sq. have not the sense which ver. 40 presupposes, B. Weiss assumes that ver. 40 contains an inexact reference to ver. 4. But ver. 4 is neither addressed to Martha, nor does it contain any allusion to belief as a condition. The point which ver. 4 and ver. 40 have in common is the idea of the δόξα τοῦ θεοῦ, which is entirely absent from vv. 23–26. But in the mind of the evangelist the same miraculous event is denoted in vv. 23 and 25 sq., which in ver. 4 and ver. 40 is regarded as a manifestation of the δόξα of God in Jesus Christ.

Now that it has become clear, however, at this one point, that in this story as in others the evangelist made use of matter taken from the Source, a clear light is thrown upon a feature of the narrative which must otherwise remain mysterious. We are told that at the grave of Lazarus Jesus "groaned in the spirit" (vv. 33 and 38), and shed tears (ver. 35). How is this deep emotion to be explained? It would be natural enough as the outcome of a deep sense of the grievous severing power of death, a sense from which even those are not exempt who have, in spite of death, the assurance of eternal life. It would be natural as the expression of Jesus' grief and longing at the loss of His friend, and of His sympathy with the sorrowing sisters. But on the presumption that Jesus clearly foresaw the immediate resurrection of Lazarus to a new span of earthly life it is unnatural. Thence arise the manifold attempts of the commentators to assign other reasons for Jesus' agitation and tears, attempts which nevertheless, in this situation, have all a remote and far-fetched appearance. It has often been said, with perfect justice, that this "truly human" trait in the portrait of Jesus cannot be due to the evangelist. It must have come to him definitively from without. But it does not follow that all the rest of his narrative was supplied to him in the same way, either by the evidence of his senses in earlier days, or by the best tradition. We have rather to conclude, from the incompatibility of this trait with the rest of the story, that it was taken over by the evangelist from an earlier record of a kind which differed substantially, in one respect, from that which we now possess. It cannot have represented Jesus, when He stood at the grave in Bethany, as clearly foreseeing and firmly intending that the dead man should be restored to earthly life. As we have already seen, the redactor-evangelist erroneously discovered this foresight and intention expressed in the words of Jesus in vv. 23 and

25 sq. The structure of his narrative framework for the words of Jesus preserved in the Source has been accommodated to that misconception. As a result, the statements taken from the Source about Jesus' emotion and His weeping at the grave will no longer fit into the narrative framework.

If the conversation in vv. 23–27 is derived from the Source, that document must also have recorded under what circumstances the conversation took place, and on what occasion. How far then, in the introduction as we have it, vv. 1–22, can the source-components be distinguished from the addition of the evangelist? Besides the reference in vv. 1*b* and 2 to the synoptic accounts (Luke x. 38, vii. 37 sq.),[1] we must certainly ascribe to the evangelist the two passages, ver. 4 and vv. 11–15, in which the prevision and intention of Jesus with regard to the raising of Lazarus are expressed. With regard to the remainder of the narrative in vv. 1–22, we can only say that there seems nothing to prevent our assigning it to the Source. Our theory that, of Jesus' conversation with the disciples in vv. 7–16, the beginning, vv. 7–10, stood in the Source, but the continuation, vv. 11–15, was added by the evangelist, is remarkably confirmed by the fact that the utterance of Thomas in ver. 16 is unintelligible unless, overleaping vv. 11–15, we bring it into direct connection with vv. 7–10. Taken after vv. 14 sq., in which Jesus declares that Lazarus is dead and that they are to go "to him," the μετ' αὐτοῦ in Thomas's words, "let us also go, that we may die with him," can only refer to Lazarus. But this is certainly not the true, original sense. The αὐτός, with whom Thomas and the other disciples will die together, must be Jesus. The remark of Thomas refers to ver. 8, in which the disciples of Jesus, in order to withhold Him from the journey into Judæa, remind Him of the attempt which the Judæans made on His life during His last visit there. In the figurative words of

[1] Cf. *sup.* pp. 40 sqq.

vv. 9 sq. Jesus then expresses His assurance that so long as He is engaged in the work to which His Father has called Him He cannot fall into any danger. This implies His decision, in spite of the danger which threatens His life, to go into Judæa. Taken immediately after this, it is clear that the words of Thomas express a resigned exhortation to the rest to perish with Jesus. By the intrusion, however, of the intimation of Lazarus' death this sense is obscured.

The narrative in vv. 17-22, which forms the transition to Jesus' words in vv. 23 and 25 sq., may in substance have formed part of the Source. After the conversation with Martha (vv. 23-27), the Source, no doubt, goes on to tell how Jesus stood with the sisters of Lazarus at the grave, and was deeply moved, and wept. I can see no indication that any further elements in the close of the story as we have it belonged to the Source. Can it be urged that the account in the Source came to an impotent conclusion, if it did not culminate in a report of the miracle of the raising of Lazarus? It records the magnificent words of Jesus in vv. 23 and 25 sq., words in which the hope and trust of Christians at the grave have found, in all ages, their support and their most sublime expression. It records these words, not as referring to an extraordinary case, in which the dead man was again to be recalled to earthly life, but to one whose nature exactly resembled those in which Christians were henceforth to take these words to their comfort. Were not these words, for their own sake, worth recording?

7. *Source-components in Chapter xii.*

In the narrative sections xi. 54-xii. 19 there are no traces which point to a use of the Source.

But in the further course of chap. xii. the Source was again employed by the evangelist, as we have already perceived from the clearness with which ver. 33 and vv. 36*b*-

43 stand out as alien additions to the contextual matter.[1] In the Source, no doubt, as well as here, the account of the inquiry of the Greeks concerning Jesus (vv. 20–22) formed the introduction to the discourse in vv. 23 sqq. In the first part of this discourse Jesus speaks of His death as the necessary precondition of His own exaltation into glory, and of the wider diffusion of the influences which went forth from Him (vv. 23–32); and in the second part, in answer to the interruption of the Jews in ver. 34, He goes on to describe His earthly ministry, which was then being wrought but soon should cease, as a light-giving manifestation of God, which men must receive with faith that they might gain eternal life (vv. 35, 36a, 44–50). As we saw above, the thought is not brought to a real conclusion in ver. 36a, where the evangelist inserts the reflection contained in vv. 36b–43. Vv. 35 and 36a only form the beginning of the thought which is carried on in vv. 44 sqq.

Besides vv. 33 and 36b–43, however, there are a few other additions to the Source to be noted in this discourse. First of all, the episode of the voice from heaven (vv. 28b–30), at least in its present form, must be ascribed to the evangelist. We are expressly told that this heavenly voice, whose miraculous character was perceived by the bystanders (ver. 29), was not intended for Jesus, but for the people (ver. 30): this remark expresses the characteristic view of the evangelist that external miraculous signs were designedly used for the arousing of faith. On the other hand, it must be acknowledged that the divine apostrophe in ver. 28b forms an important, indeed an indispensable, answer to His question and prayer reported in vv. 27 and 28a. Even if it were not recorded, we could not explain the transition from the agitated, questioning cry in ver. 27 to the triumphant utterance of vv. 31 sq. without assuming that Jesus' prayer in ver. 28a was followed by the instant assurance that His prayer had

[1] Cf. *sup.* pp. 69 and 96–99.

been heard. But since we have also to look for the occasion which led the evangelist to insert here the episode of the heavenly voice, the following theory presents itself. In the Source the prayer in ver. 28*a* was probably followed by some other words of Jesus, expressive of His assurance that His prayer was heard. They doubtless had some such form as this,—" I hear the voice of my Father saying unto me, that as He has glorified Himself in me hitherto, so will He glorify Himself yet again in my death " (cf. xiii. 31 sq., xvii. 1, 4 sq.). This word "hear" was used, in the Source, in the sense of an inner perception of the voice of God (cf. v. 30, 37, vi. 45, viii. 26, 47). But the evangelist, working on the Source, understood it as the literal hearing of a voice which actually resounded from heaven. Such a voice, however, must have been observed by the bystanders also. It formed a miraculous sign, which must indeed have been intended for this very throng, to give them a divine witness to the glory of Jesus. In accordance with this interpretation the evangelist set out in a more extended form the ideas he derived from the Source.

Then, again, in the second part of this discourse the explanatory clause in ver. 47*b* must be adjudged an addition of the evangelist, after iii. 17. The thought that Jesus came not to judge the world, but to save it, has no organic connection with the sequence of thought in this section of the speech. The sentence in ver. 47*a*, " If any man hear my sayings, and keep them not, I judge him not," seems indeed to coincide with Jesus' saying in the discourse with Nicodemus, that God had sent Him into the world, not to judge the world, but that the world through Him might be saved (iii. 17). For that reason our evangelist thought it an appropriate thing to insert that saying as an elucidation in this place. But, accurately considered, the thought in the two passages is substantially different. The antithesis which comes into play in the discourse with

Nicodemus is this,—it is not Jesus that judges the unbeliever, but *the unbeliever draws judgment upon himself*, by refusing the light of salvation. The idea that Jesus' own work is not to judge, but to save, comes in to explain that antithesis. But in our place in chap. xii. we have another antithesis, which lies in this: it is not to *Jesus in Himself* that the paramount importance for salvation belongs; He is the messenger and agent of God (vv. 44 sq.), and that which is of such decisive import unto salvation is the *divine revelation* which Jesus brings and accomplishes (vv. 47–50). To this antithesis the explanation that Jesus was not sent to judge, but to save, is inadequate.

Finally, the concluding words of ver. 48, ἐν τῇ ἐσχάτῃ ἡμέρᾳ, are in all probability an addition of the evangelist, analogous to those in ver. 28 sq. and at the close of vi. 39, 40, 44, 54.[1]

8. *Source-components in Chapters xiii.–xvii.*

There are decisive indications, which we have already discussed, for holding that the farewell discourses of Jesus in the circle of His own disciples (chaps. xiii.–xvii.), which form the third main section of the Gospel, were derived by the evangelist from his source, but were there arranged in another order than that which they now have in our Gospel.[2] The evangelist appears to have added but little to the matter from the Source.

When we have recognised that xiii. 18 sq. is an interpolation by the evangelist, we must also regard the clause in xiii. 11 and the narrative in xiii. 21–30 (besides the transition in ver. 31*a*) as additions by the same hand, inspired by the same purpose, as xiii. 18 sq.: that purpose was to lay an express emphasis on the fact that Jesus was

---

[1] Cf. *sup.* pp. 131–134 and 136 sq.
[2] Cf. pp. 99–107 and 70.

not deceived and outwitted by the traitor.[1] It cannot be held that the incident in vv. 21–30 is a necessary part of the whole, as supplying the motive for the new turn of the discourse in ver. 31. For there is indeed no definitively new turn given in this verse to the discourse. The exhortation to loving service, which Jesus adds to its exemplification in the washing of feet, vv. 12–17 and 20, is here continued in vv. 34 sq. The object of the words in xiii. 31*b*–33 is only to give to that exhortation, which has not in its earlier expression (vv. 12–20) borne any reference to Jesus' departure, the form of a farewell charge for the time when the disciples will be left alone.[2] Nor is the special wording of vv. 31 sq. dependent on the foregoing scenes with the traitor. Jesus says that now God is glorified in Him, and straightway shall He glorify Himself in Him yet more. This "now" does not indicate a moment which comes with the departure of the traitor, and the glorifying of Jesus is not a thing which is caused by Judas' treachery. By the glory which is already accomplished must be understood God's glorification in Jesus throughout the whole ministry of His calling on earth; it shall now be followed by that reception into heavenly glory, to which Jesus attains by His death (cf. xii. 28, xvii. 4 sq.). The reason for Jesus' speaking in a preterite tense of the glorifying of God in His earthly ministry, as of an event already finished, is that He knows His death to be even now imminent, and is reviewing the whole from the standpoint of the end (cf. xvii. 4). Moreover, the episode in vv. 21–30 has no internal connection with the following words; it rather interrupts the connection in which the commandment of love, ver. 34, only strengthened by the words in vv. 31–33, stands with the preceding exhortation in vv. 12–17 and 20.[3] It was the false

---

[1] Cf. *sup*. pp. 28 sqq.   [2] Cf. *sup*. p. 103.
[3] When we consider that in vv. 31–35, and then again in xv. 1–17,

impression that in vv. 31–33 the reference to that exhortation is no longer maintained which misled the evangelist to insert the episode of vv. 21–30 before ver. 31.

In the remainder of these farewell discourses the only words which seem to me to have been added by the evangelist to the Source are the closing words of xvi. 13: καὶ τὰ ἐρχόμενα ἀναγγελεῖ ὑμῖν. This function of the Spirit, to grant a miraculous foreknowledge of coming events, is neither reverted to again in the surrounding context of this place (xvi. 13), nor referred to anywhere else in the farewell discourses where Jesus speaks of the sending of the Spirit. The thought which constantly recurs to Jesus is that the Spirit shall be a substitute to the disciples for Him who is now departing from them; that He will support them in their witness for Jesus to the world (xv. 26 sq., xvi. 7–11) and instruct them further in the teaching they have received from Jesus (xiv. 26, xvi. 12–15). The object of this characteristic element in the promise of the Spirit is to cope with the misgiving, which forces itself upon the natural reflection, that the disciples are not yet ripe enough to be able to dispense with Jesus, since they do not yet fully understand the meaning and bearing of His teaching, to say nothing of their ability to carry on His work by themselves. Jesus overcomes this misgiving by the assurance that God will send His Spirit to the disciples as another Advocate. But for that very reason there is no allusion in these promises to those miraculous χαρίσματα of the Spirit, which have no relation to the special object of affording to the disciples a substitute for Jesus' own presence among them. But we can well conceive

which must have followed immediately afterwards in the Source (cf. *sup*. pp. 104 sq.), the theme of xiii. 1–20 is continued, we are precluded from concurring in Spitta's hypothesis (*Zur Gesch. u. Litt. d. Urchristentums*, i. pp. 186 sqq.) that in the original state of the farewell discourses a place after xiii. 31*a* and before xv. 1 sqq. must have been occupied by an account of the Supper.

that the evangelist thought it necessary that the Spirit's functions of this kind should also be referred to, and that this was his ground for inserting a short allusion, at least, to the apocalyptic prevision of the future which the Spirit should effect.

9. *Source-components in Chapters xviii.–xx.*

In the history of the passion (chaps. xviii.–xx.) it is only, so far as I can see, in the conversation between Pilate and Jesus (xviii. 33–38a and xix. 9–11) that any trace of the Source can be discerned.[1] On the one hand, the words

[1] Spitta (*op. cit.* i. pp. 158 sqq.) maintains that in the account of Jesus' examination before Annas and Caiaphas, and of the denial of Peter (xviii. 12–28), a displacement of the original order can be seen. The story of Peter's denial, which should, he holds, form one connected whole, has been broken up into two sections, vv. 15–18 and 25–27. The original state of the text, he thinks, must have been vv. 12, 13, 19–23, 24, 14, 15–18, 25b–27, 28. From this order it appears that the examination before the "high priest" (vv. 19 sqq.) was really held before Caiaphas, who is denoted high priest in ver. 13, although it took place in the house of Annas. Then what is meant in ver. 24 is the transfer of Jesus to the high priest's palace, in which the Sanhedrin assembled. In vv. 15 sq. too, then, it is Caiaphas who is to be understood by the high priest. But this explanation comes to wreck on the words of ver. 24. If the hearing in the house of Annas had really been held before the high priest Caiaphas, the further transfer of Jesus to the *house* of Caiaphas could not have been simply described in the words "Annas sent him bound unto Caiaphas the high priest."—The opinion of Spitta that a displacement has come about in this section has certainly been confirmed in a remarkable way by the fact that the Syrus Sinaiticus also shows another order of the text, in which ver. 24 does indeed stand before ver. 14, and the two pieces treating of Peter's denial are joined together (cf. A. Merx, *Die vier kanon. Evang. nach ihrem ältesten bekannten Texte*, 1897, i. p. 223). The order is here:—vv. 13, 24, 14, 15, 19–23, 16–18, 25–28. According to this, therefore, the proceedings in vv. 19–23 also took place in the *house* of Caiaphas. In this rendering it is clear that the ἀρχιερεύς in vv. 15, 16, 19, 22 is always Caiaphas, and this whole Johannine tradition may easily be harmonised with the synoptic. We cannot but suspect, however, that the form of the text in Syr. Sin. has been induced by the desire for such a harmony. The separation of the two pieces

of Jesus addressed to Pilate have the closest affinity, in thought and expression, with earlier sayings derived from the Source (cf. viii. 23, 32, 40, 42, 45–47, x. 27). On the other hand, we have in xix. 11 another case where a saying of Jesus has a distorted meaning, which no longer suits the context. To Pilate's question, "Knowest thou not that I have power to release thee, and have power to crucify thee?" (ver. 10) Jesus replies, "Thou wouldest have no power against me, except it were given thee from above (ἄνωθεν): therefore he that delivered thee unto me hath greater sin" (ver. 11). In its relation to the words of Pilate the first part of this reply can only bear the sense that Pilate has that power, with which he seeks to impress Jesus, not from himself, but ·from God. But presuming this to be the sense, we cannot understand—unless, indeed, we eke out the thought by interpolating a complicated chain of ideas[1]—how the judgment expressed in the second part can be brought into sequence with the fact asserted in the first part. That judgment is pronounced on him who had delivered Jesus to Pilate, that is to say, on Caiaphas, as the head of the Jewish nation and the chief priests (cf. xviii. 35). The sequence only becomes clear if the granting unto Pilate of power against Jesus, in the first part of the answer, is understood in the same sense as the giving over of Jesus unto Pilate in the second part,—that is to say, if it refers to the delivery of Jesus by the Jewish high priest into the power of the heathen Procurator. The ἄνωθεν in ver. 11 is used, in that case, in a temporal, not a special sense. This meaning for ver. 11*a* certainly does not accord with the original sense of the words. The fact that it seems to be presupposed in ver. 11*b* must

relating to Peter's denial, vv. 15–18 and 25–27, presents no difficulty. There is, of course, an internal connection between the two; but their severance was prompted by the literary motive of suggesting an interval of time between the first and second denial.

[1] Cf. Meyer-Weiss, *ad. loc.*

lead us to believe, on the analogy of other similar cases, that the evangelist is, in vv. 7–11*a*, employing foreign material, taken from his source, to which ver. 11*b* is an addition of his own. We have no data on which to decide further what were the narrative introduction and framework which belonged to this conversation between Pilate and Jesus in the Source.

C. THE CHARACTER OF THE SOURCE AS A WHOLE

Now that we have decided which of the several components of our Gospel are probably derived from the Source, we can obtain an idea of the character of that Source as a whole.

Our first and foremost conclusion is that the Source contained discourses and conversations of Jesus, and therefore, as regards the matter recorded in it, substantially resembled the Logia of Matthew, the source employed in our First and Third Gospels. It does not seem to have included any pieces of a purely narrative character. The several passages of discourse, however, were introduced, as in that synoptic source, by short notices on the historical occasion and situation. In this way the cleansing of the Temple, which gave occasion for the significant utterance of Jesus in ii. 19, was described (ii. 13 sqq.); so also the nocturnal visit of Nicodemus (iii. 1 sq.), the meeting with the Samaritan woman at the well (iv. 4 sqq.), the work of healing which Jesus wrought on the Sabbath at the Pool of Bethesda (v. 1 sqq.), His encounter with a man blind from his birth (ix. 1), His coming to Bethany after the death of Lazarus (xi. 1 sqq.), the inquiry of the Greeks (xii. 20–32), the washing of feet at the last meal (xiii. 1 sqq.). But the real purpose of the text was not to record these historic events, but to record the words of Jesus to the utterance of which they gave occasion. On that account the narrative introduction had not always a corresponding narrative conclusion. Nothing is told concerning the conduct of Nicodemus after his speech with Jesus, or the further course of the affair with the Greeks (xii. 20-22). Exactly in the same way, we are not told in the Logia of Matthew how the three men afterwards behaved who would follow Jesus, but were first warned by Him of the full and instant renunciation which such a choice involved (Luke ix. 57-62), or what that man did whose prayer to Jesus to settle a dispute about an inheritance gave occasion for Jesus' warning against covetousness, and against restless anxiety about earthly goods (Luke xii. 13-34).

Did the passages of discourse follow one another in the Source in the same order in which the fourth evangelist has employed them in his narrative? In one case we are able definitely to recognise a displacement effected by the evangelist: he has removed the passage in vii. 15-24 from its original place at the close of chap. v. It follows that in other places he can hardly have confined himself strictly to the order of the Source. The places where we have best reason to suppose that pieces of the Source have been rearranged are those where the evangelist's independent root-ideas betray themselves in the grouping of the matter. This is specially the case in the first part of the Gospel (i. 19-iv. 54), where the initial attestation of Jesus' Messiahship by the Baptist and by Jesus Himself, and the taking up of the Messianic work of Jesus in the various parts of Palestine are depicted.[1] Did the pieces from the Source made use of in this section of the Gospel,—the words of Jesus to the chief priests after the cleansing of the Temple, the conversation with Nicodemus, and that with the Samaritan woman, besides the conversation with the disciples which is attached to it,—did these pieces stand in this order at the beginning of the Source, so that the evangelist, in his own disposition of matter, was able to adopt them exactly

[1] Cf. *sup.* p. 117.

as they stood?[1] There are clear indications pointing to the fact that these pieces really belonged to the close of Jesus' ministry. The cleansing of the Temple, according to Mark xi. 15 sqq., took place in Jesus' last visit to Jerusalem.[2] In the conversation with Nicodemus Jesus glances at the misunderstanding and rejection which befell His message of salvation, as at a fact already decided and complete: "We speak that we do know, and bear witness of that we have seen; and ye receive not our witness" (iii. 11); "this is the judgment, that the light is come into the world, and men loved the darkness rather than the light : for their works were evil" (ver. 19). In the words which Jesus addresses to the disciples after the conversation with the Samaritan woman He speaks of the full harvest of His labour as even now at hand (iv. 35), and proclaims, moreover, that it is not He, but His disciples who are entering into His labour, that shall gather that harvest in (vv. 36–38). This is the expression of a state of mind at the close, not at the beginning, of Jesus' ministry. Probably, then, these three pieces had in the Source a later place, and were moved forward by the evangelist to suit his literary scheme.

The discourses and discussions recorded in the Source stood closer together in time on the showing of that document than in the account of our evangelist. He has distributed the discourses of the Source over the whole course of Jesus' public ministry; and he certainly considered that ministry as extending over several years. But we have seen that he has several times dissevered passages which formed one context in the Source, and distributed them in different situations. Not only vii. 15–24, but the whole

[1] Compare the way in which our first evangelist, in the first part of his account of the ministry of Jesus (chaps. iv.–xiii.), has displaced the order of Mark to suit his own independent ideas, whereas later, from chap. xiv., he keeps to the order of Mark.

[2] On the correctness of this synoptic tradition, cf. *sup.* p. 12.

discussion in vi. 27 sqq., belonged, according to the Source, to the situation in Jerusalem of v. 1 sqq.[1] The utterances in vii. 28 sq., 33 sq., 37 sq. belonged to the passage of discourse in viii. 12 sqq.[2] The discussion in x. 24–28 was the continuation of the passage made up of ix. 4 sq., 39–41, x. 1–18.[3] In the Source three visits of Jesus to Jerusalem appear to have been noticed. The healing on the Sabbath at the Pool of Bethesda (v. 1 sqq.), with the discussions that followed (v. 17 sqq., vii. 15–24, vi. 27 sqq.), belonged to the first. All the discourses from vii. 25 to the end of chap. x. fell in the second, at the Feast of Tabernacles. The third was that which closed with the death of Jesus.

The whole of the matter recorded in the Source referred to these visits of Jesus to Jerusalem. As a single exception must be noted the conversation with the Samaritan woman in chap. iv. Still, even this took place on a journey of Jesus either from or to Jerusalem. Reference was made in vii. 1–7 to Jesus' stay in Galilee; but there was no record, so far as we can see, of Jesus' work of preaching either here or on His other journeys.

The conclusion that the Source contained Logia of Jesus may then be defined more narrowly: it recorded specifically discourses and conversations of Jesus during His visits to Jerusalem. The author of the Source wished thoroughly to set forth two groups of material: the first describes how Jesus, again and again, confronting the representatives of Judaism in the capital itself, testified with especial emphasis concerning His inner communion with God and His unique importance for human salvation, but was opposed in this testimony by an utter lack of understanding, which quickly grew into deadly enmity; the second tells how, again in Jerusalem, at His last meal with His disciples, He opened to them His whole heart, exhorted

[1] Cf. pp. 78 sqq. and 85 sqq.   [2] Cf. pp. 92 sq.
[3] Cf. pp. 148 sqq.

them, comforted them, prayed for them. The author has not, indeed, pedantically confined himself to the treatment of these two themes, but has also recorded some other important discourses of Jesus, which were very closely related to these visits to Jerusalem: the conversation with the Samaritan woman, that with His brethren, that with the sisters in Bethany sorrowing over the death of Lazarus, that with Pilate.

CHAPTER IV

THE SOURCE OF THE FOURTH GOSPEL IN ITS RELATION TO OTHER LITERATURE

A. THE JOHANNINE EPISTLES

BEFORE we proceed to inquire into the value and origin of the Source, we must take into consideration the fact that some writings of the earliest Church exhibit a close affinity with this Source, but no relation to its redaction in our Fourth Gospel. This fact affords an important, if indirect, piece of external evidence that the distinction between the source-components and the narrative framework supplied by the evangelist, the distinction which we have effected by means of internal evidence, corresponds also with the facts of literary history.

The close affinity of the First Epistle of John with the Fourth Gospel is evident. It shows itself in a widespread coincidence of thought and expression, and in the peculiar stamp of the style. On the ground of this affinity a common authorship has been almost universally assumed for the Epistle and the Gospel. But alongside this conformity, there is also a not inconsiderable divergence between these writings. We need not attach much weight to the fact that certain terms which do not occur in the Gospel are of prominent significance in the Epistle (especially παράκλητος applied to Christ, ii. 1; ἱλασμός, ii. 2; χρῖσμα, ii. 20, 27; σπέρμα τοῦ θεοῦ, iii. 9; ἀντίχριστος, ii. 18, 22, iv. 3; ψευδοπροφῆται, iv. 1; παρουσία, ii. 28), and that certain thoughts are emphasised in the Epistle which are not brought out so much in the Gospel (*e.g.* that God is light, i. 5; that he who says he has no sin deceives himself, i. 8; that God is love, iv. 8, 12; that he who does not love his brother does not love God, iv. 20 sq.). Such differences only imply that the one writing is not merely derivative, not a bald reproduction of the thoughts of the other. But it is a point of great importance that in the Epistle there is absolutely no allusion to the "signs" of Jesus, as having testified aforetime to His Messiahship, and as affording the true basis for faith in it. The emphasis which the fourth evangelist lays on these signs is his most characteristic feature, and of fundamental importance in his Christology. It cannot be held that this difference is incidental to the different purpose of the two writings,—historical in the one, hortatory in the other: that the Epistle is not concerned with the historical events reported in the Gospel, and has therefore no need to mention the signs. On the one hand, the practical object of the historical presentation in the Gospel is to induce its readers to believe in the Messiahship of Jesus, and through that belief to win eternal life (xx. 30 sq.). On the other hand, the author of the Epistle has the consciousness that all that he writes is a preaching of Jesus as the historical Messiah, who has appeared in the flesh, in whom his readers may have eternal life (I i. 1–4, v. 10–13). The practical rules of conduct which he exhorts them to follow are but the necessary guide to true communion by faith with the Christ whom he preaches. Gospel and Epistle agree, then, in the preaching of faith in the historical Jesus Christ. We should therefore expect to find some hint in the Epistle of that which is to the evangelist the essential manifestation of the divine glory of Jesus Christ, and the conclusive ground for faith in Him; some hint of His miraculous signs when He walked the earth and His miraculous appearances after His resurrection (cf. Acts x. 38–41),—if the evangelist were indeed the author of the Epistle.

The true relation of the Epistle to the Gospel comes to

light as soon as we distinguish between the source-components in the Gospel and the additions of the evangelist in his redaction of the Source. It then instantly appears that it is specifically to the passages from the Source that the Epistle is related. All affinities which the Epistle shows with the Gospel in expression and thought are affinities with the passages taken from the Source; while the difference between the Gospel and Epistle is exactly that which subsists, in the Gospel itself, between the passages of discourse derived from the Source and the narrative passages of the evangelist. The Second and Third Epistles of John, too, range themselves not with the fourth evangelist, but, by the side of the First Epistle, with the Source of the Gospel.

The discourses of the Fourth Gospel are characterised, as we saw above,[1] by the ever-recurring claim of Jesus to be the God-sent bearer of a revelation which leads those who accept and observe it to eternal life (v. 24, vi. 63, vii. 16 sq., viii. 51, xii. 44–50, xvii. 2 sq., 6, 8, 14). Attested as He is in this character by the quickening effects of His teaching, He has no need of further attestation by means of "signs," such as the unbelieving Jews demand of Him (vi. 30–36, 63). That which corresponds in the Epistles to this claim of Jesus in the Gospel-discourses is the writer's certainty that there has been given to himself and to the Christian community, in the historical Jesus Christ, a revelation of life (I i. 1–3), a new and perfect apprehension of God (I i. 5, v. 20), and that the all-important matter for Christians is that they should cleave to that revelation, and follow it (I ii. 3–6, 27 sq., iii. 24; II 9 sq.). It is the writer's living sense of the worth of this revelation of God given in Jesus Christ which yields the intrinsic reason why he is never prompted to speak about the signs of Jesus.

He does not make the import of the revelation of Jesus Christ the object of any theoretical speculation; but he

[1] Cf. pp. 58–64.

draws from it the true, practical conclusion, by appealing constantly to Jesus as the rightful authority for himself and the Christian readers of his Epistle. The nature of this appeal is very significant. The author does not cite detached, sententious utterances of the Lord, as Paul does occasionally, though, relatively speaking, in very few cases (1 Cor. vii. 10 sq., ix. 14, xi. 23–25; cf. Acts xx. 35), and as the Christian writers of the second century quote Logia of Jesus, sometimes synoptic, sometimes obtained from oral tradition. But he lays stress on the fact that the main thoughts which he wishes to impress on his readers take their origin from Jesus. And these are indeed the simple, fundamental ideas of the gospel of Jesus, which together constitute His epoch-making advance on Judaism. "And this is the message which we have heard *from him* and announce unto you, that God is light, and in Him is no darkness at all" (I i. 5),—that is to say, as the following words show, that God is the sum of moral perfection, and can have no communion with sin and wickedness. "Beloved, no new commandment write I unto you, but an old commandment which ye had from the beginning: the old commandment is the word which ye heard. Again, a new commandment write I unto you, which thing is true *in him* and in you; because the darkness is passing away, and the true light already shineth. He that saith he is in the light, and hateth his brother, is in the darkness even until now. He that loveth his brother abideth in the light, and there is none occasion of stumbling in him" (ii. 7–10). "And this is the promise which *he* promised us, even the life eternal" (ii. 25). "As *he* taught you, abide in him" (ii. 27). "And this is His (God's) commandment, that we should believe in the name of His son, Jesus Christ, and love one another, even as *he* (Jesus) gave us commandment" (iii. 23). "And this commandment have we *from him*, that he who loveth God love his brother also" (iv. 21). "We know that the Son of God is come, and hath given us an understanding, that we know him that is true" (v. 20). Nowhere else in the New Testament Epistles and the rest of the ancient Christian literature do we meet this αὐτὸς ἔφα, in reference to Jesus, so frequently and impressively as in the First Epistle of John. Another unique point in this Epistle, especially remarkable in contrast with Paul, is the absence of any reference to the "Scripture." The reason for this is certainly not that the author had any gnostic animus against the Old Testament, but simply that, in view of the primary authority of Jesus, he did not feel the need of appealing to any scriptural authority.

If the Epistles of John and the Source of the Fourth Gospel are to be classed together as writings of the same author, it follows that we have no right to see, as critics generally do see, in the earliest traces of a use of that Epistle, an indirect testimony to the use of the Fourth Gospel also. This applies, in the first place, to the passage in the epistle of Polycarp (vii. 1): πᾶς γὰρ ὃς ἂν μὴ ὁμολογῇ Ἰησοῦν Χριστὸν ἐν σαρκὶ ἐληλυθέναι, ἀντίχριστός ἐστιν where the words of 1 John iv. 2 (2 John 7) have clearly been appropriated. In the second place it applies to the statement of Eusebius, *Hist. Eccl.* III. xxxix. 16, that Papias made use of the First Epistle of John. We are at liberty to infer from these passages that the author of the Source of the Fourth Gospel, but not that the fourth evangelist himself, was regarded by Polycarp and Papias as a Christian authority.

B. CHRISTIAN WRITERS OF THE SECOND CENTURY

1. *Ignatius*

The relation of the epistles of Ignatius to the Johannine writings is very interesting. These epistles strongly suggest the Johannine world of thought and phrase. It is true that no passage from the Fourth Gospel or the First Epistle of John is cited with verbal exactness; but not only is the general Christian position of Ignatius closely related in many respects to that laid down in the Johannine writings: there also occur in detail several characteristic Johannine conceptions, even though sometimes in a slightly modified form of expression, and, on the other hand, several characteristic Johannine expressions, though sometimes with a slight shifting of the sense.[1] The following are adduced as specially important points of contact:—Ignatius says of Christ, *ad Magn.* vii. 1, ὁ κύριος ἄνευ τοῦ πατρὸς οὐδὲν ἐποίησεν (cf. John v. 19, viii. 28), ἡνωμένος ὤν (cf. John x. 30); in vii. 2, Ἰησοῦν Χρ., τὸν ἀφ' ἑνὸς πατρὸς προελθόντα καὶ εἰς ἕνα ὄντα καὶ χωρήσαντα (cf. John xiii. 3, xvi. 28); in viii. 2, ὅς ἐστιν αὐτοῦ λόγος (cf. John i. 1), ἀπὸ σιγῆς προελθών, ὃς κατὰ πάντα εὐηρέστησεν τῷ πέμψαντι αὐτόν (cf. John viii. 29). Again, *ad Rom.* viii. 2, τὸ ἀψευδὲς στόμα, ἐν ᾧ ὁ πατὴρ ἐλάλησεν ἀληθῶς (cf. John viii. 28, xii. 49 sq.). With reference to himself, he says, *ad Rom.* vii. 1, ὁ ἄρχων τοῦ αἰῶνος τούτου (cf. John xii. 31, xiv. 30, xvi. 11), διαρπάσαι με βούλεται (cf. John x. 28 sq.). In vii. 2, ὕδωρ δὲ ζῶν καὶ λαλοῦν ἐν ἐμοί (cf. John vii. 38). In vii. 3, οὐχ ἥδομαι τροφῇ φθορᾶς (cf. John vi. 27), ... ἄρτον θεοῦ θέλω, ὅ ἐστιν σὰρξ Ἰησοῦ Χρ., τοῦ ἐκ σπέρματος Δαβίδ, καὶ πόμα θέλω τὸ αἷμα αὐτοῦ (cf. John vi. 33, 35, 51–58). With reference to the communion of the society with their bishop, he says, *ad Eph.* v. 1, ὑμᾶς μακαρίζω, τοὺς ἐνκεκραμένους αὐτῷ ὡς ἡ ἐκκλησία Ἰησοῦ Χριστῷ καὶ ὡς Ἰησοῦς Χρ. τῷ πατρί, ἵνα πάντα ἐν ἑνότητι σύμφωνα ᾖ (cf. John xvii. 21, 23). In v. 2, πάντα γὰρ ὃν πέμπει ὁ οἰκοδεσπότης εἰς ἰδίαν οἰκονομίαν, οὕτως δεῖ ἡμᾶς

---

[1] Cf. the thorough exposition of Ed. von der Goltz, "Ignatius von Antiochien als Christ und Theologe" (*T. U.* xii. 3), 1894, pp. 118 sqq., and the synopsis, pp. 196 sqq.

αὐτὸν δέχεσθαι, ὡς αὐτὸν τὸν πέμψαντα (cf. John xiii. 20): He says of the πνεῦμα in *ad Phil.* vii. 1, οὐ πλανᾶται, ἀπὸ θεοῦ ὄν. οἶδεν γὰρ πόθεν ἔρχεται καὶ ποῦ ὑπάγει (cf. John iii. 8). Such coincidences of thought and wording cannot be accidental.

But by their side the fact must be considered that Ignatius never refers to the historical notices in the Fourth Gospel, even where they would have been most apposite to his purpose. He knew the facts of the Gospel history only according to the synoptic tradition; and, indeed, makes special use of the Gospel of Matthew. At one place, *ad Smyrn.* iii., he shows an acquaintance with a peculiar version of the resurrection story, perhaps that which belonged to the κήρυγμα Πέτρου.[1] Now in this place the absence of any reference to the narrative of the Fourth Gospel is especially striking. Ignatius wishes to show that the risen Christ appeared to the disciples not in an incorporeal state, but in the flesh. If John xx. 19–27 had been known to him, the recollection of the passage must here have forced itself upon him. But he only refers to that apocryphal account and to Acts x. 41.[2]

How is this ignoring of the Johannine narrative, by the side of considerable use of the Johannine thought and expression, to be explained? Ed. von der Goltz deduces from his examination of the matter the conclusion that our Fourth Gospel was not known to Ignatius, but that he must have been influenced by a valuable tradition, going back to the Apostle John; that this was used in our Fourth Gospel, but had already exercised a great influence before that Gospel became known, and independently of it.[3] How perfectly this conclusion agrees with the result of our

---
[1] Cf. von Dobschütz, "Das Kerygma Petri" (*T. U.* xi. 1), 1893, pp. 82 sq.
[2] Cf. Ed. von der Goltz, *op. cit.* pp. 137 sq.
[3] *Op. cit.* pp. 140, 165–177.

investigation of the Source employed in the Fourth Gospel! All the coincidences between Ignatius and the Fourth Gospel concern the discourses which are derived from that Source. That of which Ignatius never takes cognisance is the historical framework in which the fourth evangelist set the pieces from the Source. The relation in which Ignatius stands to the Fourth Gospel is exactly the same as that of the First Epistle of John. In fact, Ignatius was not acquainted with our Fourth Gospel. He must, however, have been acquainted either with the Source of which that Gospel is a redaction or with an oral tradition which reached back to the author of that Source, the writer of the First Epistle of John.

2. *Justin*

Again, the relation in which Justin stands to the Fourth Gospel is quite analogous to that of Ignatius. He too has points of contact only with those elements of the Gospel which derive from the Source. It has several times already been noticed as a remarkable fact, by the inquirers who have investigated his relation towards the Gospel, that while he is acquainted with the religious cycle of thought in this Gospel he nevertheless makes no use of the Johannine narrative, but always keeps to the Synoptics.[1]

Certain thoughts from the Johannine prologue are used by Justin, *Apol.* I. lxiii. 13, ὃς λόγος καὶ πρωτότοκος ὢν τοῦ θεοῦ καὶ ὑπάρχει (cf. John i. 1); *Apol.* II. vi. 3, ὁ υἱὸς ἐκείνου, ὁ μόνος λεγόμενος κυρίως υἱός, ὁ λόγος πρὸ τῶν ποιημάτων καὶ συνὼν καὶ γεννώμενος, ὅτε τὴν ἀρχὴν δι' αὐτοῦ πάντα ἔκτισε καὶ ἐκόσμησε (cf. John i. 1–3, 18); *Apol.* I. xxxii. 10, υἱὸς ὁ λόγος ἐστίν· ὃς σαρκοποιηθεὶς ἄνθρωπος γέγονεν (cf. John i. 14). John iii. 3 sq. is quoted in *Apol.* I.

[1] Cf. Thoma, "Justins literar. Verhältnis zu Paulus und zum Johannesevang.," *Zw. Th.*, 1875, pp. 490 sqq., esp. pp. 555 sqq.; von Engelhardt, *D. Christentum Justins d. M.*, Erl., 1878, pp. 347 sqq.; Ed. von der Goltz, *op. cit.* pp. 140 sqq. and 198 sqq.

lxi. 4, καὶ γὰρ ὁ Χριστὸς εἶπεν· ἂν μὴ ἀναγεννηθῆτε, οὐ μὴ εἰσέλθητε εἰς τὴν βασιλείαν τῶν οὐρανῶν. ὅτι δὲ καὶ ἀδύνατον εἰς τὰς μήτρας τῶν τεκουσῶν τοὺς ἅπαξ γεννωμένους ἐμβῆναι, φανερὸν πᾶσίν ἐστι. In spite of a slight alteration of the wording, caused by recollection of Mark xviii. 3, it is evident that the passage meant is this passage from the discourse with Nicodemus. The Christians are denoted in *Apol.* I. vi. 2 as, λόγῳ καὶ ἀληθείᾳ τιμῶντες (cf. John iv. 24); in *Dial.* 69 and 114 Christ is called πηγὴ ὕδατος ζῶντος and τὸ τῆς ζωῆς ὕδωρ (cf. John iv. 14, vii. 38). As in these cases, so everywhere else in Justin where coincidences with the Fourth Gospel occur, they relate to those passages which are derived from the Source. There is besides an obvious use of the First Epistle of John in *Dial.* 123, ἡμεῖς ἀπὸ τοῦ γεννήσαντος ἡμᾶς εἰς θεὸν Χριστοῦ . . . καὶ θεοῦ τέκνα ἀληθινὰ καλούμεθα καὶ ἐσμέν, οἱ τὰς ἐντολὰς τοῦ Χριστοῦ φυλάσσοντες (cf. 1 John iii. 1 sq., v. 1 sq.).

A reference to the narrative part of the Fourth Gospel can hardly be found in *Dial.* 69, τοὺς ἐκ γενετῆς καὶ κατὰ τὴν σάρκα πηροὺς καὶ χωλοὺς ἰάσατο. It is true that the expression ἐκ γενετῆς here reminds us of John ix. 1; but it strangely happens that it is precisely the τυφλοί, of whom in any reminiscence of John ix. we should expect to hear, that are not mentioned. Justin has clearly in mind the passage in Matt. xv. 30 sq. Moreover, as we saw above,[1] the words in John ix. 1 certainly belonged to the Source, as an introduction to the passage of discourse beginning in ix. 4 sq, and continued in ix. 39. So that even if the ἐκ γενετῆς in Justin is derived from John ix. 1, this does not indicate any acquaintance with the narrative point of our Fourth Gospel. Nor can such an acquaintance be inferred from the wording of the quotation (Zech. xii. 10) in *Apol.* I. lii. 12, *Dial.* 14, which differs from the LXX, and agrees with John xix. 37, ὄψονται εἰς ὃν ἐξεκέντησαν. Justin is

[1] P. 150.

not referring to the thrust of the spear, but means the piercing of the crucifixion. The cause of this agreement in citation may be that the verse of Zechariah was customarily used throughout the Christian community in this wording of the Greek, which brought clearly out its oracular application to the death of Jesus (cf. Apoc. i. 7). The single passage in Justin which perhaps refers to the Johannine narrative is in *Dial.* 88, where the words of the Baptist are quoted as follows: οὐκ εἰμὶ ὁ χριστός, ἀλλὰ φωνὴ βοῶντος, οὗ οὐκ εἰμὶ ἱκανὸς τὰ ὑποδήματα βαστάσαι (cf. John i. 20, 23, 27). But the last clause in these words, at anyrate, is not given in accordance with John i. 27, but with Matt. iii. 11, and the beginning also may have been shaped merely on Acts xiii. 25. It cannot be decided with certainty from this passage that Justin was acquainted with the work of our fourth evangelist.

The whole question, so much discussed, of the external testimony to the Fourth Gospel in the second century takes a new and altered form when we are forced to distinguish between the Gospel and the Source of which it is a redaction. Are the apparent traces of a literary relation to the Fourth Gospel really traces of the employment of the Gospel itself, or are they not rather signs of the use of the Source, or of a verbal tradition derived from its author? On the other hand, are not the traces of the "Johannine" element before the Gospel of John,—that is to say, early echoes of the Johannine world of thought, which we can hardly venture to explain by the theory of a literary use of our Gospel [1] —are they not in reality traces of the influence of that document or of its author? In fact the "Johannine" echoes which have been detected in the so-called apostolic fathers [2]

---

[1] Cf. *sup.* p. 51.
[2] Cf. H. Holtzmann, *Zw. Th.*, 1871, pp. 336 sqq., 1875, pp. 40 sqq., 1877, pp. 187 sqq.; Th. Zahn, *Geschichte des neutestamentlichen Kanons*, i. 2, pp. 897 sqq.

and in the Didache[1] are always echoes of the passages derived from the Source or of the prologue. That does not, of course, preclude the possibility that the knowledge of these sections derived from the Source was communicated to the authors in question by means of our Fourth Gospel. But this is by no means certain. It remains an exceedingly remarkable fact that the thought-material belonging to that element in the Fourth Gospel which came from the Source was employed in other Christian literature so much earlier than the narrative matter in the Fourth Gospel which did not come from the Source. The first use of this narrative matter—the first use, in fact, of the Gospel as we have it—which can be recognised with certainty occurs, so far as I can see, in the *Diatessaron* of Tatian.[2]

[1] Cf. A. Harnack, "Prolegomena z. Didache" (*T. U.* ii. 2), 1886, pp. 79 sqq.; Th. Zahn, *Geschichte des neut. Kanons*, i. 2, pp. 909 sqq.
[2] Cf. A. Harnack, *Z. K. G.*, 1881, pp. 476 sqq.; Th. Zahn, *Forschungen zur Geschichte des Kanons*, i. pp. 112–219.

CHAPTER V

THE HISTORICAL VALUE OF THE SOURCE AS A RECORD

A. THE RELATION OF THE HISTORICAL NOTICES IN THE SOURCE TO THE SYNOPTIC TRADITION

FROM the task of establishing the fact that an older document was used as a source in the Fourth Gospel, we now proceed to test the historical value of the contents of that document. We must apply to this test the same standard which we used in testing the narrative element in the Fourth Gospel, namely, the primary synoptic tradition.

We must first realise and weigh the extreme independence which is shown towards the synoptic tradition by the historical statements in the Source. The discourses and conversations of Jesus are neither fitted into the historical scheme of the Synoptics as a whole, nor attached severally to situations in the synoptic story. An entirely different set of historic scenes from the life of Jesus is set before our eyes. The tradition delivered to us by the Source is peculiar to itself. This does not preclude an acquaintance on the part of its author with the synoptic tradition. The peculiar selection of the subject-matter — the attention which is paid to the earlier visits of Jesus to Jerusalem, of which the synoptic tradition has no direct record, while Jesus' ministry of teaching in Galilee, of which there is an extended account in the synoptic tradition, is not gone into; the report of utterances delivered during Jesus' last stay in

Jerusalem, of a kind which are not contained in the synoptic tradition, while the words at the Last Supper are lacking,—this selection can be most simply explained by attributing to the author the definite intention of supplementing, in certain important points, another tradition which was known to him—that which received its final literary form in our synoptic Gospels.

In spite of their perfect independence of the synoptic record, the historical notices in the Source contain many references to it, by means of which the consistency of the two traditions is maintained; and that which is new and peculiar in the notices of the Source does not bear the stamp of intrinsic improbability.

The most striking point is that mention is made in the Source of several visits of Jesus to Jerusalem,—of two which preceded that in which He met His death. We have already shown [1] that the tradition of the Source on this point, in spite of its variance from the account of Mark, is not incredible, but rather is confirmed by certain indications in other parts of the older synoptic tradition. Then, again, it is perfectly credible that the earlier visits of Jesus to Jerusalem saw the beginning of the conflict with the high priests, which afterwards led to His death; that the arrogance of the men of Judæa was much too great for the words of an unlearned Galilean to find acceptance among them, while to this arrogance Jesus opposed His own serene religious consciousness of a life derived from God, and a saving power of which that life was the spring. Moreover, the Source expressly refers in vii. 1-7 to Jesus' abode in Galilee; and in the account of His journey through Samaria (iv. 4 sqq.) the abode in Galilee is presupposed.

The detached historical events which are recorded in the Source to introduce speeches and conversations of Jesus are in part analogous to those related in the synoptic

[1] Cf. pp. 9 sqq.

tradition, and in part serve to complete or explain, in an interesting fashion, the statements of the Synoptics. The account of how Jesus, on occasion of a work of healing on the Sabbath, was brought into conflict with the people of Jerusalem (v. 1 sqq.) forms a parallel to the synoptic notices of conflicts which Jesus sustained concerning the Sabbath (Mark ii. 23–iii. 6; Luke, xiii. 10–17, xiv. 1–6). We are told in Mark iii. 6, as well as in John v. 18, vii. 19, that in one such dispute the adversaries of Jesus quickly reached the point of plotting to kill Him. The manner in which, according to John vii. 22 sq., Jesus defends His own alleged illegal Sabbath-breach by appealing to an exception, which the law itself prescribes, to the Sabbath rest, is similar to His defence in Matt. xii. 5 sq. The demand of the Jews for a sign, and the way in which Jesus repulsed them (John vi. 30–33, ii. 18 sq.), have their analogue in the events of Mark viii. 11 sq., Luke xi. 16, 29 sq. The statement that even the brethren of Jesus had not, at the time of His earthly ministry, believed in Him (John vii. 3–5), is confirmed by the story, in Mark iii. 20 sq. and 31–35, that those of Jesus' own household ascribed His zeal to a morbid ecstasy, and sought to restrain Him from further activity. How could such a statement about the brethren of Jesus have originated in subapostolic Christendom? The notice, again, that Mary and Martha, the sisters of Lazarus, lived in Bethany (John xi. 1) is consistent with the story in Luke x. 38 sqq. Thence it follows that in this story also, which is derived from the Logia of Matthew, a journey of Jesus to Jerusalem was presupposed. The intimation that the news of Lazarus' sickness unto death was what decided Jesus to go to Judæa, in spite of the mortal danger which threatened Himself, because He regarded it as a duty of His calling to bring help and comfort to the sisters in Bethany (John xi. 7–10), affords a most valuable supplement to the synoptic record. That record only tells us that Jesus foretold to the Twelve, as they drew nigh to Jerusalem, the destiny of suffering which awaited Him there (Mark x. 32–34), but does not explain why He went straightway to meet and fulfil that destiny, and did not seek, in the first place, to continue that work of teaching to which He was called. The story of the cleansing of the Temple in John ii. 13 sqq. agrees in essentials with the record in Mark xi. 15 sqq. It supplements the record, however, by the statement that Jesus' saying about the destruction and building up again of the Temple (ii. 19) was uttered in connection with that event,—a saying which was, according to Mark xiv. 58, a mainstay of the charge against Jesus before the Sanhedrin. The report in Luke xxii. 26 sq. of how at the Last Supper Jesus exhorted His disciples to serve one another, and pointed to Himself as being in their midst as One that serveth, agrees with the statement in John xiii. 1–17, 20 that at the Last Supper Jesus gave His disciples an example of loving service by washing their feet.[1] Finally, the report of the interchange of words between Jesus and Pilate, John xviii.

[1] The scene in Luke xxii. 24–26 is clearly the parallel to Mark x. 41–44. Luke's insertion of this piece from Mark in the story of the Last Supper, instead of in the place it holds in Mark's account, can be explained by the analogy of his treatment of other notices from his sources in cases where he combines them; he found in his second source, the Logia of Matthew, among the farewell words of Jesus an utterance which resembled that passage in Mark, and he attached the incident to the saying. Besides ver. 27, which is independent of Mark, the groundwork of ver. 26 is probably also derived from the Logia of Matthew. If we separate from the sayings of Jesus at the Last Supper which are recorded by Luke (xxii. 15–38) the elements taken over from Mark (vv. 18–26a), there remains a residuum of great value which probably comes entirely from the Logia. This tradition of farewell words of Jesus, peculiar to Luke, forms a supplement, exactly analogous to that which is afforded by our farewell discourses in John xiii.–xvii., to the short account in Mark xiv. 18–25. Is it to be wondered at that in different quarters should have been preserved different sayings of Jesus at this His last intercourse with the Twelve?

33–38a and xix. 9–11, which also belongs to the Source, is a very important supplement to the short account in Mark xv. 2–5. The statement that Jesus, face to face with the Procurator, who hitherto knew nothing of Him and was now misled by the slanderous charges of the Jewish high priests, not only openly confessed that He was indeed the King of the Jews, but added the definite declaration that His Kingship was not of any temporal or political kind, —this bears a high degree of intrinsic probability. And it is equally credible that the words in which Jesus spoke of the ethical and religious character of His kingdom were received by the Procurator with a blasé scepticism, in view of which Jesus henceforth kept silence.

The detached historical notices of the Source furnish, then, in reality an appropriate supplement and enrichment of the synoptic delineation. We do not meet in them with any such contradictions of the synoptic tradition as appear in those accounts in the Fourth Gospel which did not originate in the Source.

But these historical notices are, after all, only subsidiary matter in the Source. Their main contents are the discourses of Jesus. The chief question for us must therefore be, what degree of historicity belongs to these discourses.

B. THE RELATION OF THE DISCOURSES OF JESUS IN THE SOURCE TO THE SYNOPTIC TRADITION

1. *The Characteristic Form of the Discourses*

No lengthy demonstration is needed to show that the discourses of Jesus derived from the Source differ considerably in vocabulary and style from such words of His as are preserved in the synoptic Gospels. The Source discourses make prominent use of certain characteristic terms which in the synoptic utterances occur but sparsely, or not at all.

Examples are: the life, the light, the truth, the world ; to be of God, to be of this world ; to be in God, God's being in men ; to believe in the Son of God ; the Paraclete. On the other hand, a term which takes a central place in the Synoptics, that of the kingdom of God, occurs only once in the discourses of the Fourth Gospel (iii. 3, 5). The popular style which is so pronounced a characteristic of the synoptic sayings is not found in these, nor do they follow the synoptic use of concrete illustrations, drawn out into circumstantial detail. They are quite free, not indeed from figures and similes altogether (cf. iii. 8, iv. 35–38, ix. 4 sq., x. 1–16, xi. 9 sq., xii. 24, 35 sq., xiii. 16, xv. 1–8, xvi. 21), but from extended parables, in which some temporal event is related as having once happened under definite circumstances, but with an allegorical intention. Again, single sayings of a pregnant, sententious character are much less frequent than in the Synoptics. On the other hand, these discourses exhibit a peculiar method in the progress of the thought. A thought which is expressed, at first, in a brief and figurative form, is then, after a few sentences have been added to it, taken up again once or several times, with slight modifications, in order, sometimes, to strike out by means of this repetition a clearer impression of the truth, sometimes to interpret the meaning more clearly, or to intensify the paradox (*e.g.* vi. 27, 32 sq., 35, 48–50, 51, 53–58, viii. 23, 38, 41, 42, 44, 47, x. 11, 14 sq., 17 sq., xiv. 18, 21, 23, xv. 4, 7, 9 sq., xvii. 21, 22 sq., 26). Since this form which characterises the discourses of Jesus recorded in the Source is also characteristic of the prologue and the Epistles of John, while, on the other hand, Mark and the Logia agree in ascribing to Jesus another manner of speech, no doubt can exist that the discourses preserved in the Source are, with respect to the form in which they are cast, unhistoric.

But, of course, this does not settle outright the question of the historic value of the discourses. When the discourse of one man is preserved through the medium of another, who possesses a strongly marked individuality, and, in consequence, an individual style of thought and speech, it is possible for the second to assimilate the manner of the discourse to his own, while the matter, the real meaning of the original, is correctly reproduced. He has perhaps a deeper apprehension of the spirit of the speaker than a third man, who transmits more accurately the detailed wording of the discourse. Has this happened here? Has the author of the Source merely impressed the stamp of his own manner upon real utterances of Jesus? How are the thoughts contained in these discourses related to the cycle of ideas ascribed to Jesus in the synoptic Gospels?

2. *The General Religious Attitude and Conception in the Discourses*

Here, too, that which comes first into notice is the independence which these discourses exhibit of the synoptic tradition. Separate sayings of Jesus in our Source may, it is true, be found in a very similar form in the Synoptics. There are the words which we have already ranged together on pp. 43 sq.: John xii. 25 = Mark viii. 35 (Matt. xvi. 25, Luke ix. 24) and Matt. x. 39, Luke xvii. 33; John xiii. 16 and xv. 20 = Matt. x. 24; John xiii. 20 = Mark ix. 37, Matt. x. 40, cf. also Luke x. 16, Matt. xxv. 40; John xiii. 38 = Mark xiv. 30, Matt. xxvi. 34, Luke xxii. 34; John xiv. 31 = Mark xiv. 42, Matt. xxvi. 46. But these coincidences with synoptic expressions are not of a kind which need be traced to a literary dependence on the synoptic writers. Just as the undoubtedly historical prediction of the denial of Peter is recorded in its characteristic form by more than one tradition, so also the pointed, sententious words in John xii. 25, xiii. 16, 20, xv. 20, and the exclamation in xiv. 31*b*, may well have been independently preserved by different reporters, or even spoken by Jesus on various occasions. It is worthy of note that the parallels to the words in John xii. 25 and xv. 20 (xiii. 16) not only appear in Mark and in those sections of Matthew and Luke which are dependent on Mark, but also in passages of our First and Third Gospels which have plainly been derived from the Logia. In the same way several other sententious sayings of Jesus, which are recorded by Mark, must also have been contained in the Logia of Matthew (*e.g.* Mark iv. 22 = Matt. x. 26, Luke xii. 2; Mark iv. 24 = Matt. vii. 2, Luke vi. 38; Mark iv. 25 = Matt. xxv. 29, Luke xix. 26; Mark ix. 42 = Matt. xviii. 6 sq., Luke xvii. 1 sq.; Mark ix. 47 = Matt. v. 29; Mark x. 11 = Matt. v. 32, Luke xvi. 18; Mark x. 31 = Matt. xx. 16, Luke xiii. 30; Mark xi. 23 = Luke vii. 6). But it is, in my judgment, a false conclusion to infer from these cases the literary dependence of Mark on the Logia. With reference to our Johannine passages we make one proviso, that perhaps the evangelist, working upon the Source, has been influenced in his reproduction of these words of Jesus by reminiscences of the cognate synoptic passages. In particular, we might suppose that in xiv. 31, where the evangelist found in the Source a final sentence forming an ellipse, ver. 31*a* (cf. xv. 25, 1 John ii. 19), he completed the principal sentence after Mark xiv. 42. But it is not necessary to assume so much.

Apart from these detached coincidences, the discourses of our Source are obviously, in the selection and treatment of their several themes, independent of the synoptic tradition. But at the same time there is a great affinity between the contents of these and of the synoptic discourses. They stand nearer to the preaching of Jesus as presented in the Synoptics than to any other known cycle of ideas of the apostolic or subapostolic age. As I can refer to the more exact exposition of this matter in my

Teaching of Jesus, I confine myself here to a short review of the chief points.[1]

It is first of all to be observed that in these discourses Jesus takes up the same attitude towards the Old Testament revelation as in the synoptic utterances. He takes His stand here, as decidedly as He does there, on the ground of that revelation (John iv. 22, x. 35). His piercing glance was able to discern those scattered passages of Scripture which bear witness to His own views (vi. 45, vii. 22 sq., x. 34 sqq.; cf. also v. 17). But in His recognition of the Old Testament Scripture He is not pharisaically bound, like the Jews, by the letter of the record. He expresses as clearly in His words to the Samaritan woman, John iv. 21–24, as in Mark ii. 25–28 and vii. 15–23, His perception that the Old Testament law of worship does not constitute an insuperable barrier of ordinance: that He, following His spiritual apprehension of the true will of God, may supersede this law of worship for Himself and His followers. Moreover, He is quite free from the effort to slur over, by the artificial device of allegorical meaning, the difference between His own views and those of the Old Testament. When we reflect how readily every sect of that age which had to do with the Old Testament—scribes of Palestine and philosophers of Alexandrine Judaism, a Paul and a writer to the Hebrews, and subapostolic Christianity likewise—resorted to allegory as a means for introducing new

---

[1] In my *Lehre Jesu*, 1890 (2nd ed. 1901), I did not attempt to make forthwith, out of the synoptic and Johannine discourses and utterances of Jesus, a unified synthesis of His preaching. Such a performance would be open to a doubt whether the unity attained meant anything more than a predetermination to impose upon the synoptic sayings a significance really foreign to them, that of the Johannine ideas. I preferred to explain the synoptic utterances by means of themselves alone, to exhibit the synthetic picture of the gospel of Jesus which they portray, and then, and not till then, to raise the question with respect to all the main points in this composite result, how the analogous problems are treated and answered in the Johannine discourses.

ideas into the old Scriptures, and making them appear to be registered there already, we must recognise the high significance of the fact that such allegorical interpretation of Scripture is as strange to the Johannine as to the synoptic utterances of Jesus. He is satisfied with the knowledge that in spite of His innovation on Old Testament teaching He still remains in harmony with the kernel of the Old Testament revelation, and is bringing it into a purer, a more perfect manifestation than before. Just as His knowledge of this is expressed in the Sermon on the Mount in the aphorism that He is not destroying the law and the prophets, but fulfilling,—that is to say, bringing them to perfection (Mark v. 17),—so it is expressed in John v. 37–47 in His contention that the Scripture and Moses, by which His opponents support themselves against Him, are really on His side, and testify for Him.

The essential affinity of these discourses with the synoptic teaching comes very clearly to light in the farewell series, John xiii.–xvii. The charges and words of consolation which Jesus here gives to His disciples, breathe throughout the spirit of the gospel of Jesus as revealed to us by the Synoptics. The agreement does not here show itself merely in certain general ideas, which are the common property of all Christian exposition, but also in particular characteristic thoughts. The one great commandment which Jesus gives His disciples is the commandment to love,—that is, to serve each other in unselfish and kindly ways (John xiii. 12–17, 34 sq., xv. 12–17; cf. Matt. v. 38–48, Mark ix. 33–37, x. 42–45). He seeks to illustrate this duty of love by His own example, in Mark ix. 35 sq. by His kind reception of a child, and so again in John xiii. 1–17 by washing the feet of His disciples. Here, in John xv. 13 sq., just as in Mark x. 45, He points to the pledging of His own life for the salvation of those that are His, as the highest example of this kind of love—the love that serves. His consciousness of the newness of this commandment, which enjoins a love so defined, is expressed in John xiii. 34 sq. as well as in Matt. v. 43 sq.; and the absolute worth of such loving service is laid down in John xiii. 20, as it is in Mark ix. 37. He does not demand of His disciples, besides the fulfilment of that commandment, any additional overt activity of any kind, or any special kind of common worship, but only trust in God and confident prayer in the name of Jesus (John xiv. 1, 12-14, xvi. 23 sq., 33). In John xiv. 13 sq., xv. 16, xvi. 23 sq. He promises, with the same assurance as in the synoptic sayings, Matt. vii. 7-11, xviii. 19 sq., Mark ix. 22 sq., xi. 22 sq., Luke xvii. 5 sq., xviii. 2-8, that their trustful prayers will be heard. His conclusive ground for this assurance is described in John xvi. 27, just as in Matt. vii. 9-11, as the fatherly love of God. The true goal to which the salvation of His disciples leads is in heaven (John xiv. 1-4, xvii. 24). He speaks in John xiv. 2 and xvii. 4 sq., 24, of the abodes prepared there for them, and of the glory laid up for Him by His heavenly Father before the creation of the world, as the reward for His completion of the work of His calling on earth, in the same sense in which He speaks in Matt. vi. 20 sq. of the treasures that should be laid up in heaven, or declares in Luke x. 20 that the names of His disciples are written in heaven (cf. also Matt. xxv. 34). But He does not regard the state of salvation into which He brings His own merely as a future, heavenly state. During the rest of their life here on earth, if only they remain in spiritual communion with Him and keep His commandments, His disciples shall possess a perfect joy, which cannot be taken away from them (xv. 11, xvi. 22-24). Just as in Matt. xi. 28 sqq. He promises to all the weary and heavy laden, if they will but come to Him and learn of Him, that refreshing rest of the spirit which He Himself enjoys in His humble submission to the will of God, so in John xiv. 27 He bequeaths His own inner peace to His disciples, and in xvi. 32 sq. bids them take courage in face of the persecutions which await them in the world, because He has overcome the world. The description which Jesus gives of these persecutions in John xvi. 1–4 is exactly similar to that of Mark xiii. 9–13. He compares them in John xv. 18–20, just as in Matt. x. 24 sq., with the hatred with which He has Himself been pursued. For an aid amid these assaults, which shall enable them to make true confession before their foes of their faith in Messiah, He promises them, in John xv. 26 sq., xvi. 8–11, as in Mark xiii. 11, the Holy Spirit.

3. *The Sayings of Jesus concerning Himself*

But is not this fact—that the discourses derived from the Source exhibit, in their general religious character and attitude, an unmistakably close affinity with the synoptic preaching of Jesus,—robbed of its significance by another fact, that in the sayings of Jesus about Himself they depart all the more markedly from that synoptic preaching? While the affinity shows itself very really in the farewell discourses to the disciples, is not this divergence to be seen with especial clearness in the polemical discourses addressed to the hostile inhabitants of Jerusalem? These are characterised by an ever-recurrent emphasis on Jesus' claims to have come and to have been sent from God, to stand as a son in the most intimate communion with God, and to be Himself of unique significance for the salvation of mankind. In the synoptic records these claims of Jesus are by no means equally prominent. In them Jesus maintains a remarkable reserve in what He says about Himself. His preaching is concerned first and chiefly with the kingdom of God, its incomparable worth and the requirement for entering into it. On the other hand, according to the discourses in our Source His preaching is concerned first and chiefly with His own Messianic person. In His person men must believe; through Him shall they obtain eternal life.

While we cannot make light of this difference, yet if we consider it more exactly it does not involve an irreconcilable antithesis. Even according to the Synoptics Jesus had, from His baptism onwards, the assurance given by revelation that He was, in a special sense, the well-beloved Son of God (Mark i. 11). In the passage from the Logia, Matt. xi. 25–30, Luke x. 21 sq., He speaks with enthusiastic joy of His filial communion with God, of the perfect mutual understanding which exists solely between the Father and the Son, of His unique power to reveal God aright to men, and of His readiness to bestow on all seekers after salvation who should come unto Him an inner quickening, based on lowliness of spirit. And it is narrated in Mark xi. 27–xii. 12 how Jesus, during His last stay in Jerusalem, after the cleansing of the Temple, engaged in sharp conflict with the leaders of Judaism who challenged His authority; and gave Himself out before them as the one beloved Son of the Lord of the vineyard, while they were the faithless, usurping husbandmen. These synoptic passages exhibit the closest analogy to the sayings of Jesus recorded in our Source concerning His relation to God. It is very remarkable, in contrast with the narrative portions of the Fourth Gospel, that in the discourses of Jesus taken from the Source, just as in those synoptic passages, Jesus never denotes Himself directly as Messiah, King, or Son of David. Even to the direct question of the Jews about His Messiahship (x. 24) He does not reply with a direct affirmative. But He does claim to be the Son of God, the Son in a special sense. It is true that to Jewish conceptions this title was also an attribute of the Messiah: but the most important and characteristic designation of the nature and rank of Messiah was that He should be a king of the house of David. To Jesus, on the other hand, the only important and decisive token of Messiah was His Sonship, not of David, but of God (Mark xii. 35–37). And this religious token was one which, according to those synoptic witnesses, He knew Himself to possess. But all that He says about Himself in the discourses taken from our Source comes always to this—His knowledge of His own direct and perfect filial communion with God.

Nor can it be said that the nature of His filial relation to God, and of the claim to saving power which He bases upon it, is conceived here in another and a higher sense than in Matt. xi. 27 sqq. Jesus speaks here, it is true, of His origin in God, of His mission from God, of His coming down from heaven, of His knowledge and experience of God and heavenly things, in such terms as might well make it seem at first sight that he asserted His pre-existence in heaven, before His life on earth, and denied His natural, human origin and nature (iii. 11–13, v. 19–23, 30, vi. 33–38, vii. 28 sq., viii. 23, 38–58, x. 30–38 ; cf. xiv. 9 sq., xvi. 27 sq.). The Jews interpreted them so, and, holding that they could only be true and justifiable if they held good in this external sense, declared it mere madness and blasphemy for a man of notorious human origin to speak of Himself in such a way (v. 18, vi. 41 sq., viii. 48, 52 sq., x. 33). But Jesus, in the face of such changes, only reiterates and intensifies His assertions concerning Himself. The sense in which He makes them is plain from His employment of the same words, which He uses about Himself, about His disciples also: they are not of this world (xv. 19, xvii. 14–16 ; cf. i. 12 sq.), they hear and learn of God (vi. 45), and are beloved of the Father (xiv. 21, 23, xvii. 26). On the other hand, He makes it a reproach to the unbelieving Jews that they do not hear and see God (v. 37 sq.), contests their claim, in spite of their natural descent from Abraham, to be in truth Abraham's seed, and declares that they are from beneath, of the devil (viii. 23, 37–44). The only existence which He will consider is the spiritual, the ethical. It is of the nature and origin of this that He speaks. It is from His own spiritual, inner life that He knows and asserts that He is not of this world, but of God, that it is from God that He receives His revelation and His impulse to proclaim it, that He stands in permanent and intimate union with God, and in so true a sense that what He says and does is a direct word and act of God (vii. 16 sq., viii. 28, x. 37 sq., xii. 49 sq., xiv. 10). The reason why His Jewish opponents do not understand His manner of speech is that they judge "after the flesh" (viii. 15). Yet He cannot and may not assume their standpoint. He judges Himself and other men according to that which is of real import, their genuine inner state of being. He knows His own life from God, and His inner fellowship with God, as a reality, and it is indeed the only real and precious reality, the only reality that matters (vi. 63). It would be a denial of the highest that He has within Him, a denial of God Himself, if He consented to speak of this reality otherwise than as He does (viii. 54 sq.).—To my thinking, these testimonies of Jesus to Himself carry the very stamp of historicity. So *must* He have thought, who was assured of His own filial communion with God, of His Messianic call received from His heavenly Father, of His endowment with the Holy Spirit of God, of His character as a prophet and revealer, of His own unique importance for men's salvation,—and of all this, even according to the synoptic testimonies, He was assured,—so must He have thought of Himself, and on due occasion so must He have spoken.

If the discourses derived from our Source do not diverge substantially, with respect to the nature and intensity of Jesus' claims, from the synoptic records, wherein consists the real difference between the two presentations? In no more than this, that in our discourses those claims of Jesus are so much more frequent, explicit, and emphatic than in the Synoptics. But the actual significance of this difference will depend on whether we consider these discourses as they stand in the historical framework of our Fourth Gospel, or in the original connection of the Source. As portions of a historical account of the whole course of Jesus' public ministry, such as our fourth evangelist offers, the sayings of Jesus concerning His divine mission and His import unto salvation occupy, indeed, a space disproportionately large. The evangelist makes them appear at the very beginning of Jesus' ministry, and recur on many occasions, even on the Galilean stage (chap. vi.). The Source, on the other hand, recorded specifically the visits of Jesus to Jerusalem. It is by no means hard to believe that Jesus had special occasion given Him here to speak repeatedly and with emphasis of His intimate filial communion with God and of the unique import of His work, and that these sayings, together with the hostile replies of the men of Jerusalem, who did not understand them, give to the Source its characteristic stamp.

A genuine historical trait may further be recognised in the discourses derived from the Source: as the burden of His calling, that to which God has sent Him, that which He knows He is faithfully carrying out, Jesus puts forward His teaching, in which, on the basis of the revelation of God which He has Himself received, He manifests God's name unto men (xvii. 6, 8, 14; cf. vii. 16 sq., viii. 26, 28, 38, 40, 45–47, xii. 44–50, xv. 15). He knows, indeed, that He is not merely a teacher (iii. 2), but rather sent of God to bestow an eternal life of salvation on those that believe (iii. 16 sq., v. 21, vi. 35, 40). But He knows also that His teaching is the means through which He imparts the eternal life to men (xii. 50, xvii. 2 sq.); for His words are spirit and life (vi. 63), and they that receive His word with faith and keep it have thereby a part in the eternal life (v. 24, viii. 51). The explanation how His teaching has this life-giving effect is given in viii. 31–36: they that abide in His teaching learn the truth (τὴν ἀλήθειαν), and are thereby made free, free from the sin in which they would otherwise die (viii. 21, 24); but, being made free by the Son, they have a right to dwell for ever in the Father's house (viii. 36; cf. xvii. 11–17). Jesus says, too, to Pilate that He came into the world to bear witness to the ἀλήθεια. They that were of the truth—men, that is to say, who had affinity with it and belonged to it—heard His voice. In this, the work of His calling and its issue, consists the Kingship which He claims (xviii. 36 sq.).

In this estimate of the teaching of Jesus as the proper work of His Messianic calling our discourses agree entirely with the synoptic presentation. According to the Synoptics, also, Jesus knows Himself called to preach and to teach (Mark i. 38 sq.; Matt. xxiii. 8, 10). He is the sower, who scatters the seed, the word (Mark iv. 3 sqq.). He reveals the Father (Matt. xi. 27). He fulfils the law and the prophets (Matt. v. 17, 21 sqq.). He calls sinners (Mark ii. 17). He preaches salvation to the poor (Matt. xi. 5). And He knows that in this teaching, wrought in the Spirit of God, He is bringing to pass the Messianic day of salvation (Luke iv. 18–21; cf. Matt. xi. 27 sqq.). The agreement of our discourses with the synoptic presentation on this point must be regarded as significant when we consider that Paul attaches no such importance to Jesus' earthly work of preaching: in his eyes the death of the cross and resurrection of Christ are the events instrumental in salvation, the foundation of the new order of grace. At first sight there seems to be a close relationship between the Johannine discourses and the Pauline view, in the emphasis which both lay upon belief in Jesus Christ as the requirement for salvation. But they are essentially distinguished by the fact that the belief of which Paul speaks relates specifically to the death on the cross and the resurrection of Christ (Gal. ii. 20, iii. 1–14; Rom. iv. 24 sq.), whereas in the Johannine discourses belief means acceptance of the words of Jesus, and observance of His commandments (v. 24, viii. 31, 51, xiv. 15, 21, 23 sq., xv. 9–12). The demand for faith in this latter sense as the means for obtaining eternal life is exactly like the demand of Jesus in the synoptic discourses that men should hear His words and follow them, in order to share in the salvation of the kingdom of God (Luke vi. 46–49, xi. 28, xiii. 26 sq.): that men should come to Him and learn of Him, to obtain true refreshment for their souls (Matt. xi. 28 sq.); that men should follow Him, and confess Him and His words even at the greatest sacrifice, it may be of life itself, if they would obtain the heavenly life of salvation at the Parusia (Mark viii. 34–38, x. 29, xiii. 9, 13; Matt. x. 32 sq.).

It is true that the saving import of the death of Jesus is also expressed in our Johannine discourses. That the death which He must take upon Him in faithful fulfilment of the calling which God has laid upon Him (x. 11–18, xiv. 31) will help those that are His to lay hold upon salvation, to establish their communion with God,—of this Jesus is as certain, according to the utterances in John x. 11–18, xiv. 12–17, xvi. 7, xvii. 19, as He is according to the synoptic utterances, Mark x. 45, xiv. 24. That His death, apparently the annihilation of His work, will really become the means of breaking down the narrow boundaries which have hitherto enclosed it, and of developing it on a grander scale, this again He foresees in John xii. 23 sq., 31 sq., as clearly as in the synoptic sayings, Luke xii. 49 sq., Mark xii. 10. But the important point in the distinction from Paul is that the saving import of Jesus does not relate to

His death *alone*, but that the work which appears in the forefront as His work of salvation, the work of His calling, is His teaching.

It is also very remarkable that in the Johannine passages derived from the Source, when Jesus speaks of His death, He makes no reference, direct or indirect, to Isa. liii. In the apostolic community this passage of Isaiah passed current from the beginning as the decisive scriptural prediction in fulfilment of which the Messiah must needs suffer; and, in consequence, the death of Christ was regarded as being principally, in accordance with this passage, a vicarious punishment for the sins of others (1 Cor. xv. 3). So, too, the fourth evangelist, in i. 29 and 36, makes the Baptist speak of Jesus, with a clear reference to Isa. liii., as the Lamb that taketh away the sin of the world. But did Jesus Himself conceive of His death in this sense? It cannot be doubted that He found in Isa. liii. one of the scriptural allusions to His innocent suffering. But it may well be questioned whether He deduced from that passage the specific idea of vicarious punishment, and thereby explained the necessity and value of His passion. The synoptic sayings, Mark x. 45 and xiv. 24, show no sign of being influenced by those thoughts from Isa. liii. 4–6. Nor is this accidental; there is sound reason for it; the general conception which Jesus had of the fatherhood of God, and of His readiness to forgive repentant sinners (Luke xv. 11 sqq.) debarred Him from appropriating to Himself those special thoughts of Isa. liii. He declares that His death will be a ransom for many, that as a sacrifice for the sealing of the new covenant, He will avail for the salvation of many: but He does not ascribe to His death any specific relation to the forgiveness of sins.[1] In this point also the

---

[1] Cf. my *Lehre Jesu*, ii. pp. 510 sqq. (2nd ed., pp. 496 sqq.), where I have attempted to explain these synoptic words of Jesus about His death by means of the whole conception and attitude of Jesus.

Johannine utterances of Jesus about His death, which come from the Source, resemble the synoptic; they, too, are uninfluenced by Isa. liii. This is an indication of the historic truth of the essential thoughts contained in the Johannine discourses, and all the more significant since the author of the Source, when he is not reporting as a historian,—that is to say, in the First Epistle of John,—clearly ascribes to Jesus' death a bearing on the forgiveness of sins (1 John i. 7, ii. 2, iv. 10).

4. *The Absence of Predictions after the Event*

There is finally another point, negative indeed, but very important, in which the discourses from our Source agree with the older synoptic tradition,—the absence of predictions *ex post facto*; these are a characteristic note of the class of utterances which are subsequently imputed to prophetic personages, and betray a secondary origin for many parts of our synoptic Gospels.

The discourses from our Source contain no oracular foreshadowings of certain events and circumstances of the apostolic age to which the apostolic and subapostolic generation attached special importance, and which it seemed to them self-evident that Jesus must have foreseen and foretold. They fail to appear even in places where the context must inevitably have suggested them to any later artificial construction of the discourses. Often, indeed, in these discourses Jesus contemplates the future of the community of His disciples. But these forecasts are always of a kind which were the necessary outcome of His absolute assurance that His business was God's business, and that therefore, in spite of His impending death, it must advance, increase, and triumph.

There is no allusion in our discourses to the appearances of Jesus after His death. True, the fourth evangelist found in the words which Jesus used after the cleansing of the Temple—" Destroy this temple, and in three days I will raise it up"—a foreshadowing of the resurrection of His body on the third day (ii. 21 sq.). But in its original sense this saying did not refer to the resurrection.[1] There are other places in the speeches belonging to the Source where Jesus speaks as definitely as possible of the heavenly glory with God which He shall attain through His death (xii. 23, 32, xiii. 32, xiv. 28, xvii. 5, 24), but He does not add that He will appear to His disciples on the third day after His death. It is only a superficial view that can see in the two sections, xiv. 18–24 and xvi. 16–24,—where He speaks of His speedy return to the disciples, and tells that after He has been parted from them a little while they shall see Him again,— any reference to these appearances. In reality Jesus is not speaking here of separate, momentary appearances, but of a return to perpetual communion, of such a kind, moreover, that His own coming and abiding shall coincide with the coming and abiding of the Father (xiv. 23). His coming will be not only to that small circle of disciples who surrounded Him at the Last Supper, but to all those that love Him and keep His commandments (xiv. 21, 23). In these sayings Jesus can only have meant a permanent *spiritual* reunion with His true disciples, which should begin after His outward severance from them (cf. Matt. xxviii. 20). If these utterances of Jesus about His speedy return had been the irresponsible inventions of a later writer, there is no doubt that He would have moulded them into predictions of that kind of appearances which were reported to have befallen the disciples, such as our fourth evangelist himself records (chap. xx.), and regards as an important basis of faith (xx. 27–29).

Again, there is in our discourses no forecasting of those miraculous gifts of the Spirit, which played so great a part

[1] Cf. *sup.* pp. 66 sq.

in apostolic and subapostolic Christianity. Jesus does indeed give His disciples the promise that God will send them the Holy Spirit, as a champion who shall abide with them continually, to instruct them, to remind them of all the words of Jesus, to support them in their witness for Him against the world (xiv. 16 sq., 26, xv. 26, xvi. 7–15); but these effects of the Spirit are not identical with those ecstatic states—visions, speaking with tongues, prophecy—which were looked on by apostolic and subapostolic Christendom as the specific tokens of the Spirit. The single reference to the spiritual gift of prophetic prevision, at the close of xvi. 13, is so isolated, that we have good reason for supposing that it was inserted by our evangelist into the text of the Source.[1]

Once more, no definite allusion to the future external form and development of the community of disciples is to be found in our discourses. Jesus never makes any kind of reference to any future visible organisation of His followers. All that He asks of them, all that He prays God for them, is this, that they should remain spiritually united with Him and with the Father (xv. 1–17, xvii. 9–26). Just as, during His lifetime, the only bond between Himself and His disciples was the bond of love and of the Spirit, so too in His farewell discourses He gives no thought to any other kind of bond, any external link between His disciples, any visible demarcation between His own community and the Jews. He foresees that as the direct result of His death there will be a mighty development in His community, and that even among Samaritans and Greeks He will gather fruit to the life eternal (iv. 35–38, x. 16, xii. 23 sq., 32): but He speaks of this world-wide expansion only in general terms, such as He uses also in the utterances of the Logia (Luke xiii. 29; Matt. viii. 11). He neither enjoins on His disciples the mission to the heathen as a definite charge, nor

[1] Cf. pp. 163 sq.

says a word about the conditions on which the heathen can be received into His fellowship. To the question which agitated apostolic Christianity with reference to the mission no definite answer is given.¹

The predictions, too, of the persecutions by the world which await the disciples (xv. 18–xvi. 3) are intended in a quite general sense. The certainty which Jesus feels that the disciples will undergo the hatred of the world is based on the fact that He has Himself been the object of this hatred (xv. 18–21), just as in several synoptic passages He associates the future day of suffering of His disciples with His own suffering (Mark viii. 31–35; Matt. x. 24 sq.; Luke xii. 50–58, xvii. 22–25). The one concrete feature in the forecast of these persecutions,—that men shall put the disciples out of the synagogues, and think that by slaying them they are offering a service to God (xvi. 2),—simply assumes the continuance of the same Palestinian surroundings in which Jesus Himself moved. Of any change in the political conditions, of the judgment which broke upon the people of Israel in the Jewish-Roman war, of the destruction of Jerusalem and the Temple, no hint is anywhere given. Jesus, it is true, is absolutely sure that God's judgment will befall the unbelieving Jews and the "prince of this world." But that judgment of God had nothing to do with a political catastrophe.

Our discourses contain no reference to false teachers and false doctrine, which should hereafter appear in the fellowship of the disciples. Their absence is all the more noteworthy that in the Epistles of John a very emphatic warning

¹ The way in which Jesus speaks of being sent to the "world," and working for the salvation of the "world" (iii. 16-19, vi. 33, 51, viii. 12, ix. 5, 39, x. 36, xii. 46, xvi. 28, xviii. 37), does not express the Pauline idea of the universal scope of Christian salvation. In the Johannine discourses the term "world" is never used in antithesis to the people of Israel, but always to God and Heaven. It corresponds to the term $\gamma \hat{\eta}$ in Luke xii. 49, Matt. x. 34, v. 12.

is given against certain dangerous false teachers: in the first place, Antinomians, who, as it appears, made a false use of the Pauline doctrine of justification by faith (I iii. 7–12); in the second place, the teachers of a docetic Christology, who distinguished between Jesus and the Christ (I ii. 22), and taught that Christ had not come in the flesh (I iv. 2; II 7), and also that He had not come in "blood," —that is, had not undergone a real passion and death (I v. 6). These false teachers, who gave themselves out as prophets speaking in the Spirit, are proclaimed by the writer of the Epistle to be false prophets and antichrists (I ii. 18–22, iv. 1–3; II 7). Hence it may be seen that this writer, the author of the Source of the Gospel, did not fail on occasion, when the inner voice prompted him, to instruct and warn the subapostolic Christians concerning false doctrine. Had he been the untrammelled composer of the discourses of Jesus in the Source, he would have been quite sure to put such instructions and warnings into the mouth of Jesus: instructions about ecstatic speaking in the Spirit and the necessary discrimination of spirits, about the coming of Antichrist in the form of many antichrists as the last hour drew near; warnings against the imagination of righteousness where no righteousness is done, intimations of the reality of His own carnal nature and of His death. But in the discourses derived from the Source these themes are not treated.[1]

One more characteristic point: Jesus never looks for-

[1] In John vi. 51–58 Jesus does indeed allude expressly to His flesh and blood. But the context shows that there is no intention here to defend the reality of His flesh against any who, like the false teachers referred to in the Johannine Epistles, denied His fleshly nature on the ground of His heavenly origin. He is rather dealing with those who, on the ground of His notorious earthly lineage, denied the heavenly origin which He asserted (vv. 41 sq.). As against those who saw in His "flesh and blood" a contradiction of His high claims, he emphasises the value of this flesh and blood as the medium through which His quickening efficacy is transmitted to other men (ver. 63).

ward in these discourses to a prolonged earthly existence of the community of His disciples. Just as in the synoptic utterances He regards His second coming as near, and speaks of it to the disciples with Him as if they themselves should live to see it (Mark ix. 1, xiii. 28-37; Luke xii. 35-46, xviii. 7 sq.), so in John xiv. 3 He says to His disciples at the Last Supper, "I come again and will receive *you* unto myself." Of generations intervening there is never a thought.

With respect, then, to all essential points in the thought —so we sum up the result of our inquiry—the discourses of Jesus preserved in our Source agree with the earlier synoptic tradition. When these discourses are once liberated from the construction which the fourth evangelist, by means of his narrative framework and scattered interpolations, has forced upon them, they may be taken unreservedly as utterances of the historic Jesus, such as the synoptic sources reveal Him. From this fact, however, we must conclude that they are derived from a *sound* tradition, from a real memory of the historic Jesus. The form in which they are cast belongs to the author of the Source. But this will not support a decisive objection against the historicity of their essential contents. It would be a much greater marvel that a writer who had composed them artificially, apart from true, historic recollection, should have kept them so free from treacherous signs of their unhistorical character, and inspired them so successfully with the Spirit of the historic Jesus.

CHAPTER VI

THE AUTHOR OF THE SOURCE

A. SIGNS OF THE AUTHORSHIP OF THE APOSTLE JOHN

1. *The Personal Statements of the Author of the Source*

WE have now to consider a fact which corresponds with the judgment we have passed on the historic value of the record in the Source: the author of the record, both in the prologue to the Gospel and in the exordium of the First Epistle, claims to have been himself one of the eye-witnesses of the revelation of God which appeared in the flesh—"we beheld His glory" (i. 14); "of His fulness we all received, yea, grace upon grace" (i. 16); "that which we have heard, that which we have seen with our eyes, that which we beheld, and our hands handled, ... declare we unto you also" (1 John i. 1–3). The most obvious interpretation of these words undoubtedly is that the author intends to declare himself one whose eyes and ears witnessed the historical ministry of revelation wrought by Jesus Christ,—that by using the first person plural he associates himself with the other eye-witnesses of Jesus' appearance on earth.

A rival interpretation has certainly been set up as likewise possible, that the writer is speaking of a super-sensuous, spiritual, mystic kind of perception, in which he associates himself with the Christian community. After the manner of the mystic and the visionary he denotes this supersensuous perception by means of expressions which properly relate to sense-perception (so in John i. 18, v. 37, xiv. 7–9; 1 John iii. 6, iv. 14; 3 John 11).[1] This explanation seems at first to receive support from the consideration that in both places—John i. 14 and 1 John i. 1–3—that which is designated as the object of sight and hearing is not the historic Jesus Christ Himself, or His flesh, but the divine glory of the Logos made flesh, or the eternal life which was from the beginning and was manifested: something, that is to say, which in its own nature cannot be the object of sense-perception, but only of the spiritual perception of faith. But, on the other hand, since the eternal Logos of God is conceived as appearing and working in the flesh, the sense-perception which has for its direct object only the flesh of Jesus Christ may yet be validly conceived as the instrument by which the dwelling and working in the flesh of the eternal and divine revelation is perceived.[2] That the perception of the divine glory and of the revelation of life in Jesus Christ is meant, in this sense, as one which has been attained by the external, physical organs, is shown by the emphatic asseveration in 1 John i. 1—which has certainly (1 John iv. 2) an antidocetic intention—that the seeing was wrought with the eyes, and the handling with the hands. In what other terms could the writer have expressed himself more clearly, if he wished to make himself known as an actual eyewitness of the historical appearance of Jesus?

But the main question which arises is not whether sense-perception is meant, or perception of a supersensuous

---

[1] Cf. H. Holtzmann, *Hand-Comm. ad loc.* and *Einleitung in d. N. T.*, 3rd ed., p. 454; Harnack, *Chronologie d. altchristl. Litteratur*, i. p. 675; also W. Karl, *Johanneische Studien*, 1898, i. pp. 1 sq. In 1 John i. 1 Karl takes the "hearing" to mean hearing the revelation, "beholding," seeing in a vision, and "handling," the coming in contact with the elements in the Supper.

[2] Cf. Romans i. 20: τὰ ἀόρατα αὐτοῦ . . . τοῖς ποιήμασιν νοούμενα καθορᾶται.

kind, but whether that perception is intended to be taken as contemporary with the earthly life of Jesus Christ, or as one which only beheld the historical appearance of Jesus Christ in a spiritual sense, after it was past. The use of the preterite tense in the wording requires that this question should be answered in the first sense rather than the second. In John i. 14 the past events of the Logos being made flesh and dwelling among us are spoken of in the aorist; then follow immediately, also in the aorist, the two clauses, "we beheld His glory," and "we received of His fulness": these must refer likewise to past events, events which fell in the same range of time with the appearance of the Logos in the flesh. If the spiritual beholding of His glory and receiving of His gifts of grace, such as still obtained in the faithful community of the disciples, had been meant, it must have been denoted in the present tense (cf. 2 Cor. iii. 18; Heb. ii. 9) or the perfect (cf. John iii. 11, vi. 46, xiv. 7, 9).[1] In 1 John i. 1–3 again, however, the perfect tense alternates, not with the present, but with the aorist. The wording, then, clearly exhibits the meaning that the writer, as a contemporary of Jesus Christ when He walked the earth, had beheld His glory as the Son of God and experienced the tokens of His love.

Why is any effort made to evade the recognition of this meaning? Because there are various important reasons for believing that the evangelist was not really such an eye-witness of the historical work of Jesus. But when we recognise that the groundwork of the Prologue to the Gospel and of the First Epistle of John did not originate with the fourth evangelist, but with the author of the Source employed in the Fourth Gospel, there is no occasion for attempting to take these expressions (John i. 14–16; 1 John i. 1–3) in any other sense than the wording demands. For in the case of this Source, as we saw above,

[1] Cf. Fr. Blass, *Grammatik des neutest. Griechisch*, 1896, §§ 57 and 59.

the credibility of its contents is a significant sign that its author was really an eye-witness and ear-witness of the ministry of Jesus. The interpretation of John i. 14 of the spiritual vision of the Lord's glory, as it was still beheld by the community of faithful disciples, has indeed a measure of justification, for it was in this sense that the fourth evangelist adopted the words of the Source. But to this interpretation should be added that it does not give the original sense of the words, and that if the fourth evangelist had been writing with a free pen he would have denoted this spiritual beholding of Christ's glory, and receiving of His gifts of grace, by a verb in another tense.

Nowhere, in the independent writing of the fourth evangelist, does he claim to have been an eye-witness of the events he is relating. There is an appeal to eye-witness in John xix. 35; not, however, to that of the evangelist himself, but of another, on whose trustworthiness and consciousness of truth he lays emphasis.[1] How artificial and distorted the expression would be in this place, if by the eye-witness the writer meant himself, is clearly shown by a comparison with the natural style in which the author of the Prologue speaks of his own eye-witness in i. 14. The striking difference of expression between these two places is

[1] The interpretation of Th. Zahn (*Z. W. L.*, 1888, pp. 594 sq., *Einleitung in d. N. T.* ii. pp. 472 sqq.), adopted by H. Dechent (*St. Kr.*, 1899, pp. 448 sqq.), is, in my opinion, quite impossible. They take the ἐκεῖνος in xix. 35 of the ascended Jesus, who knows that "he that hath seen" saith true. But no reader could understand by the ἐκεῖνος any other person than the ἑωρακώς of whom mention has just been made.— It is, of course, possible for a writer or speaker to allude to himself in the third person as ἐκεῖνος : cf. John ix. 37. But unless he explicitly denotes the person of whom he speaks as ὁ γράψας ταῦτα, ὁ λαλῶν μετὰ σοῦ, or the like, he is deliberately leaving his readers in ignorance of the fact that he means himself. This applies here : if the fourth evangelist had really been himself the eye-witness referred to in xix. 35, he deliberately concealed the fact. It is not correct to say that his wording reveals an intention to bring his own eye-witness clearly out (Luthardt, *Kurzgef. Komm. N. T.*, 2nd ed., ii. p. 8).

simply explained by the knowledge that in the one the writer is the author of the Source, an immediate witness of the earthly ministry of Jesus, in the other the fourth evangelist, a secondary historian.

2. *The Hints of the Fourth Evangelist*

If it is as spectator and auditor that the author of the Source gives his account of the discourses and conversations of Jesus, we must seek him among the disciples who accompanied Jesus on His journeys, among His most intimate disciples, in the midst of whom He took His last meal in Jerusalem. What data have we for a more exact determination of His identity?

The fourth evangelist speaks about one of the closest disciples of Jesus, but only in a mysterious, hinting fashion. The eye-witness to whom he appeals in xix. 35 can only mean the disciple whom he has spoken of just before as standing by the cross, the disciple " whom Jesus loved," to whom He intrusted the care of His mother (xix. 26 sq.). It is the same disciple of whom he speaks in other places without giving his name: one of the two first disciples, who left the Baptist and followed Jesus (i. 35–41); the disciple who at the Last Supper reclined in Jesus' bosom (xiii. 23–25); the " other " disciple who came with Peter into the court of Annas during the trial, since he was known to the high priest (xviii. 15 sq.), and afterwards outran Peter to the empty grave of Jesus (xx. 2–8). The same disciple is denoted in the same periphrastic manner in the appendix to the Gospel (xxi. 2, 7, 20–23). This would be a very forced style of reference if the evangelist had known himself to be that disciple. It is a natural style if the disciple in question stood in a special relation, a closer relation than any other disciple of Jesus, to the Christian circle to which the evangelist and the original readers of his Gospel belonged, and if, when he wrote, it was already a cherished custom in this circle to speak of this disciple, not by name, but as "the Disciple" κατ' ἐξοχήν, or as "the disciple whom Jesus loved." The evangelist would not speak of this disciple as he might speak of some remote person, but as of one who was known and could, of course, be recognised; as an initiate in the knowledge of this disciple, speaking to his fellow-adepts. According to ancient tradition, this unnamed disciple is John the son of Zebedee. This John is not otherwise mentioned in the Fourth Gospel, although he belonged, as we know from the synoptic tradition, to the earliest and most intimate disciples of Jesus. There are no cogent reasons to be urged against this interpretation of "the disciple whom Jesus loved" as the Apostle John.[1]

If the fourth evangelist had special relations towards that apostle, it does not, of course, absolutely follow that he was also the author of the Source which the fourth evangelist employed. It is formally conceivable that many several notices in the narrative of the Gospel, such as xix. 34, refer to that apostle, while the Source for the discourses belonged to some other author. But since the author of the Source

[1] Bousset, "Offenbarung Joh." (Meyer's *Komm.* xvi., 5th ed.) pp. 44 sqq.; *Th. R.*, 1897, pp. 12 sqq., adopts the view that the disciple whom the Lord held dear was not the son of Zebedee, but the presbyter John of Asia Minor, a native of Jerusalem, of the high-priestly family (according to the statement of Polycrates *apud* Eusebium, *H. E.* v. 24 : ὃς ἐγενήθη ἱερεὺς τὸ πέταλον πεφορηκώς ; cf. John xviii. 15 sq.) who belonged to the Jerusalem disciples of Jesus. So already F. von Uechtritz and H. Delff (cf. *sup.* p. 3 n.). This explanation avoids the hypothesis that there were afterwards two different Johns in Asia Minor; but involves the hypothesis that John the son of Zebedee had a double of the same name among the most intimate disciples of Jesus, one about whom nothing further has come down to us. I cannot find that this latter hypothesis is at all easier or simpler than the former. The fact that the scenes in Jesus' ministry recorded in the Fourth Gospel are specifically those in Jerusalem does not necessarily imply that an eye-witness, a native of Jerusalem, who held aloof from the Galilean ministry of Jesus, stood behind the Fourth Gospel. That fact may be otherwise explained (cf. *sup.* pp. 182 sq.).

must himself be sought in the inmost circle of Jesus' disciples, among His companions at the Last Supper, it must be allowed as probable in the highest degree that this author is identical with that mysteriously denoted apostle, —that he who designates himself an eye-witness in i. 14, 1 John i. 1-3, is identical with the eye-witness to whom the evangelist appeals in xix. 35.

We must further observe that the author of the appendix (chap. xxi.) gives at the close an express assurance that the disciple whom Jesus loved (vv. 20-23) was he "which beareth witness of these things and wrote these things" (ver. 24). The Fourth Gospel, as we have it, was not written by the Apostle John. But it does not of necessity follow that the concluding remark is a mere wanton fancy. Its truth may lie in the fact that the Apostle John is the author of that written Source of which the Fourth Gospel is a redaction. Perhaps the writer of the appendix was no longer aware that the Gospel to which he added that chapter was not really itself the writing of the apostle, but a redaction of it. But even if he did know, he might nevertheless have used the existing form of words to express the idea that the apostle's notes formed the essential groundwork of the Gospel, and the additions of the redactor were merely a framework intended to render that material historically intelligible.

The ancient ecclesiastical tradition,—which meets us first in Theophilus of Antioch, *ad Autol.* ii. 22, and in the Muratorian fragment,—that John was the author of the Fourth Gospel, receives a natural explanation when we adopt the view that the Gospel contains the memoirs of the Apostle John, and was received and valued by its first readers as a redaction of those memoirs, provided with a historical setting.[1] The designation of this Gospel as εὐαγ-

[1] In certain circles there may nevertheless have been preserved a knowledge that our Gospel was not itself the direct work of the apostle.

γέλιον κατὰ 'Ιωάννην has in that case exactly the same ground and the same measure of justification as the denoting of our First Gospel as εὐαγγέλιον κατὰ Ματθαῖον, because it includes the Logia of the Apostle Matthew.

3. *The Tradition as to the Residence of John in Asia Minor*

The ancient ecclesiastical tradition tells us besides that the same John who reclined in the bosom of the Lord went in his old age to Ephesus, and lived on in the Christian community there until the time of Trajan. We have no direct testimony to this tradition until the close of the second century, when it is expressed by Bishop Polycrates of Ephesus in his letter to the Roman Bishop Victor (Eusebius, *H. E.* v. xxiv. 3), and also by Irenæus (*Adv. Hær.* II. xxii. 5, III. i. 1, iii. 4). But Irenæus, in the first place cited, refers to the witness of all the presbyters who had met John in Asia; and in the letter to Florinus (Eusebius, *H. E.* v. xx. 4 sqq.) he appeals to his childhood's recollection of Polycarp, and how he had spoken about his intercourse with John and other eye-witnesses of the Lord. So that Irenæus appears, in his statements about the residence of John in Asia Minor, to be following no vague rumour, but the assertions of sure witnesses.

The defenders of the apostolic authorship of the Fourth Gospel have treated the existence of this intelligence concerning the Apostle John, which reached Irenæus by way of Polycarp and the presbyters, as an important proof of the Johannine authenticity of our Gospel. How, they argue, could a writing which was spuriously ascribed to the Apostle John have found unhesitating acceptance among those who still possessed a living tradition of that apostle, going back

It is not impossible that such knowledge underlay the denial of its Johannine authenticity, which was put forward by the Alogi in the middle of the second century.

to eye-witnesses of the man himself?[1] Those, on the other hand, who contest the apostolic authorship of the Gospel on internal grounds, throw doubt on the trustworthiness of the tradition that the Apostle John dwelt in Asia Minor.[2] Indeed, the interval of a whole century between the end of the Apostle John and the first testimony we have to the tradition is so great that the possibility of some accretion, some change having befallen the tradition during that time, cannot be put aside.

We know from the fragment of Papias preserved by Eusebius (*H. E.* III. xxxix. 3 sq.) that there was a presbyter John in the Church of Asia Minor. Papias clearly distinguishes this presbyter, whom he associates with Aristion, from the original apostles, whom he mentions first, and among whom he names the Apostle John. Now Papias was obviously an important authority for Irenæus. Where Irenæus appeals to the sayings of the "presbyters," the source of his knowledge seems almost regularly to have been merely the work of Papias.[3] Irenæus asserts (*Adv. Hær.* V. xxxiii. 4) that Papias was Ἰωάννου ἀκουστής, and understands this "John" as being the apostle. But in reality what Papias says in that fragment is not that he has collected information from the Apostle John, but from the presbyter John. Nor did Eusebius (III. xxxix. 2) find any relation between Papias and the Apostle John denoted in Papias' work. Now, since Irenæus has clearly, at this point, confused the presbyter John with the apostle, the question suggests itself whether there are no other cases of a like confusion. Is it not possible that everything which Irenæus had received as traditional about the residence of John in Asia referred originally to the presbyter John?

[1] Cf. Th. Zahn, *Einleitung in d. N. T.* ii. pp. 445 sq.
[2] Cf. recently especially H. Holtzmann, *Einleitung in d. N. T.*, 3rd ed. pp. 470 sqq.; Bousset, *Offenbarung Joh.* pp. 33 sqq.; Harnack, *Chronologie d. altchristl. Litteratur*, i. pp. 656 sqq.
[3] Cf. Harnack, *op. cit.* pp. 333 sqq.

Was not that John, too, of whom Irenæus as a boy had heard Polycarp speak, John the presbyter? Was it not he also whom Polycrates meant, or confused with the apostle? This same Polycrates, in the same writing in which he appeals to John (Eusebius, *H. E.* v. xxiv. 2), also speaks of the Philip who died in Hierapolis, the father of the prophesying daughters, as one of the twelve apostles, whereas that Philip was really the evangelist and one of the seven (Acts xxi. 8 sq.). The admission of such doubts prepared the way for the hypothesis that the author of the Fourth Gospel and of the Johannine Epistles was not the apostle, but the presbyter John of Asia Minor. Is it not a striking confirmation of this hypothesis that the author of the Second and Third Johannine Epistles speaks of himself in the introduction as ὁ πρεσβύτερος?

Nevertheless these doubts which are cast on the residence of the Apostle John in Asia Minor are not, in my judgment, convincing. They point, indeed, to a certain possibility of confusion between different persons of the same name. But they do not give it the preponderance of probability. To found on Irenæus' mistake, in making Papias the pupil of the apostle instead of the presbyter, a similar conclusion with regard to everything else that Irenæus says about the John of Asia Minor, is decidedly precarious. It is much more probable that the mistake with regard to Papias was caused by the fact that Irenæus had received from other sources the tradition as to the residence of the apostle in Asia Minor, and, knowing that Papias also belonged to Asia Minor, was thereby prompted to relate him to the apostle. That Irenæus knows nothing, or rather says nothing, about the existence of two distinct Johns in Asia Minor, is not astonishing. For it is only too easily conceivable that even if the presbyter had played, in his time, a very important part in the Church of Asia Minor, he should nevertheless have been eclipsed in the tradition of the next age by the figure of his namesake the apostle, if that apostle had also made Asia Minor the scene of his later activity. But there is nothing in the slightest degree improbable in the fact that there were in Asia Minor two prominent disciples called John,— perhaps not contemporary, but, as may be inferred from Papias, belonging to two different generations. Who thinks it odd that the Apostle John once had a namesake in Palestine, in the person of the Baptist? or that besides Philip the apostle there was a Philip the deacon? or that besides the two Jameses who belonged to the Twelve, James the Lord's brother was also a member of the community at Jerusalem?[1]

Nor, again, does the manner in which the author of the Second and Third Johannine Epistles denotes himself prove that that author was the presbyter and not the apostle. The writer of these Epistles, even if he were the Apostle John, had no such special occasion to emphasise his missionary calling as Paul had in the introduction of his Epistles to the Corinthians, Galatians, Romans, and Colossians;—at the beginning of 1 and 2 Thessalonians, and the Epistles to the Philippians and to Philemon, even Paul does not denote himself as ἀπόστολος. Who could have contested his rank as an apostle called of Jesus? On the other hand, the term πρεσβύτερος had in the earliest times a very wide

[1] The notice of Dionysius of Alexandria (in Eusebius, *H. E.* VII. xxv. 16), that there were two monuments to John in Ephesus, cannot be taken as a testimony that both the apostle and the presbyter died in Asia Minor. Nor, on the other hand, can the statement which comes to us through Philip Sidetes (cf. de Boor in *T. U.* v. 2, pp. 167 sqq.) and George Harmartolos (*Chronicon*, ed. E. de Muralto, 1859, p. 336), and is referred by them to Papias, that John and his brother James were killed by the Jews, be regarded as credible evidence for the martyrdom of the Apostle John in Palestine. All the evidence tends to show that this statement, in the form in which it reaches us, is not really due to Papias. Cf. Harnack, *op. cit.* pp. 665 sq.; also Th. Zahn, *Einleitung in d. N. T.* ii. p. 465.

signification, including every kind of person in authority. There is nothing, therefore, to cause surprise if the venerable apostle denoted himself by this most general title of honour, as "the elder." The fact that he does not add his name expresses his consciousness that, for those to whom his letters were addressed, he was distinctively the elder whose authority was recognised.

The most important reason for inclining to the view that in the tradition concerning John of Asia Minor there has been a confusion between the apostle and the presbyter arises out of the internal criticism of the Fourth Gospel: the apostle cannot have been its author. The confusion seems plausibly to explain how the subapostolic Gospel came to be ascribed to the apostle. But, if we explain the title "according to John" by reference to a Source which goes back to the Apostle John and is employed in the Gospel, then that tradition supplies us with an otherwise missing link in the elucidation of the historical circumstances. All the oldest traces of an acquaintance with this Johannine Source and its redaction in our Fourth Gospel point to Asia Minor. How came the memoirs of the apostle to Asia Minor? How came it that there existed here in Asia Minor a Christian circle in which the disciple whom Jesus loved, the disciple who reclined in His bosom, was the object of a special interest, of a special, pious veneration? These questions receive their simplest answer if we accept as genuine the tradition that the Apostle John dwelt in Asia Minor.[1]

When may the apostle have taken the important step which withdrew him from what had hitherto been his call-

---

[1] Even Harnack, although he takes the notices of Polycrates, Polycarp, and Irenæus concerning a John of Asia Minor to refer to the presbyter, recognises that the circle of communities in Asia Minor, out of which the Fourth Gospel proceeded and for which it was intended, must have had a special relation towards the Apostle John. So that he too considers it probable that the son of Zebedee once spent a short time in Asia Minor (*op. cit.* pp. 677 sqq.).

ing and province, the mission to the Jews (Gal. ii. 9), and transferred him to what had formerly been the province of Paul, the mission to the heathen? Whether he took it soon after the year 70 cannot be determined; but there is certainly an intrinsic connection between that step and the catastrophe which broke, in the year 70, over the Jewish people, over Jerusalem and the Temple. To the Christians of the mother community this catastrophe must have appeared as a judgment of God upon Israel, for their rejection of the Messiah, and for their continued unbelief towards the preaching of the Messiah. Even those who had hitherto regarded it as their calling, given of God, to bring first to the chosen people the Messianic message of salvation, must look upon the catastrophe as a sign from God that this their calling was now ended. Since the destruction of the Temple rendered impossible the further observance of the Mosaic ceremonial law, it was to them a God-sent token that the duty of piously fulfilling, in the Messianic community, the Old Testament law of worship was annulled. In their hearts the leaders of the earliest community had long been prepared for such a view by the words which they had once heard from Jesus, and had faithfully stored up in memory, concerning the merely relative worth of the external cultus (John iv. 21-24; cf. Mark ii. 27 sq.; Matt. xvii. 20 sq.; also Acts vi. 13 sq.), and the future share which even those who were not Israelites should have in the Messianic salvation (John x. 16, xii. 20-24, 32; cf. Luke xiii. 28-30). This had enabled them to yield a recognition in principle even to the heathen mission of Paul, although they felt that the stronger call upon themselves was to a mission of another kind (Gal. ii. 7-9). The long reluctance of the primitive apostles, even after they had recognised the principle of freedom from Jewish ceremonial legalism (cf. Gal. ii. 15 sq.), to apply the practical conclusion to their own conduct and their own missionary methods, offers no psychological puzzle. And it is equally easy to understand how the revolution which God wrought among all existing conditions in the year 70 led the one apostle who survived the catastrophe to realise that the justification and call had come to him for another kind of work than he had hitherto pursued. The specific occasion which actuated him to emigrate into Asia Minor may have lain in the expressed needs and desires of the Christian communities there, or in his own personal relations on that point. No more precise conjecture can be offered.

B. APPARENT REASONS AGAINST THE AUTHORSHIP OF THE APOSTLE

1. *The Whilom Fisherman an Author*

But against the belief that the Apostle John was the author of the Source there arises the objection—is it conceivable that the son of Zebedee, whom Jesus once called from the fisherman's net to follow Him, turned author in his old age, and set forth in fluent Greek such profound religious speculations as form the contents of the Source employed in our Fourth Gospel, and of the First Epistle of John?

If we disregard the point, which will be considered more exactly further on, that the Prologue of the Gospel shows some relation to Alexandrian speculation about the Logos, this objection is not important. What do we know about the spiritual capacity of that fisherman by the Lake of Galilee? What do we know about his further development, after he began to walk with Jesus? Can it be said that the acquisition of a spiritual culture corresponding to the Jewish standard of that day—a thorough acquaintance with the Holy Scriptures, a vital share in the religious questions and hopes that animated the national spirit of

Judaism—was less consistent with the occupation of a fisherman than with that of a carpenter or a tent-maker? We only know definitely that Jesus called this fisherman, among the first, into His constant companionship (Mark i. 19 sq.), and afterwards accounted him amongst the most trusty of His disciples (Mark v. 37, ix. 2, xiii. 3, xiv. 33). According to our Fourth Gospel He gave him a distinctively intimate affection. The reason for such conduct on the part of Jesus must have been that He found in this simple fisherman a peculiarly rich religious life, an especially frank receptivity for His gospel, an especially deep understanding of His own aims. The disciple whom Jesus loved was assuredly not a spiritual cypher.

After the death of Jesus the whilom Galilean fisherman belonged to the enthusiastic witnesses in Jerusalem to His Messiahship. We have Paul's statement (Gal. ii. 9) that at the beginning of 'the fiftieth year he was devoting himself, as one of the pillars of the original community, to the mission among the Jews. He had been practising for decades a work of ministry which consisted in preaching the historic appearance of Jesus, in defending His Messianic character, in safeguarding and explaining the revelation of God which had come through Him. Will it be said that such an apostle could not have been able, in his old age, to give written expression, on the one hand, to His historical reminiscences of certain important disputes, conversations, and discourses of Jesus, on the other hand, to definite exhortations addressed to a special circle of Christian communities? He knew that in the one case as in the other, in the Source of our Gospel as in the First Epistle, he was giving nothing of his own, nothing new, but was only giving again to others what he himself had from Jesus. True, that which he had received into himself of the thoughts and words of Jesus had undergone redaction within his own soul. To all that he said and wrote about Jesus he gave his own individual tone.

In comparison, indeed, with the rabbinical scribes the apostle was but an unlettered laic (Acts iv. 13) like Jesus Himself (John vii. 15). In that he was distinguished from such a man as Paul. But it is characteristic of the writings which we ascribe to this apostle that they have no such flavour of rabbinical culture and logic as belongs to Paul's Epistles. They lack the allegorical, typological interpretation of Old Testament texts. They lack the attachment to rabbinical speculation. They lack the conception that until Christ came a strict legal code, the law of works, had regulated the relation between God and man.[1] Moreover, the Source passages in the Gospel and the First Epistle of John exhibit no elegance of style or rhetorical art. The report of the conversations and discourses of Jesus in the one, the composition and manner of writing in the other, are so artless and at times so uncouth as to suggest a want of literary practice in the author. That author is assuredly not lacking in depth of thought, or in the art of marshalling his thoughts sagaciously, of propounding paradoxes and resolving them. But he lacks the skill to bring out clearly for other minds the internal connection and progression of his trains of thought.[2] He thinks and writes, in spite of the

---

[1] The passage in John i. 17 is not to be understood in the Pauline sense, that the dispensation of grace, wrought in Christ, took the place of the dispensation of law, given through Moses. According to the Prologue that same divine Logos which was made flesh in Jesus Christ had aforetime been the medium of life and light unto men. But now the *form* of the revelation, the nature of the operation of the Logos upon men, had been exalted. The revelation came by Moses in the form of a law, from whose commands the nature of God was to be inferred; by Jesus Christ it came in the form of a man, in whose personal character and conduct the χάρις καὶ ἀλήθεια which make up the nature of God were directly visible to men.

[2] This is the judgment of the latest editor of the First Epistle of John, W. Karl, *Johanneische Studien*, i. 1898. Cf. esp. p. iv : " Our author, too, although it is with labour and pain that he subdues the thoughts

Greek language, in an essentially Hebrew fashion,—not combining and subordinating the members of his thought in artistic periods, but setting them simply in procession, one after another. In short, the literary style of these writings is of exactly the kind which we should have expected in the composition of a man of Palestine, in that age, who had received no scholastic education. It harmonises admirably with the idea that they were written by the erewhile Galilean fisherman, who afterwards became the disciple whom Jesus loved.

2. *The Relation of the Apostle to Alexandrian Speculation about the Logos*

There still remains, however, the point that in the Prologue to the Gospel, which must come in the main from the same pen as the great discourses of the Gospel and the Johannine Epistles, there appears a reference to Alexandrian speculation on the Logos. And this one point seems important enough to overthrow all our former reasonings and conclusions with regard to the author of the Source. Is it not, at this one point, clearly apparent that the author was a Hellenist, and, if born a Jew, did not belong at any rate to the Judaism of Palestine, but to Judaism, and later to Jewish Christianity, in the Philonist version of Alexandria; that he was a man familiar with the modern philosophy of that time, a man whose culture was definitively scholastic? Can the primitive apostle be imagined as a man of the academical stamp? Is it conceivable that in his grey old

that so powerfully move him, although his intractable pen often brings them to paper with but little felicity, has yet, with a marvellously tenacious energy of thought, victoriously, and not without system, made known the love which he had experienced as the substance, the sign, the proof of Christianity." P. 10: "The unpractised author can only become fully master of his thoughts little by little; he does not display them clearly at once, but only after several attempts and repetitions."

age, though not till then, he plunged deep into the speculative religious philosophy of Hellenism? Everything, of course, depends upon the character of the reference to Philonist speculation which appears in the Prologue. In attempting to define that character with greater precision I am able to associate myself with Harnack's position in a treatise which seems to me to be conclusive on all main points: "On the relation of the Prologue of the Fourth Gospel to the whole work."[1] Only I must, of course, from my standpoint, still distinguish between the part played by Logos-speculation in the pieces derived from the Source, and that which it plays in the presentment of the views of our fourth evangelist.

It must first be recognised that there can really be perceived in the Prologue of the Gospel some contact with that speculative religious philosophy of the Logos which was formulated by Philo, and became widely current in connection with his name. This appears from the fact that the term ὁ λόγος, in the special sense of the Logos κατ' ἐξοχήν, the Logos of God, is introduced quite at the beginning of the Prologue without any attributive or explanatory phrase. It could not have been used in this way unless it had been a well-known and current expression with the writer and among his original readers. Since it was specifically in the Philonist philosophy of religion that this term played a prominent part in that peculiar sense, we are driven to believe that its similar use in this place was caused by influence of Philonist speculation.[2] Again, that which is predicated of the Logos in the first verse of the Prologue, its primeval relation to God, its activity as the agent in the creation of the world, as the bringer of life and light to mankind, agrees with the Philonist conception

---

[1] *Z. Th. K.*, 1892, pp. 189 sqq.
[2] Cf. O. Holtzmann, *Z. Th. K.*, 1891, pp. 414 sq.; H. Holtzmann, *Hand-Comm.*, 2nd ed., iv. p. 40 ; *Neutest. Theologie*, ii. pp. 371 sq.

of the nature and work of the Logos. "There is nothing in these verses, if the terms are examined one by one, which might not have been written by a Jewish philosopher of Alexandria, and on the other hand ... it is absolutely unknown to us that in the year 100 any other than an Alexandrian philosopher could have written so."[1]

But, in the second place, we must hold, with equal definiteness, that Philonist speculation on the Logos has exerted no perceptible influence on the remainder of those passages in the Fourth Gospel which we derive from the Source. The view, frequently expressed, that the Philonist idea of the Logos is the governing and fundamental principle of the whole doctrine of the Fourth Gospel[2] is not made good by the contents of the great discourses in that Gospel. The term "Logos" in the special Philonist sense of a supramundane hypostasis, mediating between God and the world, does not occur anywhere in them. The expression "the λόγος of God" is indeed used several times in the simple sense of God's impersonal revelation, which went forth aforetime to the people of Israel and is expressed in the Holy Scriptures (v. 38, x. 35), and is now intrusted to Jesus by His heavenly Father, that He may give it again to His disciples (viii. 55, xii. 48 sq., xiv. 24, vii. 6, 14, 17). How could this fashion of using the term be understood, if the writer's manner of thought had really been dominated by Philonist speculation? It is not enough to appeal to the author's sense of historical propriety, which withheld him from putting in the mouth of Jesus a term derived from ancient philosophy.[3]

---

[1] Harnack, *op. cit.* p. 213.
[2] Cf. esp. A. Thoma, *Genesis des Johannes-Evang.*, 1882, pp. 176 sqq.; O. Pfleiderer, *Urchristentum*, pp. 742 sqq.; O. Holtzmann, *Johannesevang.* pp. 79 sqq.; C. Weizsäcker, *Apost. Zeitalter*, 2nd ed., pp. 530 sqq. (*The Apostolic Age*, vol. ii. pp. 226 sqq.) ; H. Holtzmann, *Neut. Theologie*, ii. pp. 368 sqq., 391 sqq.
[3] So Jülicher, *Einleitung in d. N. T.* § 30, 4*b* (p. 250), and H. Holtzmann, *Neut. Theologie*, ii. p. 397.

We must rather connect the fact that the term λόγος in the special Philonist sense does not occur again, with the further fact that throughout the discursive passages of the Gospel which are derived from the Source there is no appearance of those ideas which characterise Philonistic speculation on the Logos. There is no sign of the cosmological tendency with which the Philonistic speculation was indissolubly bound. There is no thought of any natural, dualistic opposition between God and the world. We do not meet with the idea that some middle term is required between God and the world to explain the origin of the world in God. Nor with the idea that the continuous operation of God on the world and on mankind can only be through the medium of such a link. To the Jesus of the Johannine discourses, although He feels Himself to be the highest agent of God's work and revelation, it is still self-evident that there is an independent work of God, to be distinguished from His own work, with reference to the world and to mankind. He co-ordinates His own work with the work of the Father, after whose example and by whose authority He labours (v. 17, 19-23). He knows the direct work of revelation which God performs among mankind, such as enables them to come to Him, the Son, and receive from Him the perfect revelation (vi. 44, 45, 65).[1] The Jesus of these discourses feels and designates Himself always the Son, the only perfect Son of God. His claim to this title expresses His consciousness of His own inner, spiritual communion with God, His fulness of the divine life and divine revelation, the support which is given Him by the paternal love of God and His own devotion of love and obedience to the Father (cf. esp. v. 19-27, vi. 63, x. 30, 34-38). His reiterated emphasis on His own origin and mission from God does not signify His emergence from a former state of celestial pre-existence, but that His

[1] Cf. Harnack, *op. cit.* pp. 208 sqq.

present earthly life is wholly founded in God, and that His work is wholly required and justified by God's commission laid upon Him.[1] In this sense it is true, likewise, of His disciples that they are not of the world, as He is not of the world (xv. 19, xvii. 14–16; cf. i. 12 sq.). Conversely, the origin from beneath, of this world, of the devil (viii. 23, 38–44), which is assigned to the unbelieving opponents of Jesus, does not signify any inborn taint of hostility to God in their nature, but their guilty addiction to a base, earthly, immoral, diabolical state of mind, which makes them incapable of understanding and accepting the revelation of God (iii. 19 sq., v. 42–44, viii. 43–47).

There are many sayings in the Johannine discourses which, taken severally, it is not hard to interpret as expressing the philosophical views of Philo. But when we consider the general view and attitude of these discourses, and try to apprehend each several part in the light of the whole, we recognise a deep-seated intrinsic difference between these discourses, steeped as they are in ethical religion, dominated by the idea of the Fatherhood of God, and the philosophical view of Philo, with its cosmological and ascetic bias. If we could assign to these discourses a definite historical connection with the Philonistic speculation, we should be forced to pronounce that in them the ideas of Philo had been transformed to something radically different. But it is a much sounder course to deny altogether that these discourses were an offshoot of Philonistic speculation.

Is there, then, an irreconcilable contradiction in the juxtaposition of these two facts, first, that at the beginning of the Prologue the term λόγος is used in the manner peculiar to Philo, and, secondly, that Philonistic speculation has exercised no perceptible influence on those source-passages in the Fourth Gospel which were written by the

[1] For the sense demanded by the true context in viii. 58 and xvii. 5, cf. my remarks in *Lehre Jesu*, ii. pp. 464 sqq.

author of the Prologue? The matter is explained by the assumption that the author of the Source (as he also was) stood himself at a great mental distance from Philonistic speculation, but finding that the identification and designation of Jesus Christ as the Logos κατ' ἐξοχήν was current and cherished in a circle of Christian communities, he associated himself with it, for that reason, in his Prologue. He was able to adopt that identification, because in a certain sense he considered it perfectly true and self-evident. But he knew that it might be, and indeed was, interpreted in a perverted sense, foreign to the true Christian conception. He associated himself with it on purpose to set it in its right bearing. Even in the Prologue he lays all his emphasis on the thought that the Logos became flesh, and in this form, as the sole-born Son of God, drew very nigh unto men, and became for them a revelation of the nature of God (i. 14, 16–18). The emphasis on this thought must be understood as a protest against any other speculation on the Logos-Christ, such as refused to know the Logos in the flesh.

Christianity was certainly penetrated very early with Philonistic speculation, and the title "Logos" applied, in the sense of Philo, to the Messiah Jesus. The first clear sign of this occurs in the Apoc. xix. 13.[1] But even here the name ὁ λόγος τοῦ θεοῦ does not make its appearance as a new and surprising title for Messiah, which calls for explanation, but as one which is well known, and solves the riddle of the celestial apparition in vv. 11 sq. As early as the time of Paul's Greek mission the learned Alexandrian

---

[1] I make use of the opportunity afforded by this reference to the Apocalypse to explain that I cannot identify the author of that writing either with the author of the Source or with the fourth evangelist. It does not seem to me altogether impossible that the John who announces himself in Apoc. i. as the author was the presbyter John of Asia Minor. I do not enter into any more exact investigation of the interesting and important question of the origin of the Apocalypse, because it would be of no advantage for the special problem of my present work.

Jew Apollos had become a Christian and a Christian teacher (Acts xviii, 24-28). How many more Alexandrians may have taken a similar step into Christianity in the following age? The peculiarity of the Christian doctrine of these Alexandrines—the peculiarity of which those Corinthians were sensible who named themselves after Apollos in distinction from those who named themselves after Paul—must have consisted chiefly in a synthesis of Alexandrian speculation with the Christian faith. Such a synthesis was not far to seek when the living memory of the nature of Jesus' historical walk on earth was no more, when in the tradition of his earthly life and work the miraculous moments were specially emphasised and intensified, and when the dogma prevailed of the pre-existence of Jesus the Messiah. This idea of pre-existence had its roots in Judaism. It was a current conception in Jewish theology that the blessings of the Messianic age, and with them the Messiah Himself, had had a heavenly existence before their earthly realisation. It is the familiarity of Paul with this doctrine in his Jewish days which explains the fact that, after the Messiahship of Jesus had been made clear to him, he regarded the pre-existence of this Messiah, and His share even in the creation of the world, as an assured dogma, which stood in no special need of demonstration and defence (cf. 1 Cor. viii. 6, x. 4; 2 Cor. viii. 9; Col. i. 15-17; Phil. ii. 6 sq.). How easily, however, could that view be converted into the conviction—the pre-existent Messiah is the Logos of whom Philo speaks, the Logos who must be regarded as the necessary middle term between God and the world. This combination was not intelligible only to the enlightened Jews. By its means the faith in Messiah was made plausible also to the philosophically educated Greeks, the adherents of Plato and the Porch.

But this combination was certainly attended with great dangers. The delight in the philosophical speculations connected with the Logos ran a risk of driving into the background the simple, practical Christian piety, which sought to show itself in active brotherly love. The cosmological proclivities which were bound up in Philo with the Logos idea were capable of submerging the appreciation of that work and those sufferings on earth by which Jesus fulfilled His calling as the Messianic Saviour. And the conviction that the Messiah was identical with the Logos might easily beget the inference that this Messiah could not have possessed real flesh, a real created human nature, because that would have been inconsistent with His nature as the Logos.

Such dangers did indeed assail the circle of communities for which the original author of our Prologue, the author of the Source employed in the Gospel, was writing: this is shown in the First Epistle of John. The whole Epistle may be understood as the testimony of a representative of the older Christian generation against the new and dangerous tendencies which were connected with the introduction into Christianity of Philonistic speculation. Hence the writer's repeated admonition to abide by the old message, which was from the beginning (ii. 7, 24, iii. 11; cf. 2 John 5 sq.); his rejection of those who pretended to a knowledge of God without keeping God's commandments in their conduct (ii. 3 sq.); his inculcation of the old commandment of love, received from Jesus, by fulfilling which the sons of God are known (ii. 7-11, iii. 11-18, 23, iv. 7-v. 2; cf. 2 John 5 sq.); his insistence that Jesus Christ was sent for the taking away and the forgiveness of sins (i. 7, ii. 1 sq., iii. 3-8, iv. 10, 14). Hence, too, especially the sharp rebuke of those Christian, or, as the writer himself pronounces, antichristian teachers and prophets, who did not confess *Jesus* as the Messiah,—did not recognise that the Messiah had come in the flesh, and had come also "by blood" (ii. 18-23, iv. 1-3, v. 6; cf.

2 John 7). Such a docetism was the inevitable result of identifying the Christ with the Philonistic Logos and maintaining at the same time the true Philonistic view of the nature of the Logos. Just as the antagonism to docetic doctrine, expressed at the beginning of the Epistle, explains the writer's emphatic assurance that for himself the revelation of God to which he witnesses was the object of immediate sense-perception (i. 1–3), so too it is by the same antagonism that we must explain the explicit emphasis in the Gospel Prologue on the idea that "the Logos became flesh." The doctrine that the Logos of God had appeared in Jesus Christ was accepted even by the writer of this Prologue as correct: but he felt called on especially to declare that the acceptance of Christ as the Logos must be associated with the acknowledgment that the Logos really became flesh, and by means of that very appearance in the flesh made the nature of God perfectly known to mankind.

This being the special sense and intent of the dissertation on the Logos in the Prologue, there is no intrinsic improbability in the opinion that the Apostle John was its author. A deep initiation into Philo's world of philosophic ideas, a direct acquaintance with Philo's works, is out of the question in the case of this writer. He merely adopted the verbal usage of the Philonist school. It was quite possible for the apostle to do so, for the terms and phrases of a Philonistic stamp which he admits into the beginning of the Prologue contained nothing that was new or strange to his mind. The thoughts — that in the beginning, at the creation of heaven and earth, there was a word of God, and that through this word all things were created; that God had then revealed Himself through His word, and that His word was the light for mankind—were familiar to him from his youth up through the Old Testament (cf. Gen. i. 1–3; Ps. xxxiii. 6, 9, cxix. 103–105). He was likewise certain, as a disciple of Jesus, that Jesus Christ had been the perfect bearer of the word of God. Jesus Himself had claimed that His word was the word of God (John vii. 17, viii. 26, 51, 55, xii. 49 sq., xiv. 10, 24, xvii. 6-8, 14). And the truth of this claim had been perceived by the disciples in the salvation which was wrought by His word (vi. 68). So that the apostle did not regard the saying that the Messiah Jesus was the primeval Logos of God as a new message.

But he certainly understood that saying in his own sense, and not in the true Philonistic sense. To Philo the Logos that mediated the work of God upon the world was a hypostasis. So, too, the Christians of the school of Philo, who combined speculation on the Logos with their belief in Messiah, conceived the primeval Logos, who had once appeared as Messiah, as the pre-existent person of Messiah. The apostle, however, understood the Logos that had appeared in Jesus Christ as the *impersonal* word, the revelation of God. To him the Logos was not simply identical with the Messiah. He called the personal Jesus Christ only the *Son*, the sole-born Son of the heavenly Father, as Jesus had designated Himself. This Son had had no personal existence before the earthly appearance of Jesus Christ. But as a man He was the bearer of the primeval revelation of God. And He communicated this revelation in a perfect way to those who accepted Him with faith.

The term "Logos" at the beginning of the Prologue must be taken as intended by its original author in this impersonal sense, unless we are willing to leave an unbridged chasm between the meaning of that term here in the Prologue, and later in the great discourses of the Fourth Gospel and in the First Epistle of John. As we remarked above (p. 225), Jesus Himself never appears in the Johannine discourses as the personified Logos; but the term "the

Logos of God," in the sense of the impersonal revelation of God, is used several times (v. 38, viii. 55, x. 35, xii. 48, xiv. 24, xvii. 6, 14, 17). In the same way the term is employed in the first Johannine Epistle (i. 1, 10; ii. 5, 14). A special importance belongs to the passage in 1 John i. 1, because of its obvious affinity in expression and thought with the Prologue of the Gospel. Here the λόγος τῆς ζωῆς is distinguished from the object which the writer declares that he once perceived by the senses. What he saw, heard, and handled, that is to say, the human appearance of Jesus Christ, was not itself the word of life; yet it stood in a special relation to the word (περὶ τοῦ λόγου τῆς ζωῆς). We must seek first of all to understand the term Logos in the Prologue of the Gospel in this impersonal sense in which it is used everywhere else by the same writer. The content of the statements made in the Prologue about the Logos does not exclude this impersonal apprehension of the term. We are told that it came into the world (ver. 9), that to those who received it it gave the right to become children of God (ver. 12), that it tabernacled among men (ver. 14). These are expressions in an easy style of personification, such as are used also in the Old Testament about the word of God, without any idea of this word being a real person (Isa. lv. 11; Ps. cvii. 20, cxlvii. 15; cf. 2 Thess. iii. 1). In much bolder and more graphic personification the Chokma literature speaks of wisdom (Prov. viii. 1–ix. 5; Wisd. viii. 1–4, ix. 4–11, x. 1 sqq.) and antithetically of folly (Prov. ix. 13–18). There is but one point in favour of a personal interpretation of the Logos in the Prologue—that the form of expression, especially the employment of the simple term "Logos" without any attributive limitation, is technical in the Philonistic school, and that Philo and his school regarded the Logos as a hypostasis. But this one point is not enough to gainsay the fact that the language of the author of our Prologue is such, everywhere else, as to require the impersonal interpretation. How many other cases are there of technical, scholastic forms of expression being adopted by extraneous writers, without being precisely understood in the original, technical sense?

But we must now distinguish from the sense in which the original author of the Prologue apprehended the term "Logos," the sense in which our fourth evangelist adopted it. The evangelist has appropriated to himself the dissertation on the Logos which stood in his apostolic source. In so doing he has naturally imposed on it his own interpretation. If the apostle found the scholastic term "Logos" in use in the circle of communities in Asia Minor, that term, as used by the apostle, was there understood in the sense of the school of Philo. The question whether our fourth evangelist regarded the primeval Logos of the Prologue in a Philonistic sense as a personal being must, in my judgment, receive an affirmative answer; for the evangelist clearly betrays further on, and indeed even in the Prologue (ver. 15), the dogma of the pre-existence of the Messiah Jesus (cf. vi. 62, xii. 41). He doubtless identified the Logos with that pre-existent Messiah. We cannot, however, be content to accept this sense of the evangelist. If we do, the riddle of the singular relation between the term "Logos" in the Prologue and the same term in the discourses of the Gospel remains unsolved.

I come to the conclusion that even in the use of the term "Logos" in the Prologue there is no decisive ground for rejecting the opinion that the Apostle John was the author of the Source employed by the fourth evangelist. If that apostle really went in his old age to Asia Minor, it is quite conceivable that he took the term, which was there much used and valued as especially important by the Christian teachers, adopted it and associated with it his own witness concerning Jesus Christ, in the manner which occurs in the Prologue.

CHAPTER VII

THE GENESIS OF THE FOURTH GOSPEL

A. THE MAIN PORTION, CHAPTERS I.–XX.

1. *The Apostolic Tradition in the Subapostolic Rendering*

HAVING now disposed of the questions which relate to the Source made use of in the Fourth Gospel, we are able to take up anew the task, which we originally undertook, of forming an estimate of the Gospel itself, and to bring it to a sound conclusion.

We have already recognised that our Gospel bears a character which is in many respects secondary, and akin to the later synoptic tradition. We have also recognised its dependence, at many points, on the synoptic Gospels. But we have satisfied ourselves that with this recognition of its subapostolic character and origin the last word has not been spoken. There flows through it a broad stream of tradition which does not rise in the synoptic Gospels. Everything depends upon the value of this separate tradition. We have seen that the main elements of this separate tradition, namely, the groundwork of the great passages of discourse, were derived from a valuable source, which according to all the signs was apostolic. Our verdict, then, on the Gospel as a whole must run: *it is the subapostolic redaction of an apostolic tradition*. The verdict, in itself, is not new. But the important result of our inquiry up to this point is this, that a judgment which has often been pronounced, but has been supported only by general impressions, has now received a detailed ratification; and in the process it has been decided how far the apostolic source-components can still be distinguished from the secondary redaction of the evangelist.

The singular manner in which apostolic and subapostolic elements are mixed in the Gospel is capable of full explanation, if the evangelist belonged to that circle of communities in Asia Minor in which the aged Apostle John had lived. We have already seen, from the way in which that apostle is spoken of as one too well known to require the mention of his name, that the Gospel must have proceeded from that circle of disciples.[1] It can hardly have originated beneath the eyes of the apostle and under his immediate influence. It was probably not written until after his death, during the first quarter of the second century. The date of its composition cannot be fixed more exactly; for the oldest evidence of the existence of the First Epistle of John cannot be admitted as indirect evidence of the existence of the Gospel,[2] and the earliest traces of the use of thoughts and words from our Gospel turn out, when more accurately considered, to be traces only of the use of the Source, or of that oral tradition of the apostle which received in the Source a fixed literary form.[3] With what love and reverence may "the elder"

[1] Cf. pp. 211 sq.   [2] Cf. p. 175.
[3] Cf. pp. 175-181. There is, however, no conclusive reason for placing the composition of the Gospel definitely as late as the close of the first quarter of the second century, or later. Such a reason would indeed be found if Corssen, "Monarchianische Prologe zu den 4 Evang." (*T. U.* xv. 1), 1896, esp. pp. 128 sqq., were right in his opinion that the gnostic Leucius, in his "Acts of John," was entirely unacquainted with our Fourth Gospel; and that conversely the author of our Gospel had before him the work of Leucius, or the traditions which it embodied, and was working in opposition to the gnosticism of these "Acts." Cf., against Corssen, James, "Apocrypha anecdota, ii." (*Texts and Studies*, v. 1), 1897, pp. 144 sqq., who points out the acquaintance of the author of the "Acts" with our Gospel of John and the first Johannine Epistle, and exhibits the motives which actuated the author, despite that acquaint-

(2 John i.; 3 John i.) have been regarded by the Christians of Asia Minor, he who had not only seen the Lord in the days of His flesh, and been His constant companion, but had been, above the rest, the disciple whom the Lord loved! With what pious eagerness may they have received the memoirs in which the apostle set down his recollections of important colloquies and discourses of Jesus! And yet in how many points must the aged John have remained strange and unintelligible to those Christians of Asia Minor! That lay in the nature of things. The very fact which made him so especially venerable to the third generation of Christendom, the fact that he had witnessed the primitive age of Christianity, imported at the same time a great distance between him and his surroundings. It was not merely a distance of age. The intellectual soil in which the Christianity of Asia Minor had grown up was quite other than the soil in which stood the spiritual roots of the apostle. And the specific influences and conditions under which Christianity had developed in Asia Minor since the time of Paul were all strange to the apostle.

There is therefore no contradiction between the two facts, that our Fourth Gospel proceeded from the circle of Christians in Asia Minor, which was closely attached by love and reverence to the Apostle John, and that there is nevertheless a significant distinction to be observed between the thoughts of the apostle and those of the evangelist.

What the apostle gave to those Christians of Asia Minor was construed by them, and so too by our evangelist,

ance, in his own peculiarly divergent doctrine.—Hilgenfeld (*Zw. Th.*, 1900, pp. 1 sqq.) agrees with Corssen's main ideas, for he too contends that the author of the Acts of John was unacquainted with the canonical Gospel of John, and that, on the other hand, the fourth evangelist makes hostile reference to the gnostic-docetic presentation of Christ. But, nevertheless, he does not believe that our evangelist had a direct acquaintance with the "Acts" of Leucius. Docetism, which in my judgment the author of the Source already had occasion to oppose, certainly goes back in its beginnings into the first Christian century.

in a sense which corresponded to their subapostolic standpoint. They already possessed, apart from the apostle, a definite body of Christian doctrine, and, in particular, of historical dogmatic concerning Jesus Christ. Of the difference between this, their established Christian tradition, and that which the apostle spoke and intended, they were not conscious. Without suspecting it they read their own ideas into the words of the apostle, and merged the historical information which they received from the apostle into the historical presentment which they had formed upon a different evangelical tradition.

Thus we recognised as a result of the subapostolic attitude of the evangelist that in his redaction of the apostolic Source he took the "works," to which Jesus appealed in the attestation of His claims, merely as miraculous signs, which Jesus had publicly performed in overpowering abundance.[1] Further, that wherever the wording of Jesus' utterances would in any wise admit of it, he construed them as hints and oracular predictions of important events in the future—of the Crucifixion, the Resurrection, the gifts of the Spirit.[2] Again, that he gave to Jesus' words about the new birth through the Spirit, without which none can enter into the kingdom of God, a reference to the baptism of water;[3] or to Jesus' assertion that the eating and drinking of His flesh and blood avail unto eternal life, a reference to the Eucharist.[4] Once more, that he tacked on to the utterances of Jesus which relate to the possession of eternal life here and now by the faithful, an explicit reference to the future resurrection and the judgment to come.[5]

The evangelist cannot, however, have made use only of the written reminiscences of the Apostle John. The circle of communities in Asia Minor amid which the apostle had lived many years in his old age must also have possessed

---

[1] Cf. pp. 58–66.   [2] Cf. pp. 66–72.   [3] Cf. p. 120.
[4] Cf. p. 139.   [5] Cf. pp. 131 sq., 136 sq., 162.

many traditions, derived from his relation by word of mouth' about the evangelical history. We do not know whether the evangelist had himself belonged to the personal disciples and hearers of John; but as a member of that circle of communities he must have had a share in that heritage of tradition which came down from oral communications of the apostle. He has certainly digested this material also into his Gospel. Many statements of a credible character in the Fourth Gospel, which do not come from the synoptic tradition, but which we have no ground for deriving from the apostolic written source, statements which rather have a closer relation to the evangelist's own characteristic additions than to the Source, may be assigned to the oral tradition of the apostle.

Naturally, however, this oral apostolic tradition also was apprehended by the evangelist according to the ideas of his own subapostolic generation. And the transforming power of those ideas must here have been exerted in a much higher degree than upon the memoirs of the apostle. It is not possible to extract the elements of this oral apostolic tradition with any confidence from the account of the evangelist. In pointing to their presence we can only bring to bear a certain intrinsic probability.[1]

It seems to me probable that no later in the Gospel than the section about the first disciples of Jesus (i. 35–52) there lurk elements of this oral tradition. It is not incredible that the first disciples of Jesus, and John among them, were previously disciples of the Baptist, and that their

[1] It would in my judgment be a mistake to assign to the written Source all statements in the Gospel which, for reasons of intrinsic probability, might pass as sound elements of apostolic tradition. But it is equally improper, from those sections of the Gospel in which what appear to be sound elements of apostolic tradition are indissolubly combined with the secondary historical view of the evangelist, to draw the wholesale conclusion that it is altogether impossible to distinguish between the apostolic material in this Gospel and the subapostolic redactory matter.

acquaintance with Jesus was brought about through their relation to that prophet. The story in Mark i. 16–20 of how Jesus, by the Sea of Galilee, simply called the two pairs of fishermen to follow Him, presupposes His previous acquaintance with those men. The exact note of the time in John i. 39*b* is most naturally explained as a fragment from the memory of that apostle for whom the hour of his first meeting with Jesus, as the epoch-making moment of his life, had the highest personal interest. The assumption that this note of time, which is otherwise so purposeless, was a mere invention of the evangelist to make a show of precision in detail, is as unsatisfactory as the idea that he was allegorically alluding to "the time by the world's clock."[1] The notice, too, that Philip was from Bethsaida, the city of Andrew and Peter (i. 44), may be a supplement, derived from sound tradition, to the statement in Mark i. 29 that Peter's dwelling was in Capernaum. In the same way the account of the meeting between Nathanael and Jesus (i. 45–51) may be founded on an oral account by the apostle. The words in ver. 51, in which Jesus figuratively asserts His communion with heaven, which His disciples shall learn to know during His life on earth, impress us altogether as a genuine utterance of Jesus,—all the more, that in the rest of the Gospel there is no mention of any of the disciples having beheld any miraculous intercourse between Jesus and the angels. On the other hand, the form of this whole initial description is conditioned by the false presumption of the evangelist that Jesus' first disciples, at their very first meeting with the Lord, in consequence of the Baptist's witness and of Jesus' own avowal, must have clearly recognised and acknowledged His Messiahship.

The story, too, of Jesus' sign at the marriage in Cana (ii. 1–11) may have been prompted by some intimation of the Apostle John, which the evangelist—if this had not

[1] H. Holtzmann, *Hand-Comm.*, *ad loc.*

already been done by the circle of communities to which he belonged—adapted to his own historical and dogmatic conceptions. The evangelist gives no sign that he assigns any symbolic meaning to his story. But it is quite possible that an utterance which the apostle originally made in a figurative sense—Jesus turned the water of legal purification into the wine of marriage joy (cf. Mark ii. 18–20)—was afterwards interpreted by the circle of Johannine disciples as recording an actual miraculous conversion of such water of purification into wine for a marriage.[1]

The oral tradition of the apostle may also have engendered the statement that the Mary referred to in Luke x. 38 sqq. and the Mary whom Mark (xiv. 3 sqq.) speaks of as anointing Jesus in Bethany were one and the same (John xi. 1 sq., xii. 1–3). Some, again, of the features in the account of the passion which are peculiar to the fourth evangelist may have the same origin. For instance, the mention by name of the servant wounded in Gethsemane (xviii. 10); the statement, too, that the trial of Jesus before the assembled Sanhedrin in the palace of Caiaphas, which is recorded by the Synoptics, was preceded by an imprisonment and preliminary hearing in the house of Annas (xviii. 12 sq. 19–24); and that the denials of Peter took place in the court of that house, to which John had procured his admittance (xviii. 15–18); finally, the intimation that Jesus had intrusted his mother to John, and that John had from that time taken her unto himself (xix. 26 sq.).

In xix. 35 the evangelist appeals expressly to the credible testimony of "him that hath seen," that is, of the Apostle John.[2] But here, in all probability, it is not the

---

[1] As a synoptic analogue to this case, the story of the cursing of the fig-tree (Mark xi. 12–14, 20 sq.) seems to have arisen out of the transformation of a simile made use of by Jesus (such as Luke xiii. 6–9, xvii. 6; cf. Mark xi. 23) into an actual history.

[2] Cf. above pp. 211–213.

oral testimony of the apostle that is meant, but the written word (1 John v. 6).[1] In the sense of the apostle this passage in the Epistle was intended to lay stress on the veritable death of Jesus Christ, as against those docetic Logos-christologists who contested the reality of Christ's carnal nature and death on the cross. Christ came not only through and in water, but also through and in blood,—that is to say, not only in His baptism, but even in His bloody death, He was betokened by God as the Messiah. The evangelist, however, interpreted the passage to mean that the earthly body of Jesus contained in a miraculous way the sacramental substance, which, when the side of the Lord was opened by the piercing with a spear, came forth into the light. In this case also the apostolic tradition underwent, in the subapostolic rendering, a substantial alteration of meaning.

2. *The Specific Aims and Prepossessions of the Evangelist*

In order, however, to understand the composition of our Gospel it is not enough to perceive that the evangelist conceived the material bequeathed to him by the apostolic tradition in the light of his own subapostolic standpoint. His manner of working upon that material, his choice of additions to be made to the apostolic tradition, are also essentially conditioned by special aims and prepossessions which actuated him in his rendering.

His chief aim was doubtless to edit in a form which should be intelligible to the communities those discourses and colloquies of Jesus which John had recorded. With this intent he sometimes interpolated such glosses as should clear up the sense of dark sayings of Jesus. Of this kind are the additions in ii. 21, v. 28 sq., vi. 62, vii. 8, 39, xii. 33, 47*b*, and his slight touches in iii. 5, iv. 11, vi. 39, 40,

[1] Cf. Ch. H. Weisse, *Die evang. Geschichte*, i. pp. 101 sq.; *Evangelienfrage*, p. 125.

44, 54, xii. 48, xvi. 13. Sometimes, again, he tried to define the historical relations of the various discursive passages more clearly and explicitly than was done in the Source. Any hint of a historical event which seemed to him to be given in the Source prompted him to recount that event in the way in which, according to his general view of the appearance and work of Jesus, it must have happened. Thus he inferred from the words of the Samaritan woman in iv. 19 that Jesus must have given her a proof of His miraculous knowledge, and from Jesus' words to His disciples in iv. 35 that He must even then have had a large following in Samaria. He gave what seemed to him an appropriate historic setting to the discourse of Jesus on the heavenly bread of life, and on the efficacy unto eternal life of eating His flesh and drinking His blood, by attaching it to the story of the miraculous feeding which he knew from the synoptic tradition. The statement in the Source that Jesus saw a man blind from his birth, and uttered on that occasion the sayings in ix. 4 sq., impelled him to a description of the miraculous healing of that blind man. On Jesus' words to Martha in xi. 23, 25 sq. he founded his account of the miraculous raising of Lazarus. The historical notices, also, in vii. 9–14, viii. 30, xii. 28*b*–30, are deduced by him from hints in the Source.

Not everything, however, which the evangelist added on his own part to the source-components is to be explained by this intention of throwing light upon the contents of the Source. He not only sought to illustrate historically the several discourses of the Source. He also supplied the contents of the Source as a whole with a historical introduction and a historical conclusion. He did not, indeed, attempt to force those contents into the framework of the synoptic tradition, as our first and third evangelists inserted the Logia of Matthew into the narrative scheme of Mark. He presupposes a knowledge of the synoptic tradition.

But he makes surprisingly little effort to establish a clear connection between his own separate narrative material and that tradition. In his historical composition he had more special ends in view.

In the first place he sought to take into account the specially vivid interest which, in the circle of communities to which he belonged and for which he chiefly wrote, attached to the personality of the Apostle John. He brought forward all he knew about the close relation of this apostle to Jesus. The sections i. 37–41, xiii. 23–25, xviii. 15 sq., xix. 26 sq., xx. 1–10 are the outcome of that interest. In all those sections, except xix. 26 sq., by the side of the disciple whom the Lord loved Peter appears. This is not unintentional. The reader was to be incited to a comparison of those two apostles, and therein to observe that John stood even nearer to the Lord than Peter, and exhibited no less zeal for Him than Peter himself. John did not, as he seemed to do in the synoptic account (Mark i. 16–20), enter into discipleship after Peter, but even before him (i. 37 sqq.). At the Last Supper John, as the disciple whom Jesus loved, reclined in the Lord's bosom, and could speak confidentially with Him, while Peter could only ask a question of the Lord through the medium of John (xiii. 23–25). Peter was not the only disciple who, at the arrest of Jesus, when all the other disciples fled (Mark xiv. 50), followed the Lord into the palace of the high priest. John did so too, and it was only through the intervention of John that Peter obtained admittance into the court of the palace (xviii. 15 sq.). It was not to Peter, who had falsely denied Him, but to the still faithful disciple whom He loved, that the dying Jesus intrusted His mother (xix. 26 sq.). And at the tidings of the empty grave of the Lord, John's eagerness to convince himself of the truth of this wonderful announcement lent wings to his speed, and he outran Peter (xx. 1–10).

But a much greater influence than that of the personal interest in the Apostle John has been exerted on the form of the narrative in the fourth evangelist by a dogmatic prepossession. The evangelist says at the close of his work that the signs of Jesus recorded in his book have been written that his readers may believe in Jesus as the Christ, the Son of God (xx. 30 sq.). However little the content of his work as a whole answers to a description of the signs of Jesus, it is decidedly characteristic of the narrative material which the evangelist has combined with the discursive material of his Source to present miraculous signs of Jesus as credentials of His Messiahship. This point of view appears no later than in the story of Nathanael, whom Jesus impels by an example of His marvellous knowledge to recognise Him as the Son of God and as Messiah (i. 46–50). The same point of view dominates the historical descriptions that follow—those in chaps. ii. and iv., no less than those in chaps. vi., ix., and xi. It also engenders the reiterated asseveration that the hostile leaders of Judaism, for the very reason that they could not assail the fact of Jesus' miracles, and the overpowering witness which they bore to His Messiahship, sought to remove Him by force (vii. 31 sq., ix. 13–34, xi. 45–53, xii. 9–19, 37–43). I have already made clear the assiduity with which the evangelist seeks to obviate such objections to the miraculous knowledge and power of Jesus as might rest upon the fact that He was deceived in the traitor and the inhabitants of Jerusalem, and that He was overpowered by His enemies without a struggle.[1] This accounts for the passages in ii. 24 sq., iv. 43 sq., vi. 64*b*, 70 sq., vii. 30, 44, viii. 20*b*, x. 39, xiii. 11, 18 sq., 21–30, xviii. 1–11. I have also remarked that if the signs of Jesus were regarded as the proper tokens of His Messiahship, the demand made upon the sub-apostolic generation must be to give credit to the *record* of

---

[1] Cf. pp. 28–31.

those miracles, without craving to *see* a miracle for themselves. This important demand is brought out by the evangelist in the stories in iv. 46–53 and xx. 24–29. Besides this dogmatic prepossession which dominates the account of the signs of Jesus, we may perceive a definite polemical bias of the evangelist. The way in which he speaks of the Baptist—the obvious intention with which he again and again lays down that the Baptist was and wished to be no more than a witness to Jesus the Messiah, and had no independent significance, was indeed incomparably beneath the heaven-descended Messiah (i. 6–8, 15, 19–34, iii. 22–36, v. 33–35, x. 41 sq.),—all this leads us to infer that he was attacking some mistaken overestimate of the Baptist. He must have had occasion to oppose certain disciples of the Baptist, who honoured him as the prophet of the final age, and would know nothing of the Messiahship of Jesus.[1] We know from Acts xix. 1–7 that in the time of Paul there was a sect of the Baptist's disciples at Ephesus.[2] The fact that twelve men of this connexion crossed over into the Christian community does not, of course, prevent others, either later in Ephesus or in other places in Asia Minor, from having still adhered to it: the connexion may very likely have carried on a propaganda inside Judaism, and, in any case, its doctrine of a Messiah still to come contradicted the Christian doctrine that the Messiah had already appeared in Jesus. The evangelist sought to deprive those disciples of John of their historical basis and justification, by laying it down that the sole function of the Baptist was to proclaim Jesus as Messiah (i. 6–8, 31–33). He had himself

---

[1] Cf. H. Holtzmann, in Schenkel's *Bibel-Lexikon*, iii. pp. 326 sqq. (where the previous adherents of this view are adduced); *Hand-Comm.*, 2nd ed., iv. p. 75; Weizsäcker, *Apost. Zeitalter*, 2nd ed., p. 529 (*The Apostolic Age*, vol. ii. p. 226); and esp. Baldensperger, *Der Prolog des vierten Evangeliums*, 1898.

[2] On the relation of Apollos (Acts xviii. 24 sqq.) to these disciples of John, cf. my "Commentary on the Acts" (Meyer's *Komm.* iii.), 8th ed. *ad loc.*

explicitly declared that he was neither the Messiah, nor Elias, nor the prophet (i. 19–21). He had directed his disciples to Jesus (i. 29, 35 sq.), and acknowledged it right and necessary that, when Jesus Himself had appeared upon the scene, men should attach themselves no longer to himself, but to Jesus, no longer seek the baptism of John, but the baptism of Jesus (iii. 25–30). His estimate of the divine origin of Jesus and His import unto salvation was the same as Jesus' own (i. 15, 30, iii. 31–36), and he had announced the suffering and death of Jesus,—which was certainly taken by the disciples of John as a disproof of Jesus' Messiahship, —as necessary, in accordance with Isa. liii. 4–7, for taking away the sin of the world (i. 29, 36). We must not, indeed, attempt, with Baldensperger, to find in the polemical, apologetic tendency against the sect of the Baptist the key to the understanding of the whole essential content of the Fourth Gospel;[1] but that this tendency is *also* at work, that it affects especially the sections of the Gospel referring to the Baptist, cannot be denied.

It is a mistake to explain the whole Gospel by doctrinal tendency, to regard the staple of its contents as a creative fancy of the evangelist, who sought to bring home religious and philosophical ideas to his Christian contemporaries by clothing them in a garment of history. Such a theory will not do justice to the character and value of the Gospel. It has to leave out of sight the many signs which point to the inclusion in the Gospel of material from a precious historical tradition. But the theory contains a kernel of truth in that certain parts of the Gospel are really the outcome of a doctrinal tendency, dogmatic and polemical. How far, when he was actuated by this tendency, the evangelist remodelled his material by means of his own imagination, how far he was

[1] Cf. what seems to me the perfectly apposite criticism of H. Holtzmann (*Th. Lz.*, 1899, pp. 202 sqq.) on the problematic historical structure on which Baldensperger builds his hypothesis.

giving a fixed and ordered form to an existing tradition, which was already dominated by the same tendency, we cannot determine. It is, however, certain that just those parts of the Gospel in which that doctrinal tendency can be traced reveal themselves, when tested by the earlier synoptic tradition, as essentially untrustworthy.[1]

B. THE APPENDIX, CHAPTER XXI.

The Gospel narrative receives its last incisive strokes in the confession of Thomas and the answer of the risen Jesus, xx. 28 sq., and the evangelist adds his formal conclusion in the words of xx. 30 sq.: but there follows an appendix, chap. xxi. Is this a subsequent addition by the evangelist himself, or the work of a later writer? In the second case we must look for the author in that same circle of Asiatic Christians, attached to the aged John, to which the evangelist himself belonged; for here in the appendix the apostle is still spoken of in that same mysterious style, designed for the initiate, which occurred in the Gospel (vv. 2, 7, 20, 23). The language of the appendix is in all essentials the same as that of the main portion of the Gospel.[2] This is a point in favour of the authorship of the evangelist. But in itself this point is not conclusive. Another writer might have intentionally imitated the language of the evangelist, in order to make his supplement as nearly uniform as possible with the rest of the work. There seems to me to be an internal piece of evidence in the appendix which shows that this has really been done.

The contents are as follow. First, in vv. 1–14, comes the story of how the risen Lord revealed Himself to several of His disciples at the Sea of Tiberias. Here we find expressed the tradition, which was not noticed in chap. xx.,

---
[1] Cf. pp. 14–32.
[2] Cf. M. Eberhardt, *Ev. Joh. C.*, 21, 1897, pp. 73 sqq.

that an appearance of the risen Lord had taken place in Galilee. Such an appearance in Galilee is presupposed in Mark xvi. 7, and in accordance with the presupposition is reported in Matt. xxviii. 16–20. The account, then, in John xxi. 1 sqq. is specially related to the tradition of Mark-Matthew, which deviates from that of Luke (xxiv.). The hypothesis, however, that the original conclusion of Mark, which is lost, and was not known even to our first and third evangelist, recorded an appearance in Galilee to the disciples, and especially to Peter,[1] is too problematical to secure my adhesion. The story of the miraculous draught of fishes in vv. 1–14 forms a doublet to Luke v. 1–9. The story had perhaps no definite date assigned to it in the oral tradition, and while Luke combined it with the first call of Peter to follow Jesus, the author of our appendix connected it with Peter's second call, the call to his office as an apostle. He has attached to it, in ver. 7, a reminiscence of the story in Matt. xiv. 28–31 of how Peter leaped into the water to come to Jesus. The account, too, of the wonderful meal of which the risen Lord partook with His disciples after the draught of fishes, vv. 9 and 12 sq., contains a reminiscence of the wonderful feeding, vi. 9–11.

After the account of this event there follow certain significant utterances of the risen Lord with reference to Peter and the beloved disciple. That these utterances had always been closely associated by tradition with that story of the meeting by the sea and the miraculous draught of fishes is matter for doubt.[2] They do not stand in any organic connection with that preceding story. The account in vv. 1 sqq. has already received its formal conclusion in ver. 14.

The earnest question which the Lord addressed three

[1] So P. Rohrbach, *Der Schluss des Marcusevang., der Vier-Evangelien-Kanon und die kleinasiat. Presbyter*, 1894, pp. 52 sqq.; Harnack, *Chronologie der altchristl. Litteratur*, i. pp. 696 sq.

[2] Cf. Loofs, "Die Auferstehungsberichte und ihr Wert" (*Hefte zur Chr. W.*, No. 33) 1898, p. 32.

times to Peter, rather than to the other disciples (vv. 15–17), has an obvious internal connection with the earlier protestation of Peter (Mark xiv. 29; Matt. xxvi. 33; John xiii. 37), and the threefold denial which immediately followed. It has been justly said that the right place for this conscience-searching question was at the *first* appearance to Peter of the risen Lord, which was the first appearance of all (1 Cor. xv. 5; cf. Luke xxiv. 34).[1] After the appointment of Peter to his new office of shepherd, there follows a further utterance of the Lord to him: in his youth, says Jesus, Peter had ranged whither he would, free from bonds, but in his old age he shall be bound and carried whither he would not (ver. 18*a*). This saying is taken by the writer as an oracular prediction of the martyr's death which Peter should die (ver. 19*a*). The analogy of the case in xii. 32 sq. suggests the question whether it really had that sense originally, or whether it was so interpreted, and accommodated to the interpretation, for the first time after Peter's martyrdom. After this oracular saying, and its assignment to Peter's death, there follows finally the word about the tarrying of the disciple whom Jesus loved (vv. 20–22). The writer remarks that this word, from which the Christians had inferred that this disciple should not die until the Parusia, was in reality only a conditional expression (ver. 23).

This last remark permits of an inference being drawn from it with regard to the author of the appendix and his relation to the main portion of the Gospel. If the Apostle John had been the author of that main portion, we should be obliged to conclude that nevertheless he had not written this appendix. The supplement clearly presupposes the death of the apostle. But since, as we saw above, the main portion was not the direct work of the apostle, there remains, with respect to the appendix, the following alterna-

[1] Cf. Loofs, *op cit.* p. 31.

tive: If the fourth evangelist was himself the author of the appendix, then the main portion of his work must have been written during the apostle's lifetime; but if that main portion was not written until after the death of the apostle, then the author of the appendix must have been some other person than the evangelist. For according to ver. 23 that utterance of the Lord concerning John was already known among the Christians during John's lifetime. The apparent contradiction given to it by the death of the apostle must have been discussed most anxiously immediately after he died. The evangelist may have been induced by that discussion to give, as a supplement to his Gospel, the true rendering of the Lord's word about the tarrying of John till He came. But it is not probable, if the whole work was written after the death of the apostle, that the duty of reporting that expression aright should never have occurred to the evangelist at the time of writing, but only at a later date when it required a supplementary addition. On the other hand, it is quite conceivable that the evangelist, writing his whole work after the death of the apostle, left out of notice the apparently unfulfilled saying of the Lord about John, and that afterwards some other member of the Johannine circle of disciples felt impelled, after all, to append to the Gospel "according to John" (xxi. 24) the true version of that saying. As I do not think it probable that the main portion of the Gospel was written during the apostle's lifetime,[1] I come to the conclusion that the appendix did *not* originate with the evangelist himself.

As members of the circle of communities in Asia Minor connected with John, the author of the appendix and his original readers doubtless felt a peculiar interest in the section, vv. 20–23, which concerns that apostle. Perhaps the real purpose of the whole appendix lay in the proper report of that saying. If we recollect that hitherto through-

[1] Cf. p. 236.

out the Gospel, whenever the beloved disciple is mentioned, Peter also plays a part, in order that the reader may draw a comparison between these two apostles,[1] we cannot but think it probable that here too, in the appendix, the account of the colloquy of the risen Lord with Peter is intended only as a foil to the word which refers to John.[2] The beloved disciple needed no such painful questioning of his conscience about his love for the Lord. His relation to the Lord had never been overclouded. The reason that he did not, like Peter, suffer a martyr's death was not that he was not, on his part, ready to endure it. Nay, he too desired, like Peter, to follow the Lord (ver. 20). But the Lord Himself disposed it otherwise: His beloved disciple should remain, for an indefinite while, His witness on earth. In the story of the draught of fishes, again, the scene in ver. 7 sets the two disciples side by side in a notable manner. In this respect it forms an obvious parallel to xx. 2–9. To the external eye it was Peter who rushed sooner and more turbulently than John to the side of the risen Lord: but the closer, inner relation of the beloved disciple to the Lord was shown in the fact that he was the first to recognise the Lord, and it was he who taught Peter to recognise Him. It was, indeed, probably with special reference to this scene between Peter and John that the author selected this story of the draught of fishes as an appropriate introduction to the record of Jesus' utterances in vv. 15 sqq. Of course, I do not mean that the author simply invented that story and the words in vv. 15–18 which refer to Peter, as an introduction to the words concerning John in ver. 22. Those passages, vv. 1–14 and vv. 15–18, certainly included older traditional material. But the author's reason for adopting from tradition this

---

[1] Cf. p. 244.
[2] Cf. H. Holtzmann, *Hand-Comm.*, 2nd ed., iv. p. 229; also Klöpper, *Zw. Th.*, 1899, pp. 365 sq.

specific material was to set the current saying of the risen Lord about the beloved disciple in the best light.

In vv. 24 sq. the author has added a second formal conclusion to the whole Gospel, and in it he denotes the apostle spoken of in vv. 20-23—that is to say, John—as the author of the preceding book. I have already observed (p. 213) that this statement need not be regarded as an intentional deception of the reader. In the mind of the writer its truth may have consisted in the fact that the Gospel was founded on the written memoirs of the apostle.

In this conclusion the author of the appendix clearly distinguishes between himself, of whom he speaks in the first person, and the apostle, of whom he speaks definitively in the third person. But while he expresses his individual opinion in the singular οἶμαι of ver. 25, he associates his own knowledge of the truth of the apostle's witness with the same knowledge in other men by using the plural οἴδαμεν in ver. 24. In this οἴδαμεν he speaks on behalf of the circle of John's disciples in Asia Minor. This attestation, in the plural, of the apostle's testimony, at the end of the Gospel, gave rise to the tradition, which we meet with in the Muratorian fragment, that John wrote the Gospel at the instance of his attendant disciples, and under their control. There is also an echo of this tradition in the words of Clement of Alexandria (in Eusebius, *H. E.* VI. xiv. 7) about the Gospel according to John.

CONCLUSION

AT the close of our work we revert to the question with which we set out, What is the truth with respect to the historic credibility of the Gospel? Our investigation of the Source employed in the Gospel, and of the genesis of the Gospel itself, shows that this question cannot be answered in any terse, rounded formula. The Gospel includes precious material of apostolic tradition. But it was not composed, any more than our other three Gospels, by an apostolic eye-witness of the Gospel history. There are in it, as in the synoptic Gospels, elements of a secondary tradition lying side by side with those of the apostolic tradition. As it is the latest of our Gospels we come face to face with its secondary character much more clearly than with that of the Synoptics. But it is possible—not indeed in every detail, but in the main—to discriminate the apostolic tradition in the Gospel from the elements of a secondary, subapostolic interpretation and tradition. And just because such discrimination is possible, the Gospel possesses for us—in spite of its subapostolic origin and the incredibility of many of its component parts—an eminent historical value. It is a real source for history, but one which must be critically used.

Are we to deplore the fact that the fourth evangelist subjected the memoirs of the Apostle John to a redaction and setting which cannot compare with them in character and value? We ought to reflect that without this redaction and setting the apostolic memoirs would perhaps have spread no further, and would have been lost altogether to later ages. Before they could be looked upon by subapostolic Christianity as fit for use, alongside the evangelical writings it already possessed, in the instruction of the communities in the life of the Lord, they required the addition of a body of important narrative material. As the Logia of Matthew have only been preserved to Christendom in the secondary redaction of the First and Third Gospels, so, too, the memoirs of the Apostle John stood in need of a redaction which should conform with the views of the subapostolic generation, in order to be rightly treasured and preserved for posterity.

We must therefore thank the fourth evangelist for assuring, by means of his work, the preservation of the Johannine Source. We must also thank him, in spite of every freedom which he assumed, for having treated the contents of the Source with so much reverence that we are still able to distinguish essentially between the components of the Source and his own work.

SYNOPSIS OF THE PASSAGES IN THE GOSPEL WHICH ARE PROBABLY DERIVED FROM THE SOURCE

CHAP.
i. Vv. 1–5, 9–14, 16–18 (*vide* pp. 110–117).
ii. The basis of vv. 13–16; vv. 18–20 (*vide* pp. 66 sq., 118).
iii. Vv. 1, 2*a*, 3, 4, 5 (except ὕδατος καί), 6–21 (*vide* pp. 118–122).
iv. Basis of vv. 4–12 (except καὶ τίς ... πεῖν in ver. 10 and οὔτε ἄντλημα ... βαθύ in ver. 11); vv. 13, 14; basis of ver. 15; vv. 19–25; basis of ver. 27; vv. 31–38 (*vide* pp. 122–128).
v. Basis of vv. 1–3, 5–7, 16; vv. 17–27 (except ἀνθρώπου in ver. 27), 30, 31, 32, 34*a*, 36*b* (from τὰ γὰρ ἔργα)–47 (*vide* pp. 73–75, 128–136). Here followed in the Source, vii. 15–19, 21*b*–24 (*vide* pp. 85–92).
vi. Vv. 27–58 (except the refrain in vv. 39, 40, 44, 54), 60, 61, 63, 64*a*, 65–69 (*vide* pp. 75–85, 136–141).
vii. Vv. 1 (2 ?), 3–7, and the basis of vv. 10–14 (*vide* pp. 142–145); vv. 15–19, 21*b*–24 (*vide* pp. 85–92); basis of vv. 25–27; vv. 28, 29, 33, 34 (35 sq. ?), 37, 38, 40–43 (*vide* pp. 67–69, 92–96, 146 sq.).
viii. Vv. 12–20*a*, 21 (22 ?), 23–29, 31*b*–59 (*vide* pp. 92–96, 146–148).
ix. Vv. 1, 4, 5, 39–41 (*vide* pp. 148–151).
x. Vv. 1–18; basis of vv. 19–21*a*, 23; vv. 24–38; basis of ver. 40 (*vide* pp. 150–153).
xi. Basis of vv. 1, 3, 5, 6; vv. 7–10, 16; basis of vv. 17–22; vv. 23–27; basis of vv. 28–35, 38 (*vide* pp. 153–158).
xii. Vv. 20–28*a*, 31, 32, 34, 35, 36*a*, 44–47*a*, 48 (except the final words ἐν τῇ ἐσχ. ἡμέρᾳ), 49, 50 (*vide* pp. 69, 96–99, 158–161).
xiii. Vv. 1–10, 12–17, 20, 31*b*–35 (here followed in the Source, chaps. xv. and xvi.), vv. 37, 38 (*vide* pp. 99–107, 161–163).
xiv.–xvii. All except the final words of xvi. 13: καὶ τὰ ἐρχόμ. ἀναγγ. ὑμῖν (*vide* pp. 69 sq., 101–107, 163 sq.).
xviii. Vv. 33–38*a* (*vide* pp. 164 sq.).
xix. Vv. 9–11*a* (*vide* pp. 164–166).

INDEX OF PASSAGES CITED FROM THE JOHANNINE BOOKS

THE GOSPEL ACCORDING TO ST. JOHN

CHAP.	PAGE	CHAP.	PAGE
i. 1–18	110–117, 223–234	iv. 1–3	120
i. 1–5	115–117, 224–234	iv. 4–9	122–124, 166, 183
i. 6–8	14, 115–117, 246 sq.	iv. 9	83
i. 9–11	115–117, 233	iv. 10–12	122–124, 242
i. 12, 13	115 sq., 120, 195, 227, 233	iv. 13, 14	122–124, 126
i. 14	110–116, 207–211, 213, 228, 233	iv. 15	126 sq.
i. 15	14, 111–115, 234, 246 sq.	iv. 16–18	22, 124–127, 243
i. 16–18	112–116, 207–211, 222, 228	iv. 19–24	124–127, 190, 219
i. 19–28	14 sq., 34, 111, 117, 246 sq.	iv. 22	83, 190
i. 29–34	14 sq., 35, 111, 117, 200, 246 sq.	iv. 25, 26	18, 127
i. 35–41	15, 117, 200, 211, 239 sq., 244	iv. 27–30	22, 125, 127 sq.
		iv. 31–33	127
		iv. 34	61, 127
		iv. 35–38	61, 127 sq., 168, 187, 203
i. 41, 42	18, 239	iv. 39–42	18, 22, 125, 128, 243
i. 44	240	iv. 43	11, 128, 245
i. 45–50	18, 22, 30, 83, 117, 240, 245	iv. 44	30, 37, 128, 245
		iv. 45	21, 24
i. 51	240	iv. 46–54	21, 24, 31, 33, 37 sq., 117, 128, 246
ii. 1–10	11, 22, 83, 117, 240		
ii. 4	145, 146	iv. 48	22, 31
ii. 11	21, 24, 117 sq.	iv. 54	33
ii. 12	11, 117 sq.	v. 1–16	23, 73 sq., 85, 129, 166, 169, 184
ii. 13–17	9, 12, 36 sq., 83, 117 sq., 166, 185	v. 1	9, 83, 85
ii. 18–20	36, 66 sq., 71, 84, 117 sq., 166, 185	v. 8, 9	38, 73 sq.
		v. 17	73, 87, 129, 190, 226
ii. 21, 22	12, 22, 66 sq., 71, 117 sq., 202, 242	v. 18	73, 184, 195
		v. 19–27	23, 73, 79, 87, 129–134, 142, 195, 197, 226
ii. 23	21, 24, 118 sq., 148		
ii. 24, 25	29, 92, 118 sq., 245	v. 24, 25	59, 79, 120, 131–134, 198 sq.
iii. 1–21	117 sq., 166–168		
iii. 2	24, 119, 197	v. 26, 27	129–134
iii. 3–8	68, 120, 121	v. 28, 29	131–134, 238, 242
iii. 5	120, 238, 242	v. 30	87 sq., 133 sq., 195
iii. 8	187	v. 31–35	134, 246
iii. 11–13	195	v. 36	61, 79, 87, 135
iii. 14–17	68, 120, 160, 197, 204	v. 37, 38	79, 87, 135, 191, 195, 225, 233
iii. 18–21	117 sq., 168, 204, 227		
iii. 22, 23	120 sq.	v. 39–47	79, 87–89, 191, 227
iii. 24	33, 120 sq.	vi. 1	11
iii. 25–36	15, 111, 120 sq., 246 sq.	vi. 2	21, 24, 39

17

INDEX

CHAP.	PAGE	CHAP.	PAGE
vi. 3-13	23, 39, 75-78, 83, 139	viii. 24	94, 198
vi. 14, 15	18, 21, 24 sq., 40, 76	viii. 25-27	197
vi. 16-21	40	viii. 28	63, 69, 196 sq.
vi. 22-24	84, 139	viii. 30, 31a	92, 147 sq., 243
vi. 26	24, 27, 58, 76 sq., 78-81	viii. 31b-36	94, 147 sq., 198 sq.
vi. 27-58	23, 58-60, 77-85, 136-139, 142, 168 sq.	viii. 37-41	147, 187, 195 sq., 197
		viii. 42-44	94, 121, 147, 187, 195 sq., 227
vi. 27-29	58, 68, 81-83, 187		
vi. 30, 31	58, 77 sq., 136, 184	viii. 45	147 sq., 197
vi. 32-38	58-60, 68, 136, 138, 184, 187, 195, 197, 204	viii. 46	64 sq., 197
		viii. 47	187, 227
vi. 36	79-81	viii. 48	195
vi. 39, 40	136, 138, 197, 242	viii. 51	59, 94, 195, 198 sq.
vi. 41, 42	83 sq., 138, 195	viii. 52, 53	195
vi. 44	136, 243	viii. 54-58	195 sq., 225-227, 233
vi. 45-50	59, 68, 136-138, 187, 190, 195	ix. 1	150, 166
		ix. 2, 3	148 sq.
vi. 51	138 sq., 187, 204, 205	ix. 4, 5	149 sq., 187, 204
vi. 52-58	59, 83 sq., 137-139, 141, 187, 205, 243	ix. 6, 7	23, 149, 243
		ix. 8-34	23 sq., 149, 245
vi. 59	136	ix. 35-38	18, 23, 149
vi. 60, 61	139, 143	ix. 39-41	23, 149 sq., 204
vi. 62	139-141, 234, 242	x. 1-9	149 sq., 187
vi. 63	59, 68, 79, 120, 138, 140, 198, 205, 226	x. 10-18	149 sq., 187, 199
		x. 16	203, 219
vi. 64	28, 141, 245	x. 19-21	24, 152
vi. 65	226	x. 22	9, 152
vi. 66-69	59, 141	x. 23	152
vi. 70, 71	28, 141, 245	x. 24-38	151 sq., 169, 194
vii. 1, 2	11, 83, 85, 143, 169, 183	x. 25	60, 64, 81
vii. 3, 4	64, 142 sq., 184	x. 26-28	151
vii. 5	142 sq., 184	x. 30	60, 195, 226
vii. 6, 7	143 sq.	x. 32	60, 64, 195
vii. 8-10	9, 143-145, 242 sq.	x. 33	195
vii. 11-14	145, 242 sq.	x. 34-36	190, 195, 204, 225 sq., 233
vii. 15-18	84, 85-92, 168, 196 sq.	x. 37, 38	60, 64, 195 sq.
vii. 19-24	73 sq., 85-92, 168	x. 39	30, 153, 245
vii. 19	86, 92, 184	x. 40-42	111, 153, 246
vii. 20	86, 92	xi. 1-44	23 sq., 153-158
vii. 21	64, 92	xi. 1, 2	40, 157, 166, 184, 241
vii. 22-24	73 sq., 86, 184, 190	xi. 3-6	25, 153, 157
vii. 25-27	92, 146	xi. 7-10	157 sq., 184, 187
vii. 28, 29	92-95, 121, 146, 195	xi. 11-14	157
vii. 30	30, 146, 245	xi. 15	25, 153, 157
vii. 31, 32	24, 92, 95, 146, 245	xi. 16	157 sq.
vii. 33, 34	92-95	xi. 17-22	158, 166
vii. 35, 36	84, 146	xi. 23-27	156-158
vii. 37, 38	67-69, 71, 92-95, 126, 146	xi. 28-44	25, 153-155
vii. 39	67-69, 71, 147, 242	xi. 40	153-155
vii. 40-43	30, 83, 93, 95, 126, 147	xi. 45	21, 23 sq., 153 sq.
vii. 44	30, 146, 245	xi. 46-53	24, 154, 245
vii. 45-52	30, 83, 93, 95, 146	xi. 54-57	83, 158
vii. 53	93	xii. 1-8	9, 40 sq., 158, 241
viii. 1-11	93	xii. 9-11	21, 23 sq., 154, 158, 245
viii. 12-59	93-96, 146-148, 169, 204	xii. 12-16	42, 158
viii. 15	196	xii. 17-19	21, 24, 43, 158, 245
viii. 20	30, 146	xii. 20-22	159, 166
viii. 21	94, 198	xii. 23, 24	69, 159, 187, 199, 202 sq., 219
viii. 22	84, 146		
viii. 23	94, 121, 187, 195 sq., 227	xii. 25	43, 159, 188 sq.

INDEX

CHAP.	PAGE
xii. 26, 27	159
xii. 28–30	159 sq., 243
xii. 31, 32	69, 71, 159, 199, 202 sq., 219
xii. 33	69, 71, 159, 242
xii. 34	159
xii. 35, 36a	96–98, 159, 187
xii. 36b–43	96–99, 158 sq.
xii. 37	24, 158 sq.
xii. 41	234
xii. 42, 43	148, 158 sq.
xii. 44, 45	96–98, 160 sq., 197
xii. 46	97 sq., 160 sq., 197, 204
xii. 47, 48	98, 148, 160 sq., 197, 225, 233, 242 sq.
xii. 49, 50	59, 98, 160 sq., 196 sq.
xiii. 1–10	24, 161, 166, 185, 191
xiii. 11	28, 161, 245
xiii. 12–15	99, 162, 185, 191
xiii. 16	44, 99, 187, 188 sq.
xiii. 17	99–101, 185, 191
xiii. 18, 19	28, 99–101, 161, 245
xiii. 20	44, 100, 185, 188, 192
xiii. 21–30	28, 43, 103, 161–163, 211, 244, 245
xiii. 31–33	103 sq., 107, 161–163, 202
xiii. 34, 35	103 sq., 107, 161 sq., 191 sq.
xiii. 36, 37	102, 105 sq., 107
xiii. 38	44, 105 sq., 107, 188
xiv. 1–4	103, 105 sq., 107, 192, 206
xiv. 5, 6	103
xiv. 9–11	60–62, 195 sq.
xiv. 12–14	61, 192, 199
xiv. 15	199
xiv. 16, 17	199, 203
xiv. 18–20	187, 202 sq.
xiv. 21–24	148, 187, 195, 199, 202 sq., 225, 233
xiv. 25, 26	103 sq., 163, 203
xiv. 27	103 sq., 192
xiv. 28–31a	103 sq., 199, 202
xiv. 31b	44, 103 sq., 188
xv. 1–17	104 sq., 107, 187, 203
xv. 4–6	104 sq., 187, 203
xv. 7–10	104, 187, 199
xv. 11	192
xv. 12–17	104, 191 sq., 197, 199
xv. 18–27	104 sq., 193, 204
xv. 19	195, 227
xv. 20	44, 188 sq.
xv. 22–24	60, 61–64
xv. 26, 27	163, 193, 203
xvi. 1–4	193, 204
xvi. 5	103

CHAP.	PAGE
xvi. 6–12	102, 105, 163, 193, 199, 203
xvi. 13	163, 203, 243
xvi. 14, 15	102, 163, 195, 197, 203
xvi. 16–22	105, 202 sq.
xvi. 21	187
xvi. 23, 24	105, 192, 202 sq.
xvi. 25–28	105, 192, 195, 204
xvi. 29, 30	105
xvi. 31–33	105, 192
xvii. 2, 3	59, 63, 197
xvii. 4, 5	61, 162, 192, 202, 227
xvii. 6–8	61, 197, 225, 233
xvii. 9–11	203
xvii. 12	69
xvii. 14–16	122, 195–198, 203, 225, 227, 233
xvii. 17	198, 225, 233
xvii. 18	61
xvii. 19	199
xvii. 20–23	187, 203
xvii. 24	192, 202
xvii. 26	187, 195, 203
xviii. 1–8	30 sq., 245
xviii. 9	70, 71
xviii. 10, 11	30, 44 sq., 241, 245
xviii. 12–14	30, 164, 241
xviii. 15–18	45, 164, 211, 212, 241, 244
xviii. 19–24	46, 164, 241
xviii. 25–27	45, 164
xviii. 28	13, 46, 164
xviii. 32	69, 71
xviii. 33, 34	46, 83, 164, 185 sq.
xviii. 35	83, 164, 185 sq.
xviii. 36, 37	164, 185 sq., 198, 204
xviii. 38, 39	46
xix. 2, 3	46
xix. 9–11	46, 164, 186
xix. 19	46
xix. 26, 27	211, 241, 244
xix. 34, 35	210, 211, 241
xix. 37	179
xix. 38–42	83
xx. 2–10	47, 211, 244
xx. 11–18	47
xx. 19–28	47, 177, 202
xx. 29	31, 202, 246
xx. 30, 31	21, 31, 50, 65, 117, 245, 248
xxi. 1–14	211, 248 sq., 252
xxi. 15–17	250, 252
xxi. 18, 19	250, 252
xxi. 20–23	211, 250–252
xxi. 24, 25	213, 253

THE EPISTLES OF ST. JOHN

CHAP.	PAGE
I i. 1-4	172, 173, 207-209, 213, 231, 233
i. 5	172, 173, 174
i. 7	201, 230
i. 8	172
i. 10	233
ii. 1, 2	171, 201, 208, 230
ii. 3-6	173, 230, 233
ii. 7-11	174, 230
ii. 14	233
ii. 18, 19	171, 205, 230
ii. 20	171
ii. 22, 23	171, 205, 230
ii. 24	230
ii. 25	174
ii. 27	171, 173, 174
ii. 28	171, 173
iii. 3-6	208, 230
iii. 7, 8	205, 230
iii. 9, 10	171, 205

CHAP.	PAGE
I iii. 11, 12	205, 230
iii. 13-18	230
iii. 23	174, 230
iii. 24	173
iv. 1-3	171, 205, 230
iv. 7-9	230
iv. 10	201, 230
iv. 11-16	208, 230
iv. 17-21	172, 175, 230
v. 1, 2	230
v. 6	205, 230, 242
v. 10-13	172
v. 20	173, 175
VER.	
II 1.	216, 217 sq., 237
5, 6	230
7	205, 230
9, 10	173
III 1	216, 217 sq., 237
11	208